The Star-Stone Ones

a journey from the stars unto the stones

by

Mary Saint-Marie/Sheoekah

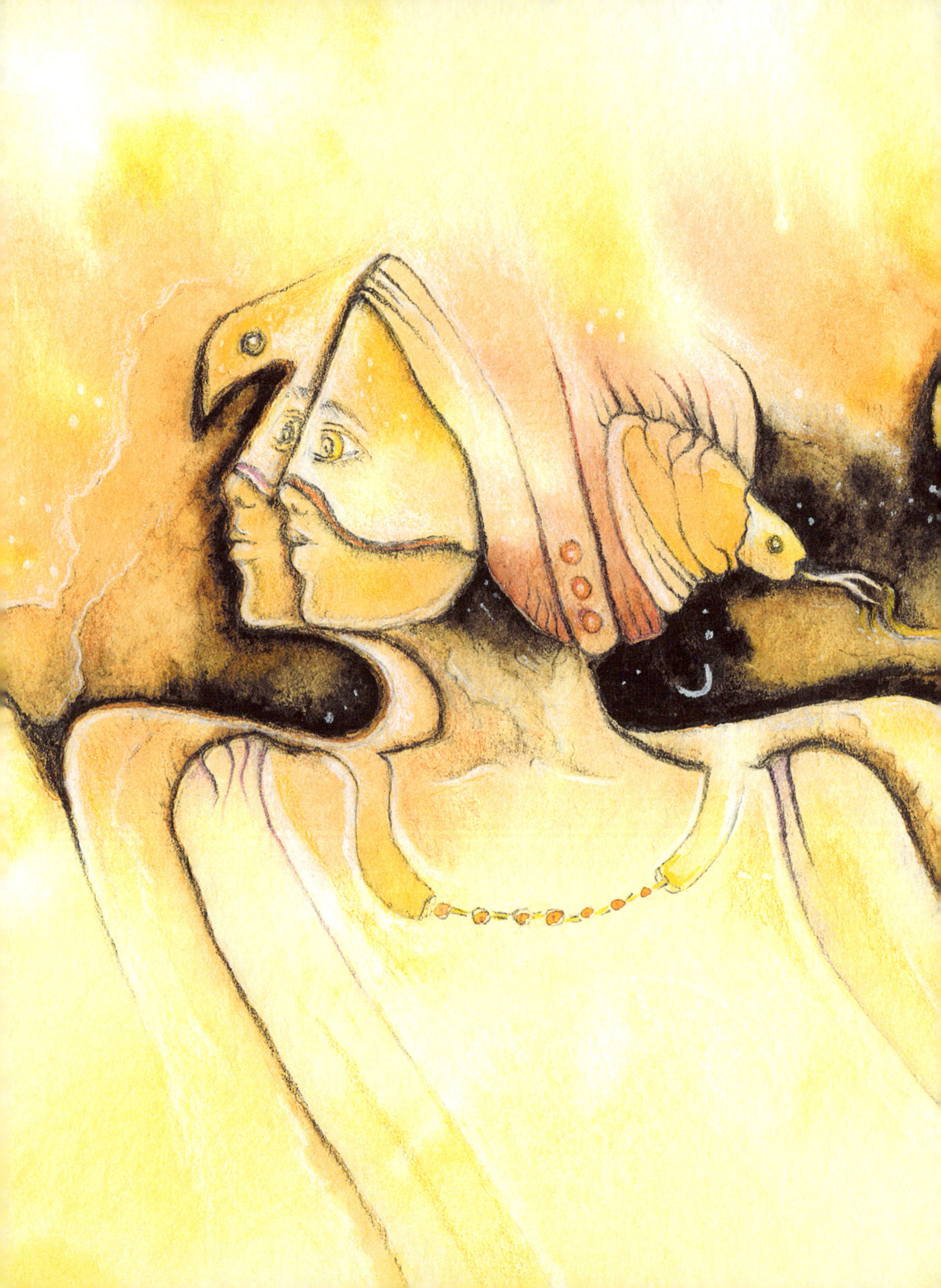

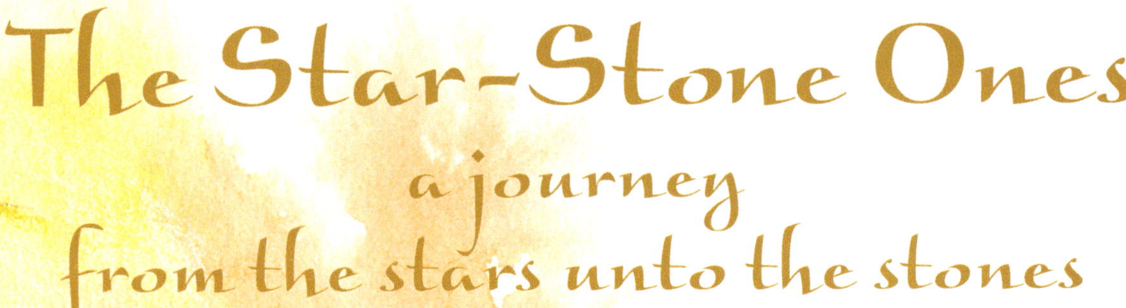

ye are the very star-stone Essence of Infinity...
ye are the very Consciousness of Creation's Dance...
ye are the Sacred Dance...

Mary Saint-Marie/Sheoekah

Published by Ancient Beauty Studios, www.marysaintmarie.com

ISBN: 978-0615778211 (sc)

All artwork by Mary Saint-Marie

Front Cover Art: *Embraced by the Beloved*

Back Cover Art: *Owl-Ceremony-HE*

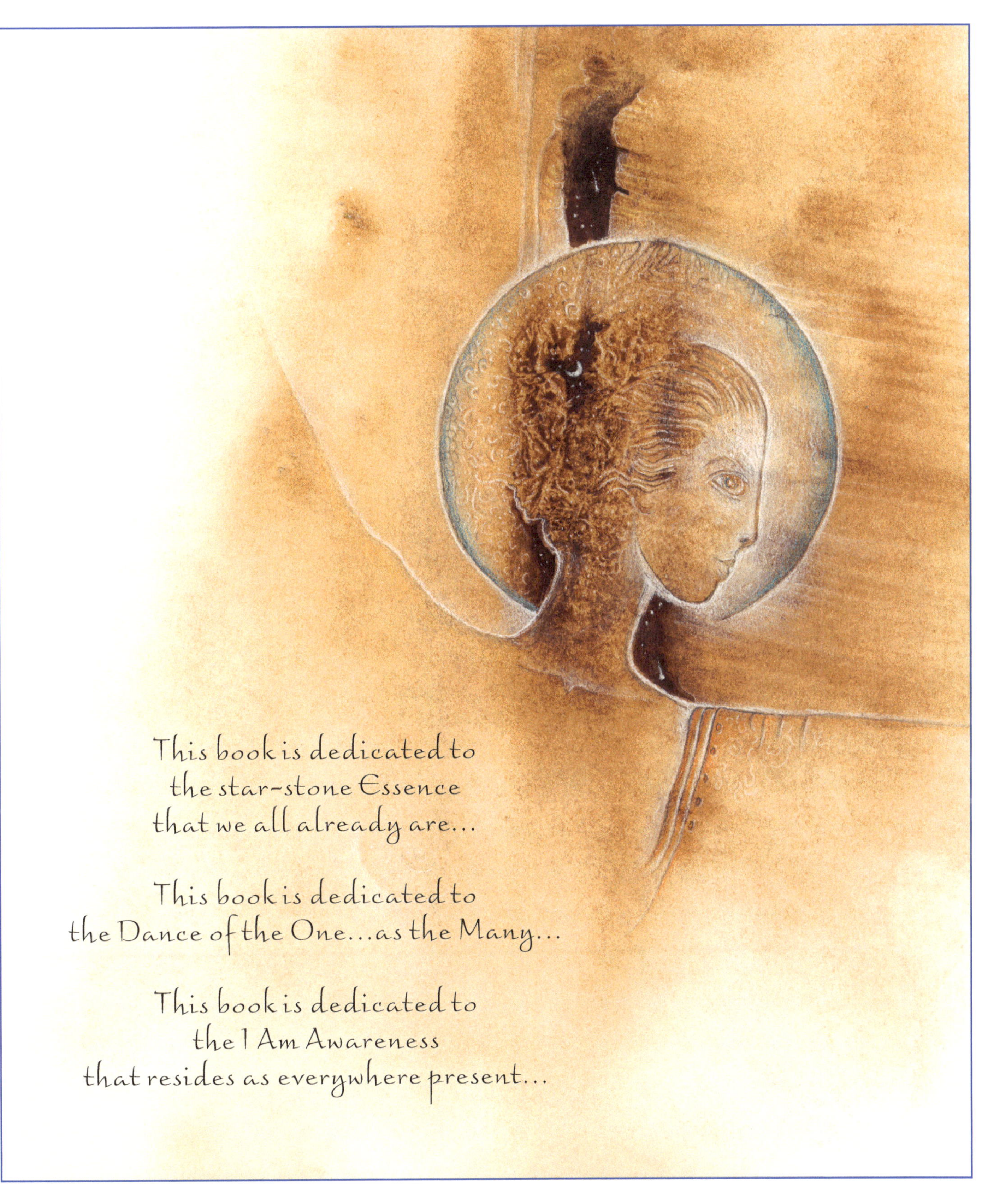

This book is dedicated to
the star-stone Essence
that we all already are...

This book is dedicated to
the Dance of the One...as the Many...

This book is dedicated to
the I Am Awareness
that resides as everywhere present...

Acknowledgments

I thank my daughters, Kimberly Backes and Rebecca Allen. Your presence in my life continues to catalyze dimensions and essence for soul awakening. I love being mom and nana beyond measure.

I thank my friends in Mount Shasta and around the globe for the support in spiritual friendship. I thank Heidi Merkins for her blessed support of this book's creation. I thank Cheryl Yambrach Rose-Hall for her continued inspiration in my life. I thank Laura Daen for the gift of creative and sacred friendship and for holding space for this manifestation.

I thank all those who have come to me for Soul Sessions, retreats and workshops. It is ever illumined moments to reflect with you your Soul Self.

I am in gratitude to the I Am Awareness, the essence that inspires this mystic and visionary art and poetry, and our very lives, as we allow.

I am grateful for Love and Wisdom that may manifest through us all as Beauty.

I am grateful for the arrival of these images over the course of many years. They continued to appear as visitors. Precious guests. They became "illumined whispers on the desert wind" while living in the high desert on the north side of Mount Shasta, amidst junipers and sage, deer and rabbits and on.

I am grateful for Mother Earth. Nature, in many forms, is a source of Inspiration for the art and poetry.

I thank Lewis Mitchell and Aaron Rose for both their aesthetic and technical support. You are such a bridge for this creation.

I thank the following ones for technical support:

Art scanning by Light Source Creations, Lewis Mitchell, Medford, Oregon

Art scanning by Swanson Images, Bob Swanson, Weed, California

Design and Layout by Aaron Rose, Mount Shasta, California

Editing by Mary Saint-Marie and Laura Daen

Photography by Laura Daen

Contents

The Divine Masculine Principle in Man and Woman

The Sacred Two: Partners in Divine Purpose… the SHE and HE of creation…in Man and Woman

Passages

Invitation: Star-Stone Essence

This book is an offering…and an invitation to be more deeply in one's True Identity as Essence. As the presence of divine being.

It is an invitation to realize that.

It is an invitation to allow Essence to Live as our very being.

It is an invitation to realize the Impersonal as the Life of what we call the personal. The personal and Impersonal as One. Wholeness IS.

Now is the time to identify with our true nature, our Essence Self…alone.

In that True Identity, we will begin to release and let go of false identities, which are roles and functions and sometimes even habits of society.
We are transcendence Itself. The roles, of mother, sister, husband, uncle, owner of house, position in career and on, are roles in the Play.

Realization of our Essence-Self. This is the way of freedom. Freedom lived.
Not freedom from disease, disorder, dysfunction and on. Freedom as the Light of Consciousness. Freedom as the I Am Awareness.

Essence-Self is I Am Awareness. It is pure Consciousness. It is the unconditioned love.

IT knows how to live a non duality life in a world of opposites, but no opposition. It opens out a way.

It is the Isness which flows as the River of Life toward the River of Convergence.
The Undivided One.

Come.
Come into this world of Essence. Star-Stone Essence.

We are all artists.
Artists animated and danced by Essence, the very Fire of Life.
In that, we are all bringers of beauty.
Beauty…expressed…

Introduction:
Whispers on the Wind

Like whispers on the wind these visitors do come unannounced.
Images arriving like a lover in the night.
Purity does sing her song.
Beauty smiles from everywhere.

Far from the clamor of the world these images
appear…dressed in colors of the desert floors.
So subtle are they that Sing of Light.
A word, sometimes even a thought, and they vanish.
Images forgotten, like a long lost dream.

These visitors do come in silence, in stillness and
with the call of a pure heart. They seem to be
visitors from another world. Illumined world that
speaks only in the tongue of joy. Abiding joy does sing.

These visitors of the wind do dance across my page,
from the paint, the water and even from my heart.
They do dance through the veil of separation.
They do dissolve the sense of separation.
They do reveal the inner and the outer only as the One.
Light and manifestation. One.

These visitors do fire upon our hearts…gladness.

O visitors…it is I.
I receive you.
Beloved that you are.
Beckoning me always and ever to play in fields of light.

Gossamer. Illumined. You call me inward again and yet again.
Realms of the Real revealed.
Visitors standing naked.
Dances of light appearing, receding, disappearing.

I stand.
I dance.
I whirl.
Head thrown back; laughter fills my soul.
Dancing alone and with everything.
Ecstatic paradox.

The phone rings.
You, my visitors, disappear.
Veiling your nakedness.
Veiling your purity.
Ever vigilant.
Ever the gargoyle at your door.

I return. And you reappear.
A whisper on the wind.
A visitor on the wind.
Silent image riding a wave of light.

The Invisible AS visible.
Formless AS form.
Whispers ride on waves.
Light and manifestation…One.

Beyond thoughts, beliefs and concepts
do you dwell as if visitors of another world.

You whisper sweetly that you dwell everywhere.
You whisper of a world that glistens always.

Silence grants me passage.
Here exaltation never leaves.
Here love chants endlessly.
The Soul…a brush stroke only.

Moments cease; the timeless opens its grand door.
You dance upon my page. You are here.
Ever…a whisper on the wind.

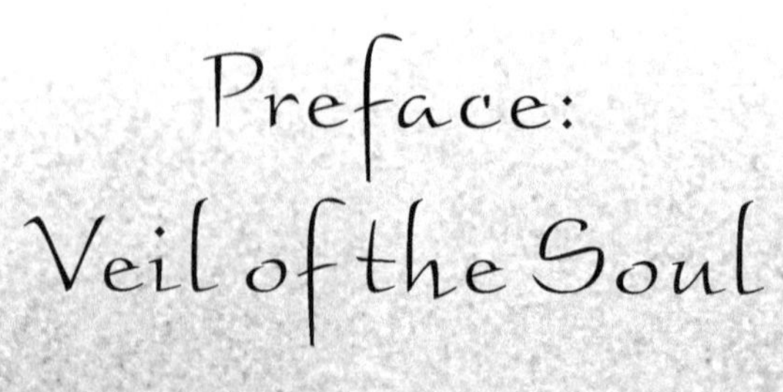

Preface: Veil of the Soul

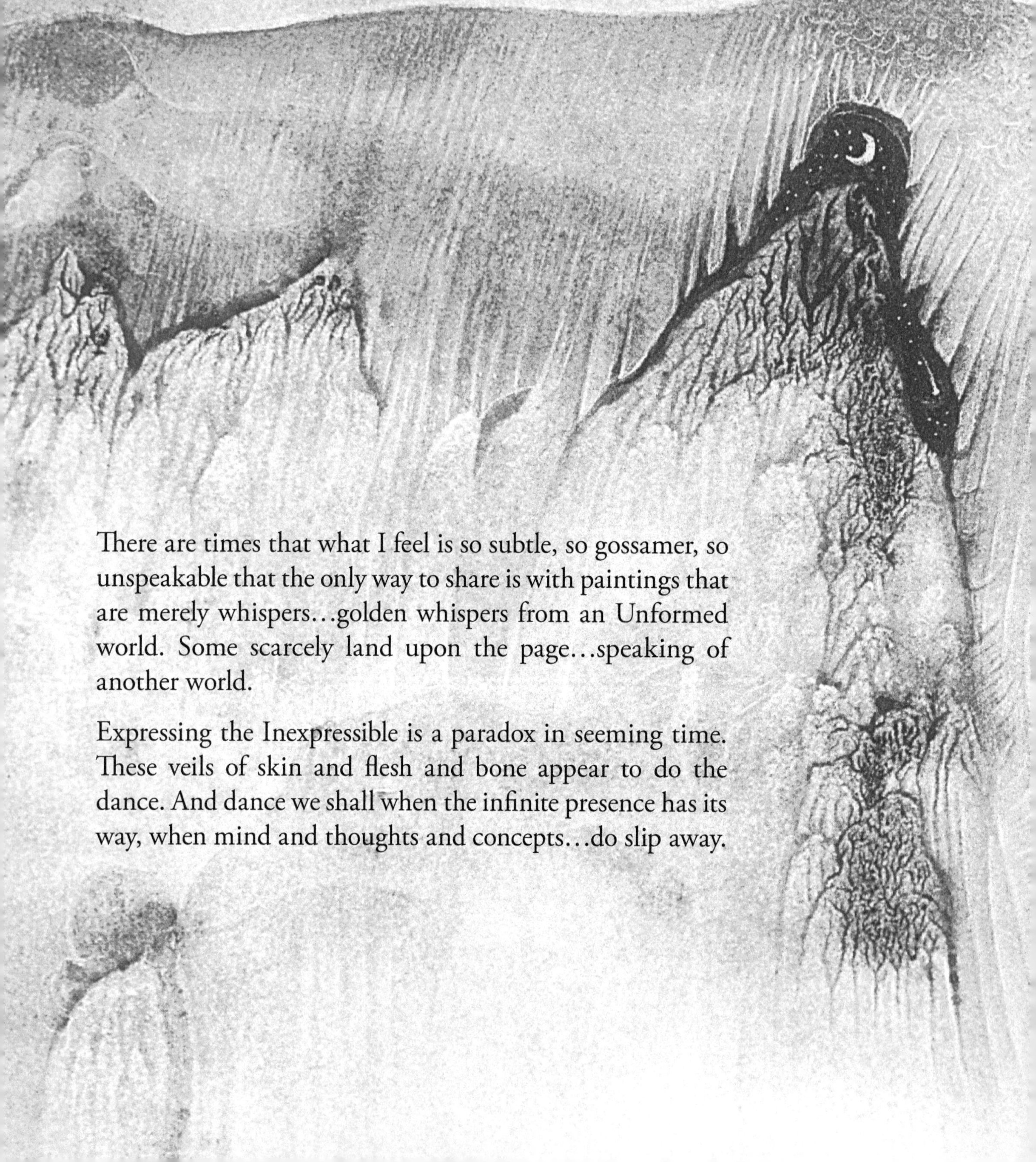

There are times that what I feel is so subtle, so gossamer, so unspeakable that the only way to share is with paintings that are merely whispers…golden whispers from an Unformed world. Some scarcely land upon the page…speaking of another world.

Expressing the Inexpressible is a paradox in seeming time. These veils of skin and flesh and bone appear to do the dance. And dance we shall when the infinite presence has its way, when mind and thoughts and concepts…do slip away.

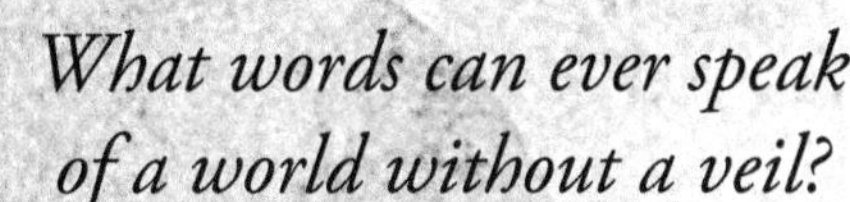

What words can ever speak
of a world without a veil?

What words can sing this song?

I tell here a story of essence dancing
from Formless to form and back again.

I tell here a story of essence acting out
the never ending story of love…

Here is a story of this world as a trysting place…
drawing us together again and yet again…
to smile, to give, to dance
and open wide our hearts…

Here the feelings of the soul are transmitted…

Veils…upon veils shall fall…
and love shall have its way…

Subtle is the space when we realize
I Am awareness…
and the sense of separation…it does cease…

The Divine Feminine Principle
in
Man and Woman

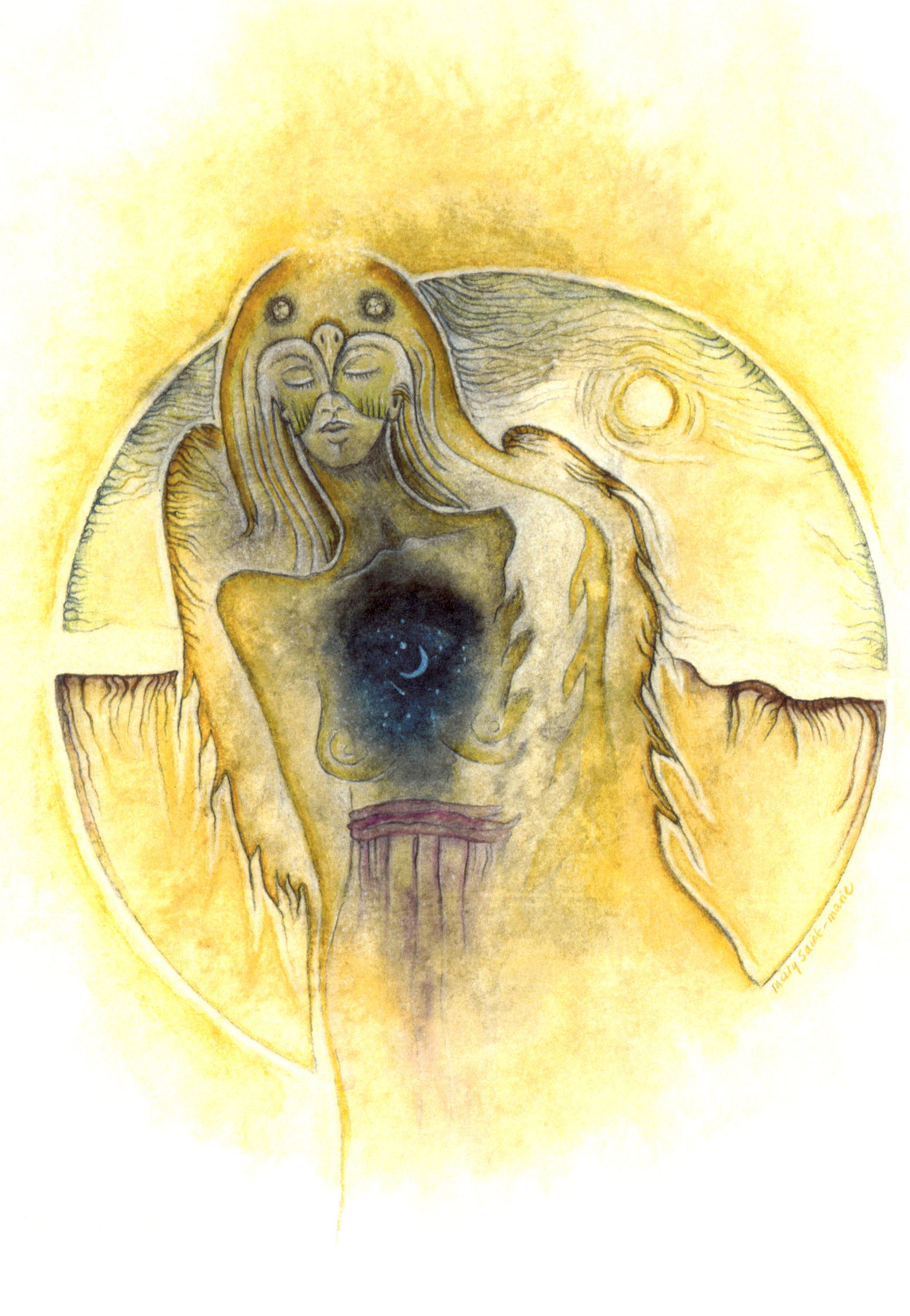
mary Saint-marie

Embraced by the Beloved

embraced by beloved one…
embraced by infinity's arms…

Here grace stands naked.

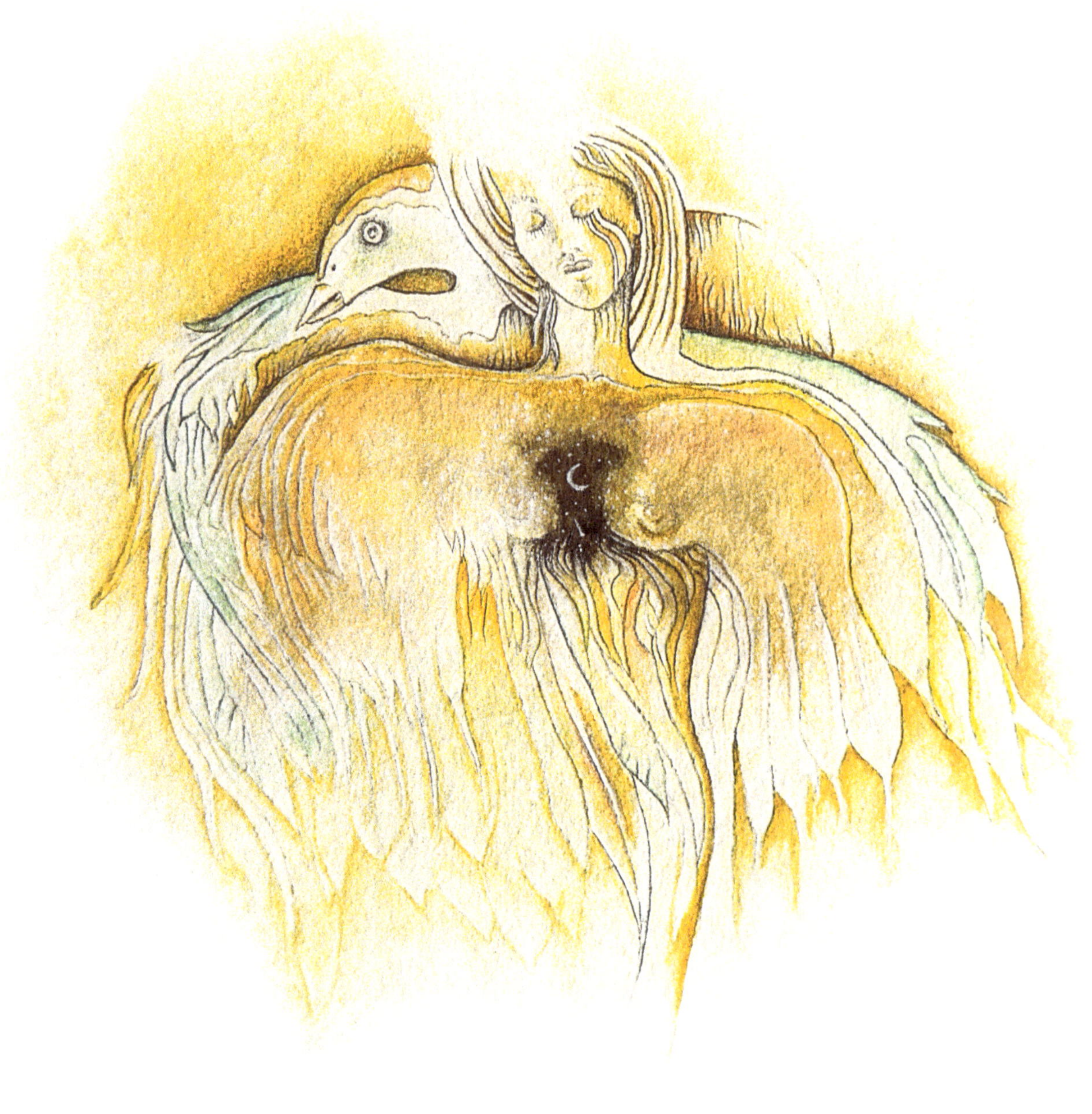

Messenger-SHE...of the winged Ones

a messenger of light-SHE...
pouring heart's peace upon the lands...

Imaged is the dwelling place that is the heart.

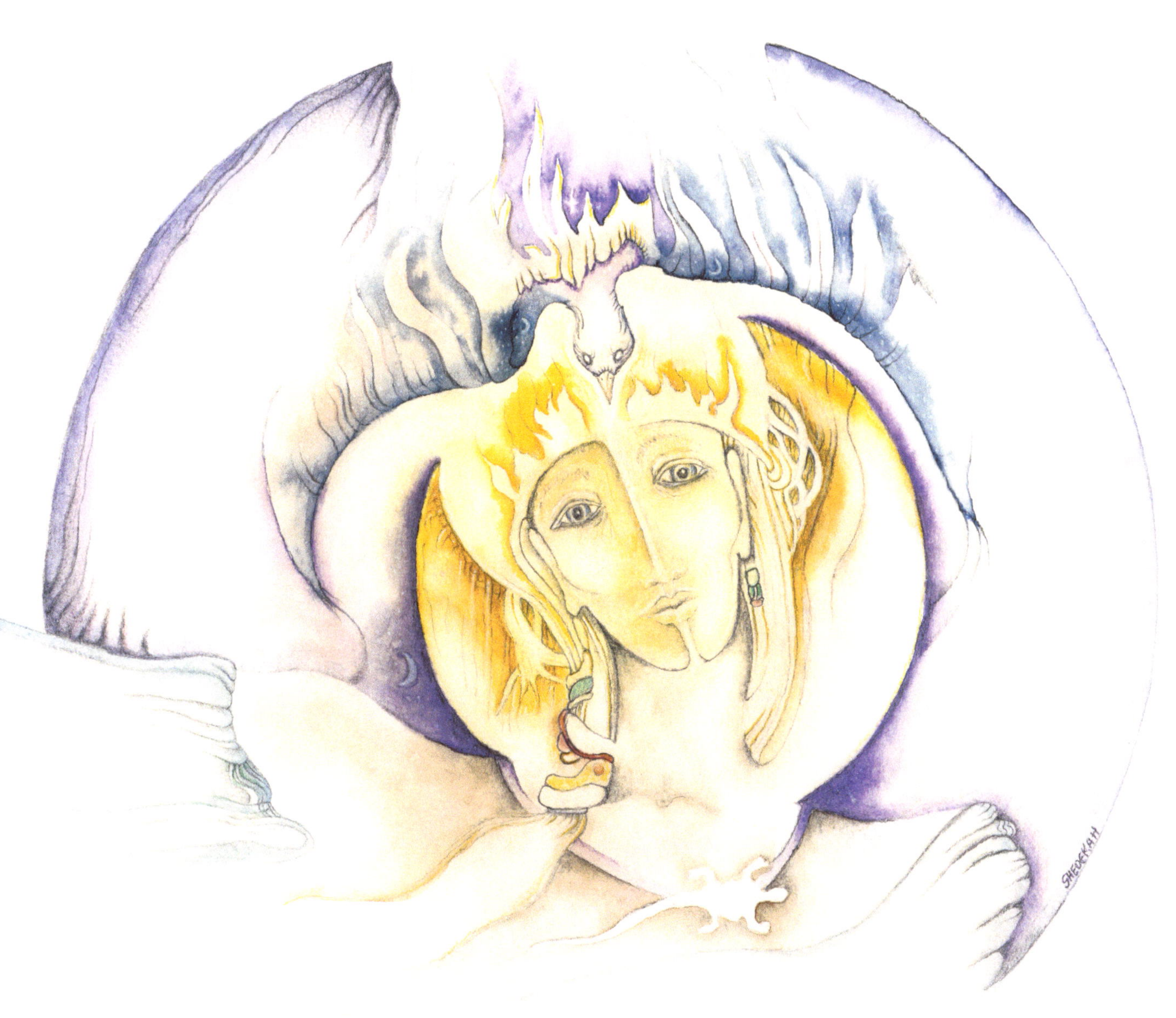

Starry-Realm-SHE

infused with peace…
she walks upon the earth…
lizard at her foot…

The realm depicted is one of being in the world, but not of the world.

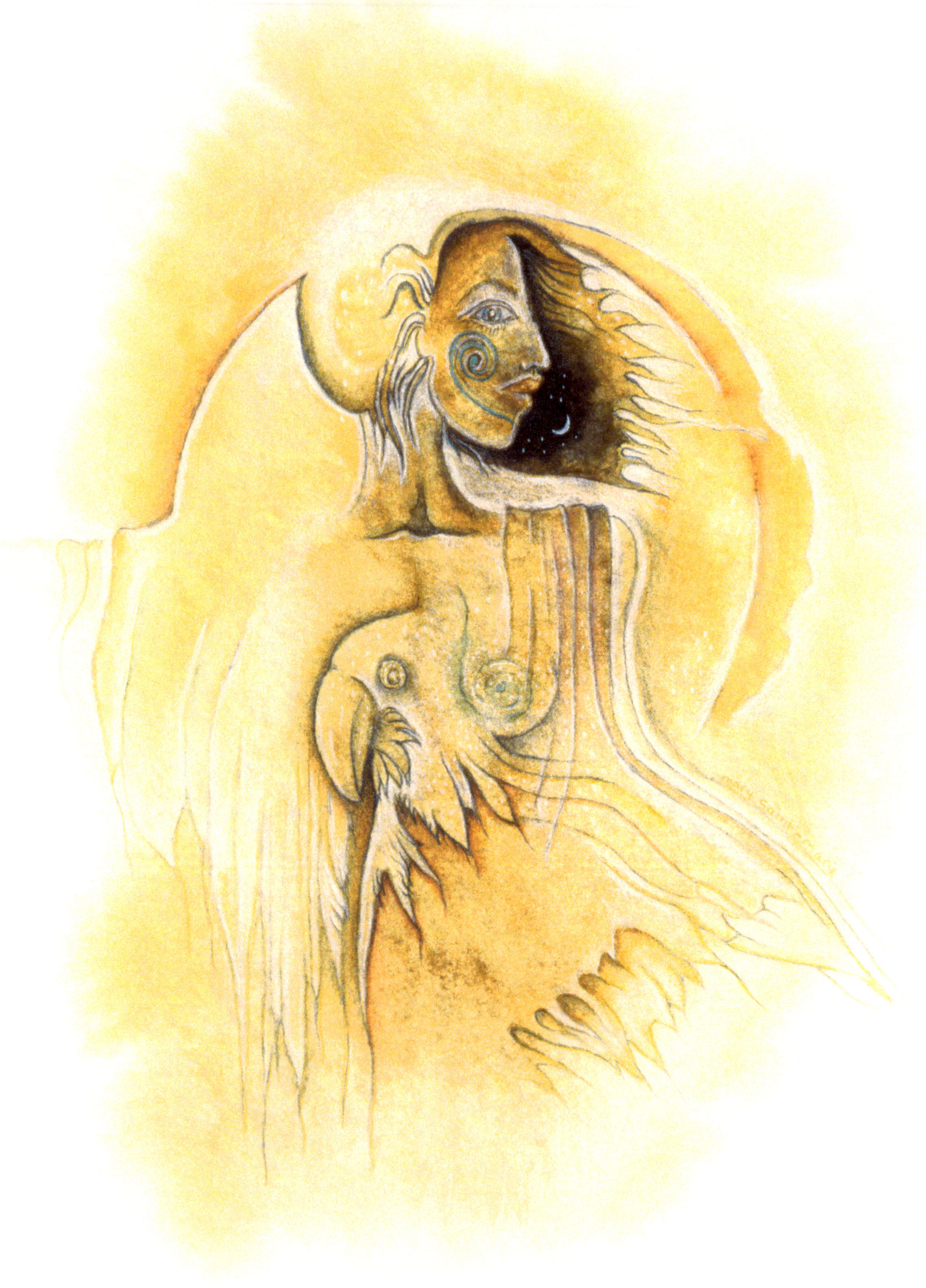

SHE remembers...
the ceremony...
with the birds...

SHE remembers...
the ceremony...
with the birds...

SHE remembers...
the Christed realms...

A visual poem announcing
purity and wholeness
as Consciousness that already Is.

SHE…is the Dancer of the Sun… and of the Moon…

SHE does dwell in sun and moon…
ever dancing yin and yang…
ever birthing stars and suns…
and universes unspeakable…

A dance emerges as visual prayer.
Balance reveals itself as joy that never
need leave the lips…yet ever sings…

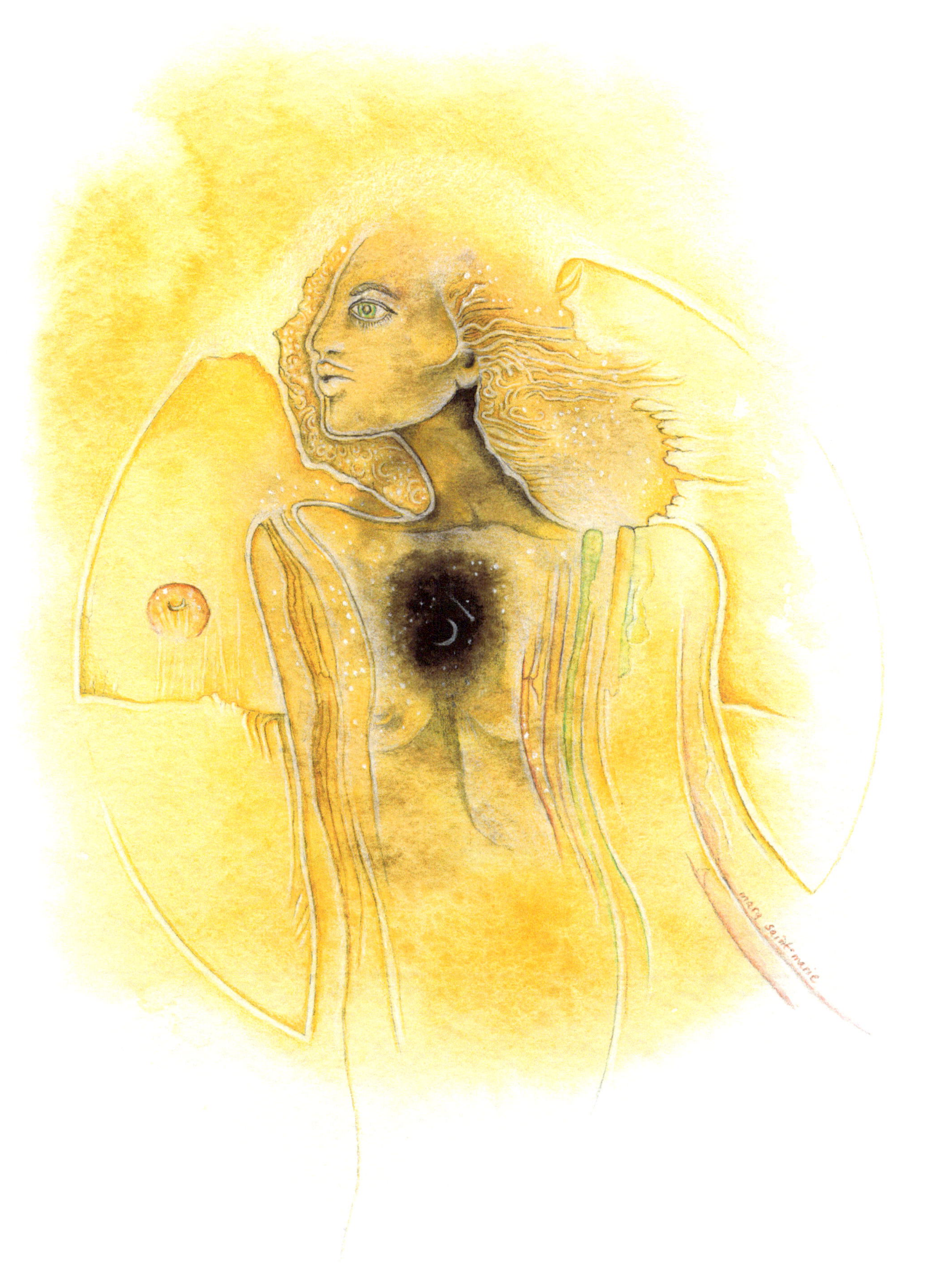
mara saint-marie

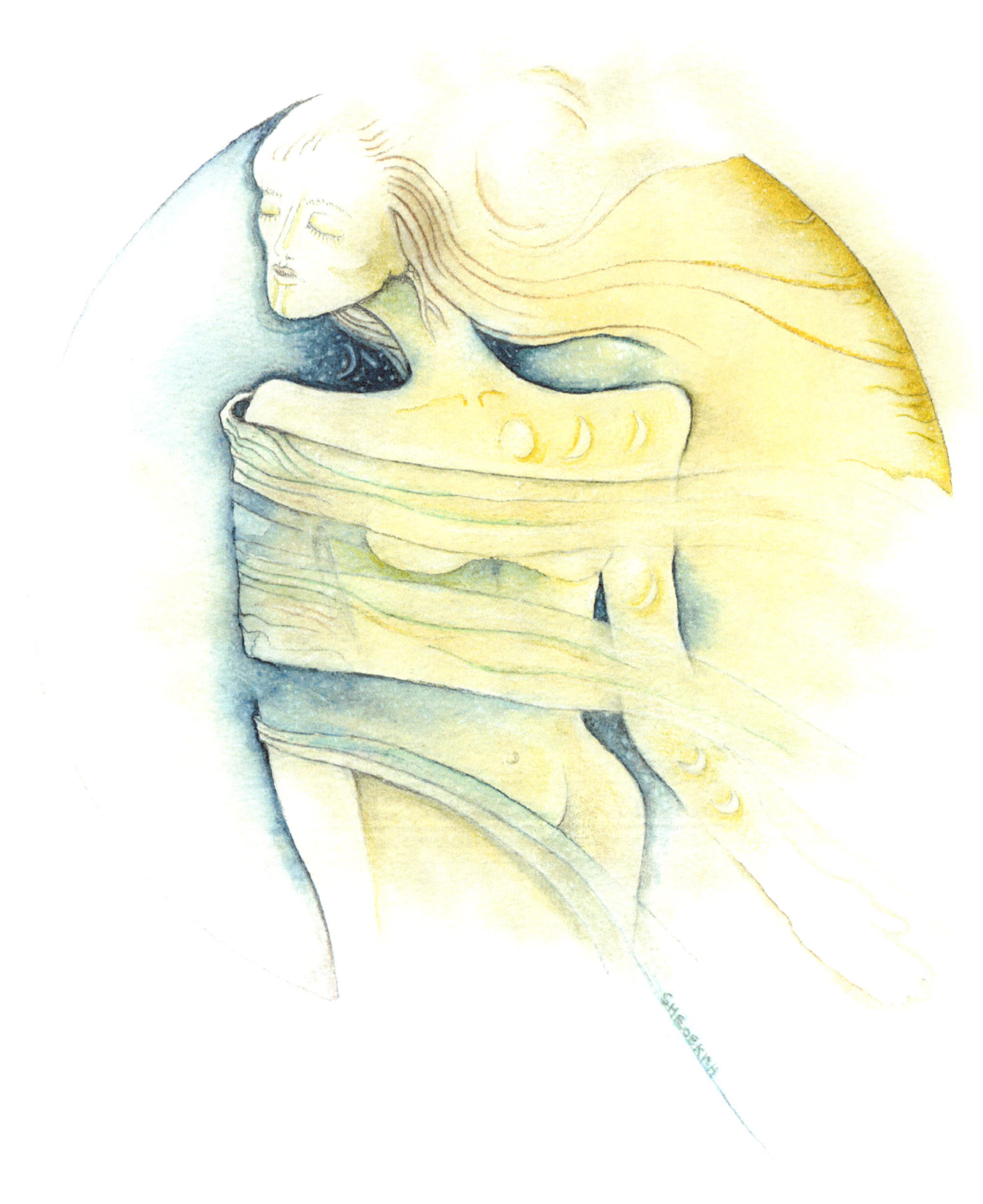

Says SHE…"O the stars am I…"

Says SHE…"O the stars am I
and the wind that blows
and the counting
of the many moons…"

In this painting is realization of the vast Infinitude that is our Being.

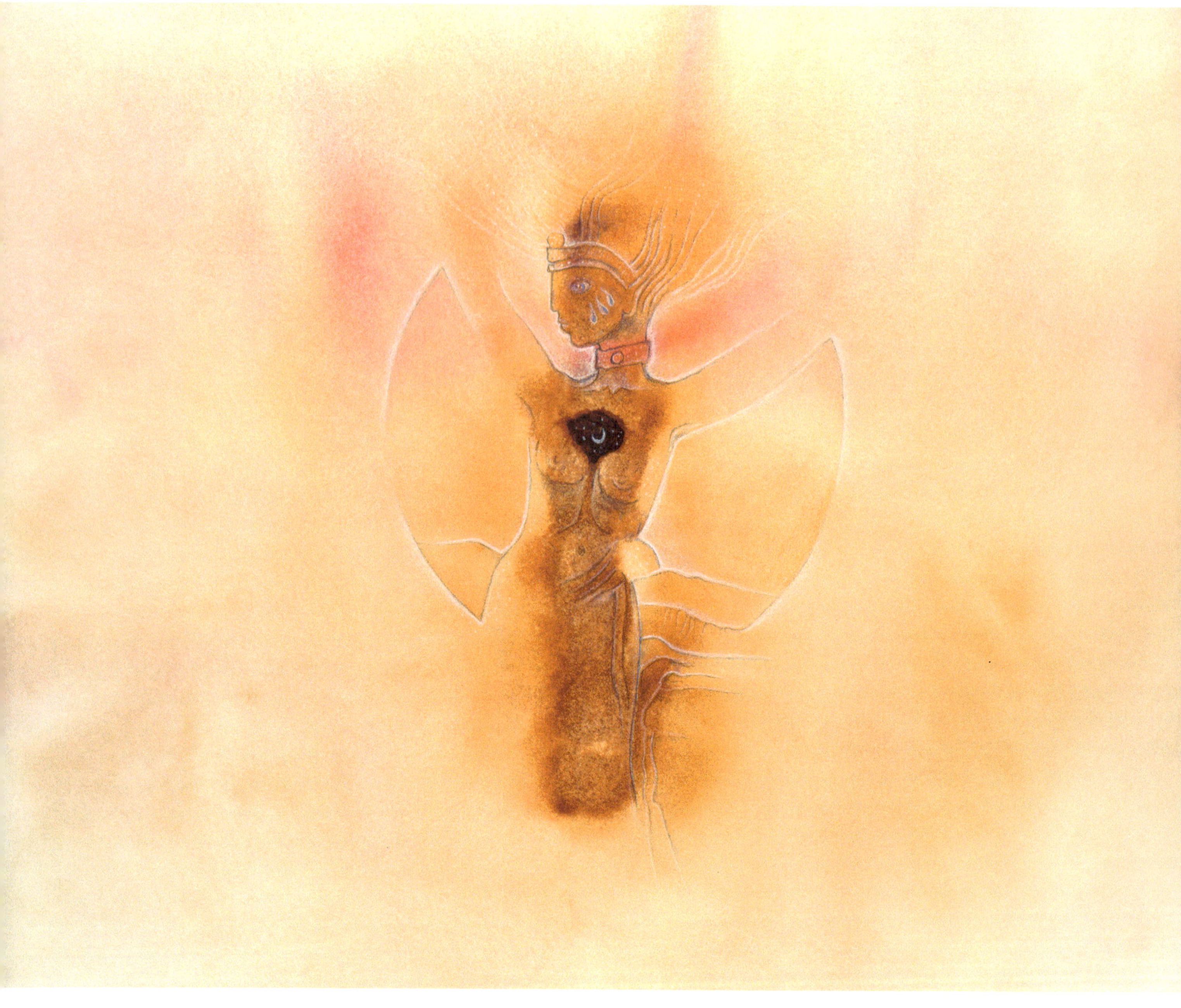

Sacred Dancer of Life-SHE

the light does dance...
galactic stars revealing ever...
the world is within...

Here we find remembrance...
of the eternal and its appearance
as sacred dancer of life.

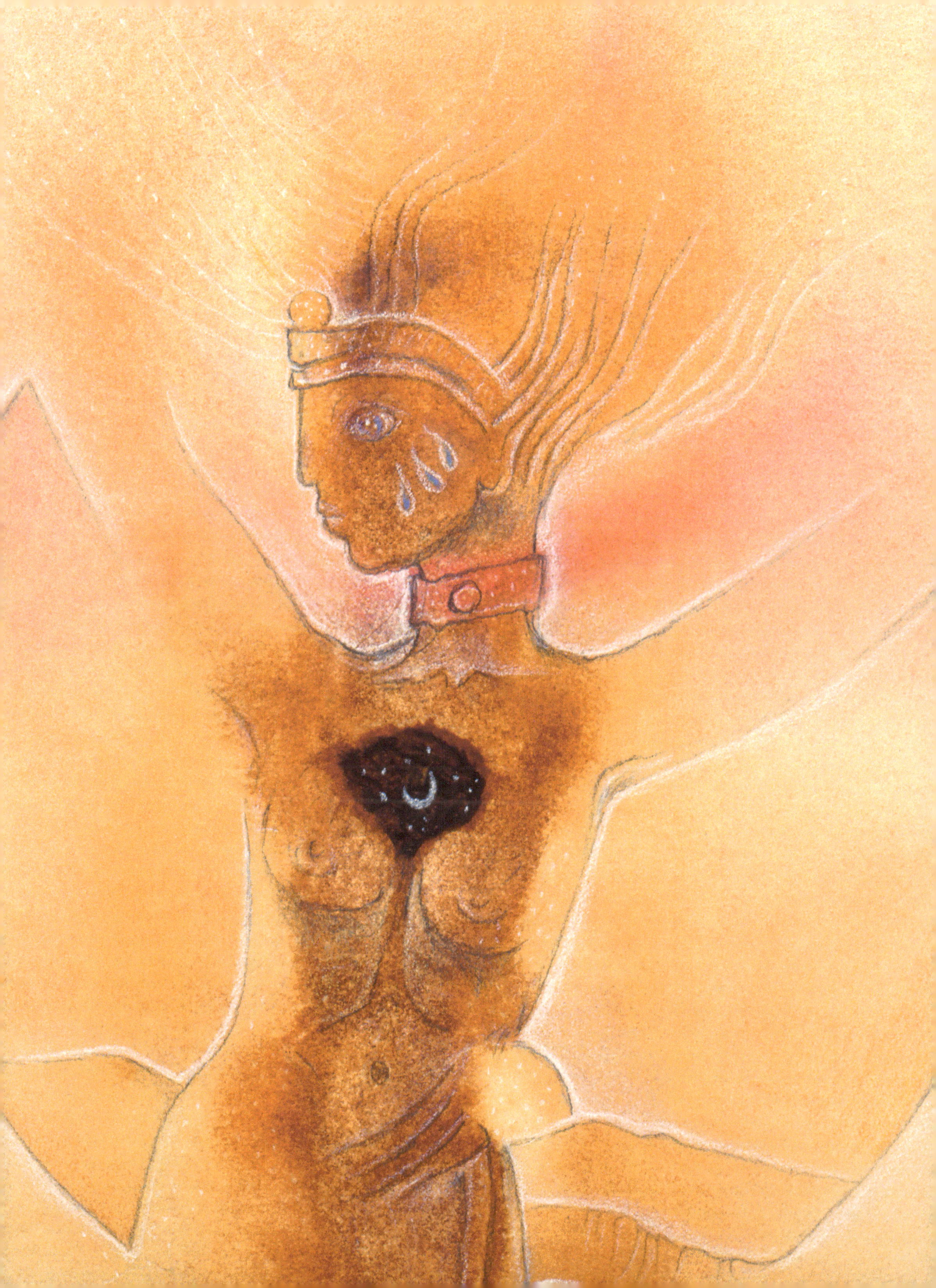

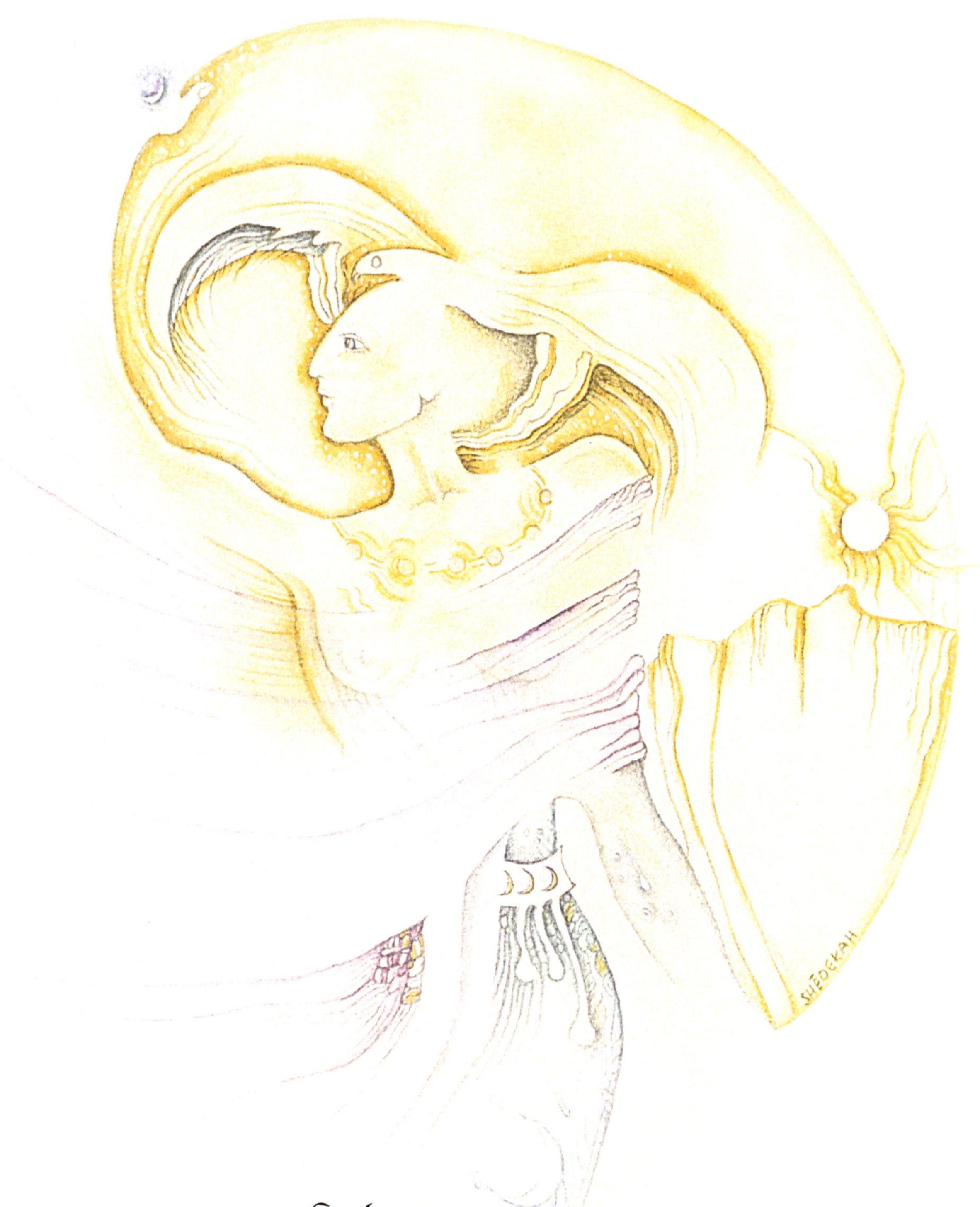

Dancer of the ever present One…

Dancer of the ever present one…
a skirt of stars…
a scarf of light…
and finder of rapture's home…

Rapture is revealed to us as an emanation of home.

SHE…who journeys with the birds…

This painting elucidates the as above…so below.
It is the invitation to be open.

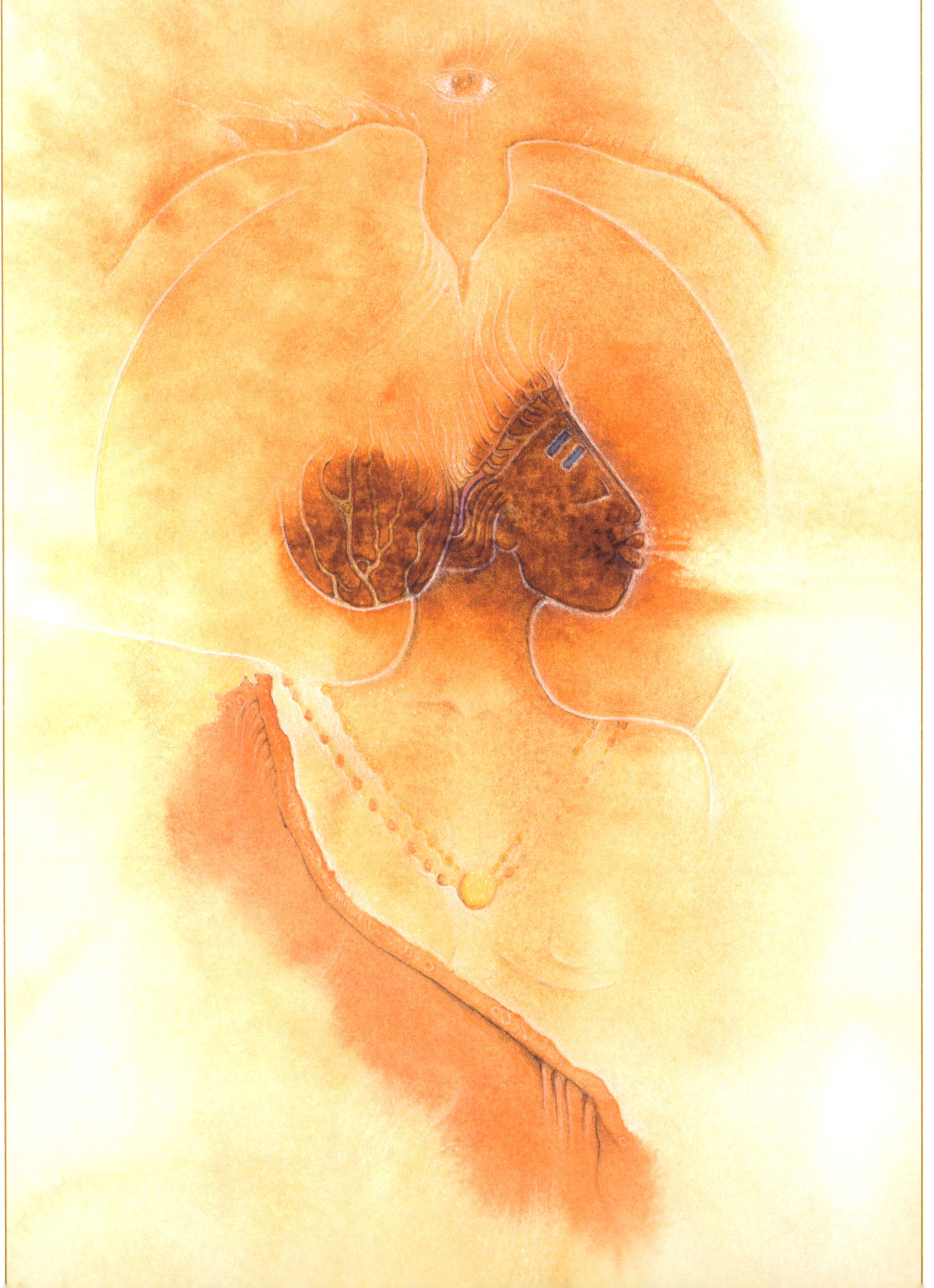

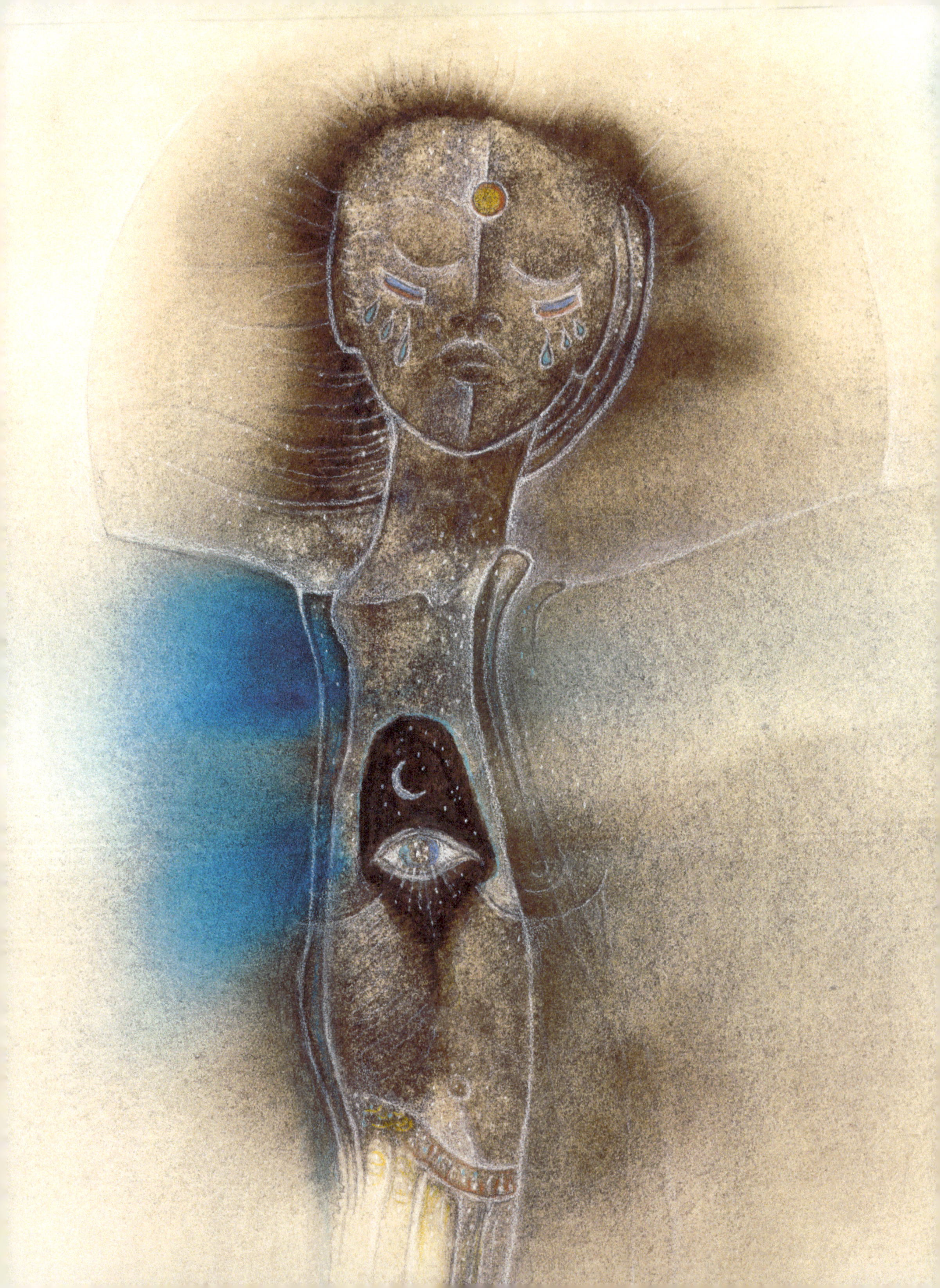

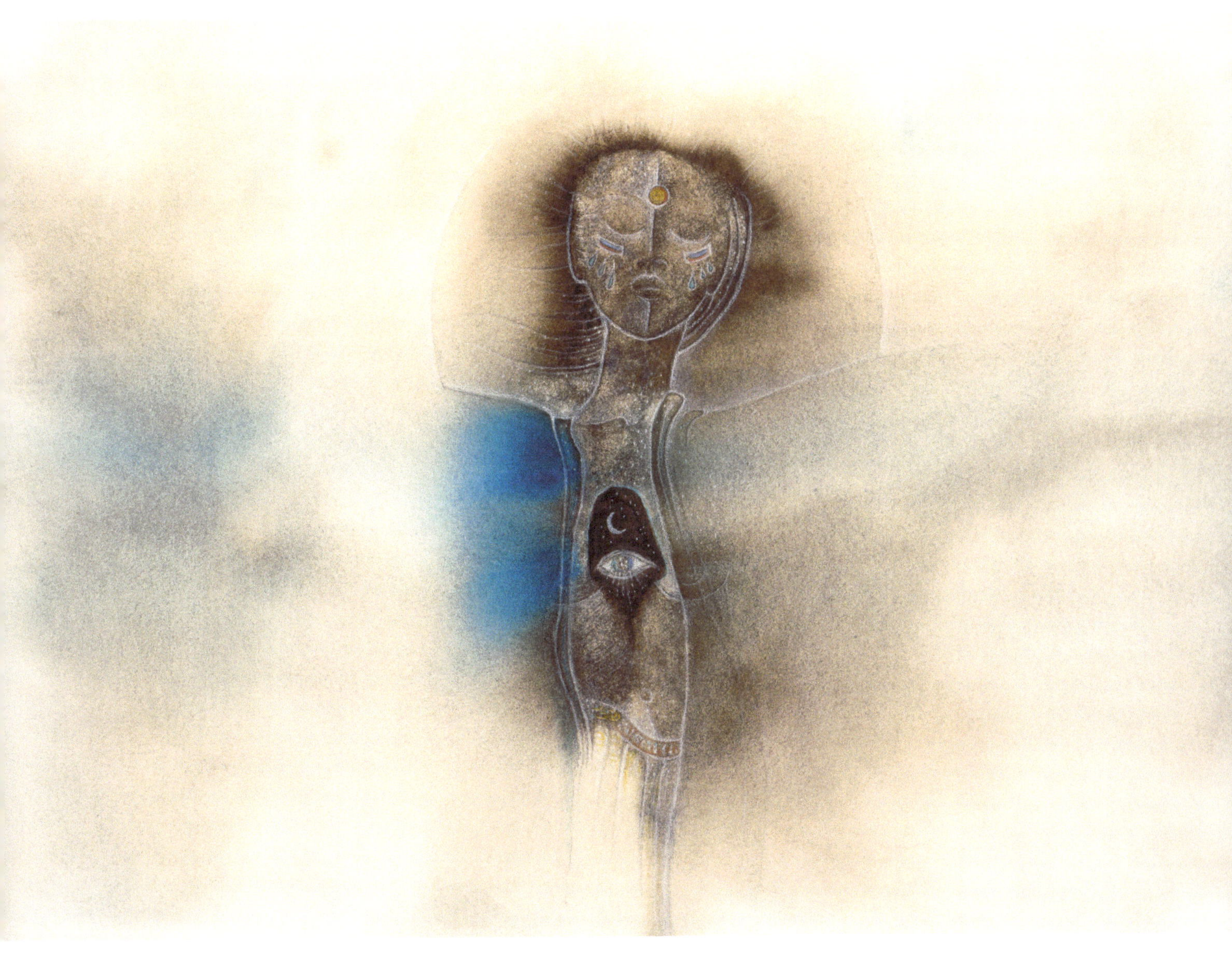

SHE...it is...who Remembers...

SHE...it is...who Remembers...
SHE is...the very web of Life...

This painting reveals the Invisible
and the visible as one.

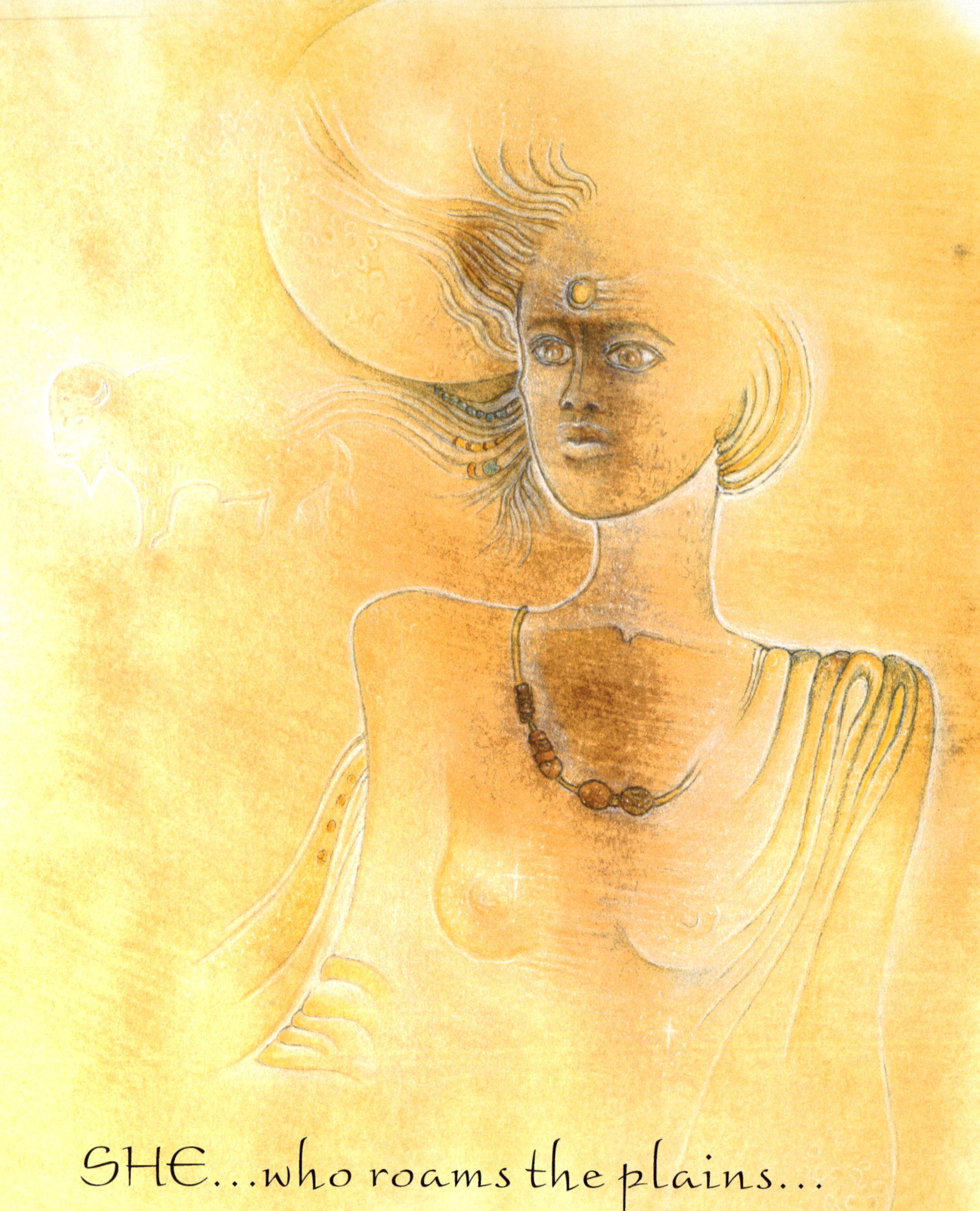

SHE…who roams the plains…

SHE…who roams the plains…
robed in Light…
and Remembers…

The garment of light stands forth
symbolizing the luminous Consciousness.

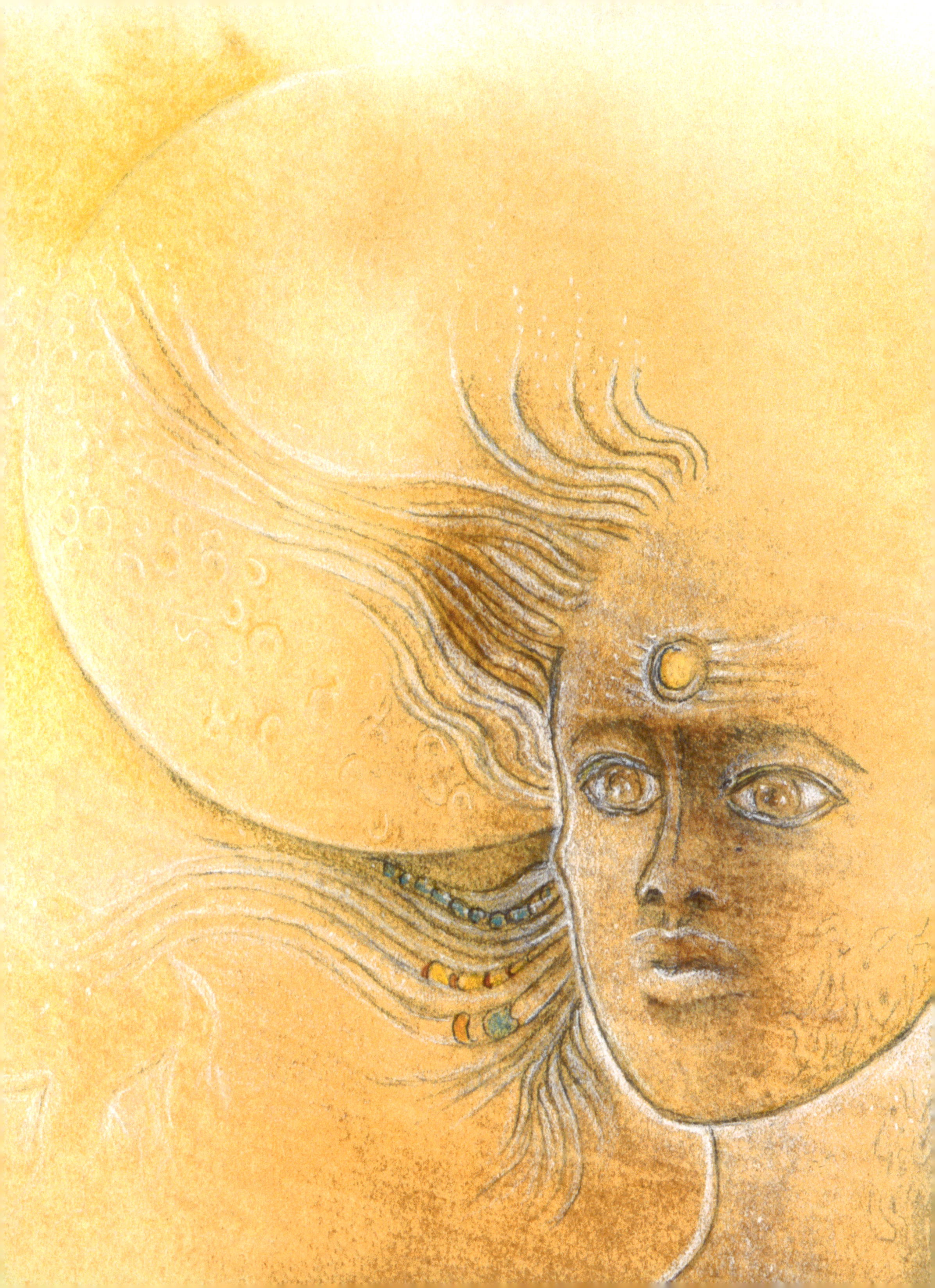

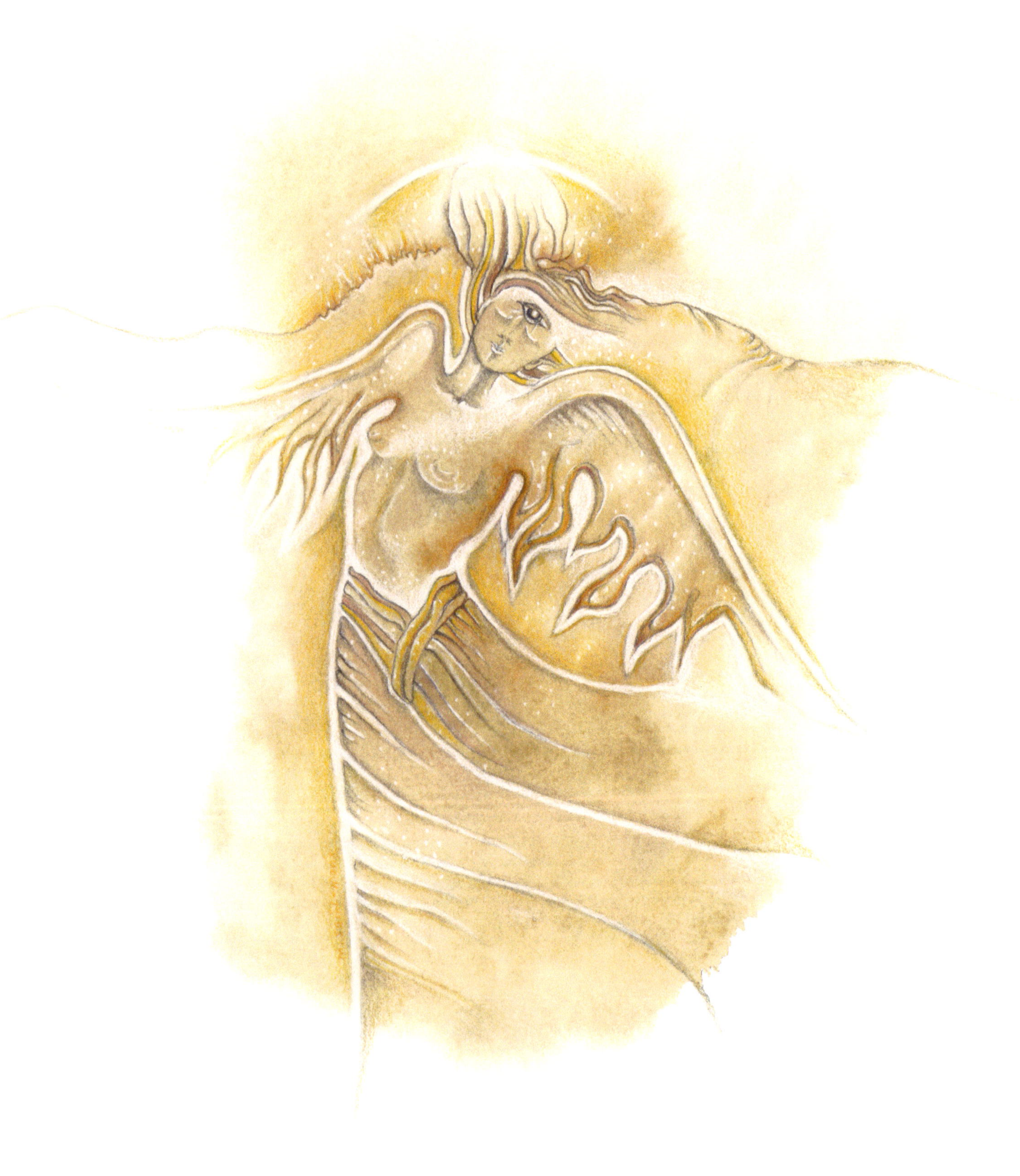

SHE…it is…who remembers her wings…

flight of illumined awareness…
flight of exaltation…

Remembering brings Awareness
in its wake.

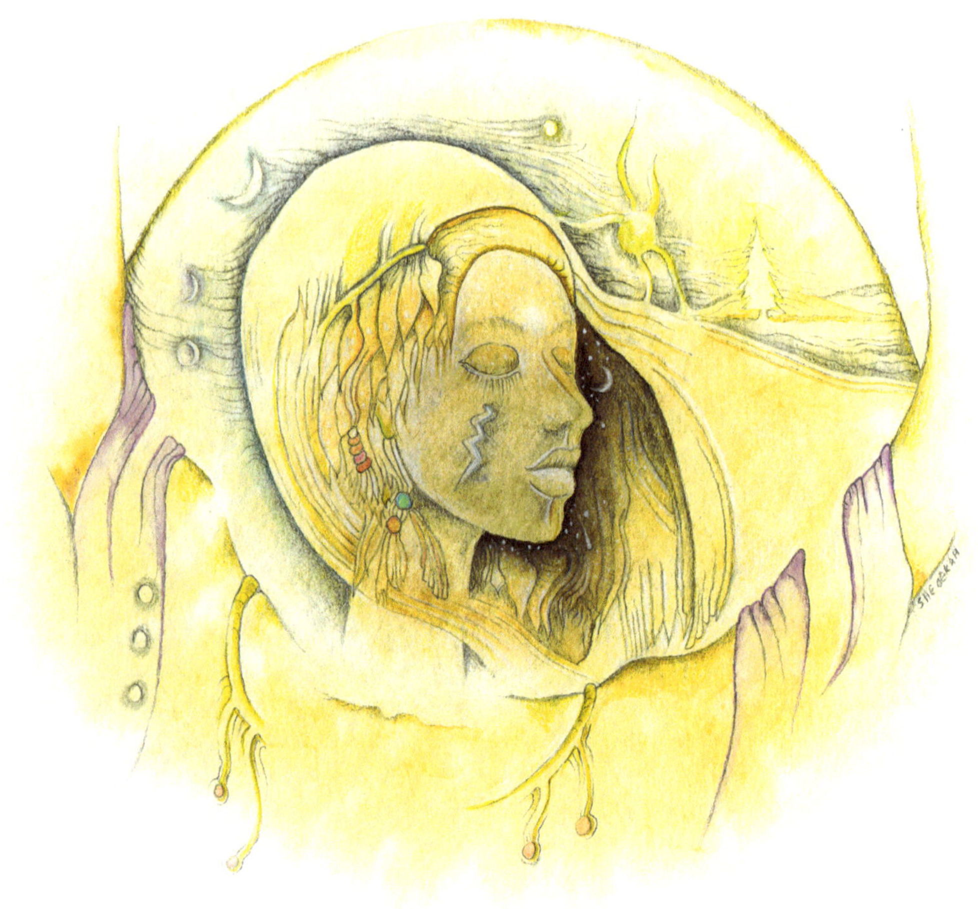

Dreams-SHE...beyond the tree...

Dreams-SHE...
beyond the tree...
the sun...and
the many moons...

Here SHE remembers her starry origins.
Here SHE realizes Self as Spirit Itself.

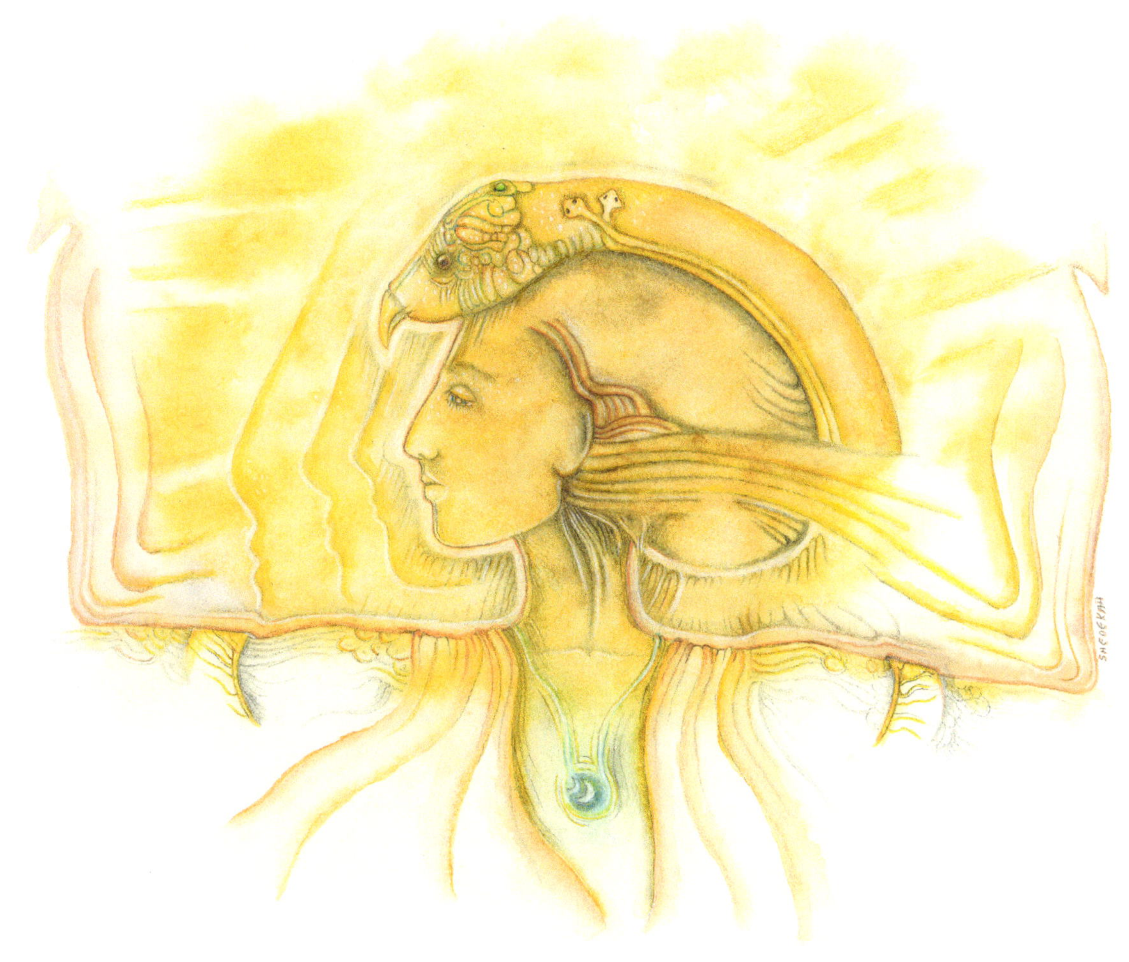

SHE…who dances…with the Inner One…

SHE…who dances…
with the Inner One…
robed in golden light…

In this reflection…the treasure…
Eternal's grace of withinness.

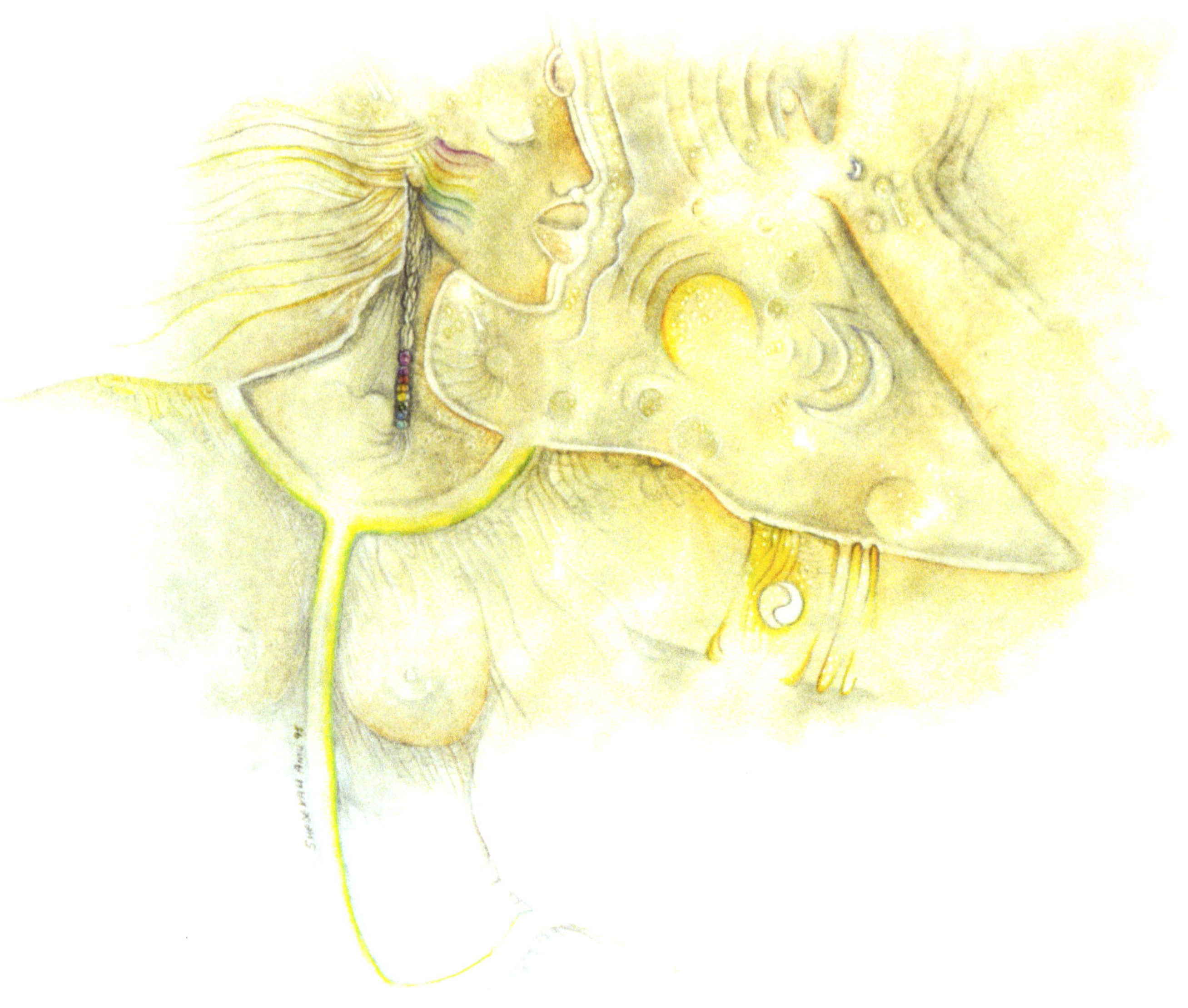

HER-dance of the Rainbow Nation

Her-dance of the Rainbow Nation
does call the very elements
and everywhere is seen the yin and yang
and singing it is heard from in the skies…

This painting is a visual image of equality.
The very universe does sing the law of balance.

HER-dance...
with the stars...and the moon...

Imaged is the grand embrace
of our infinite being.

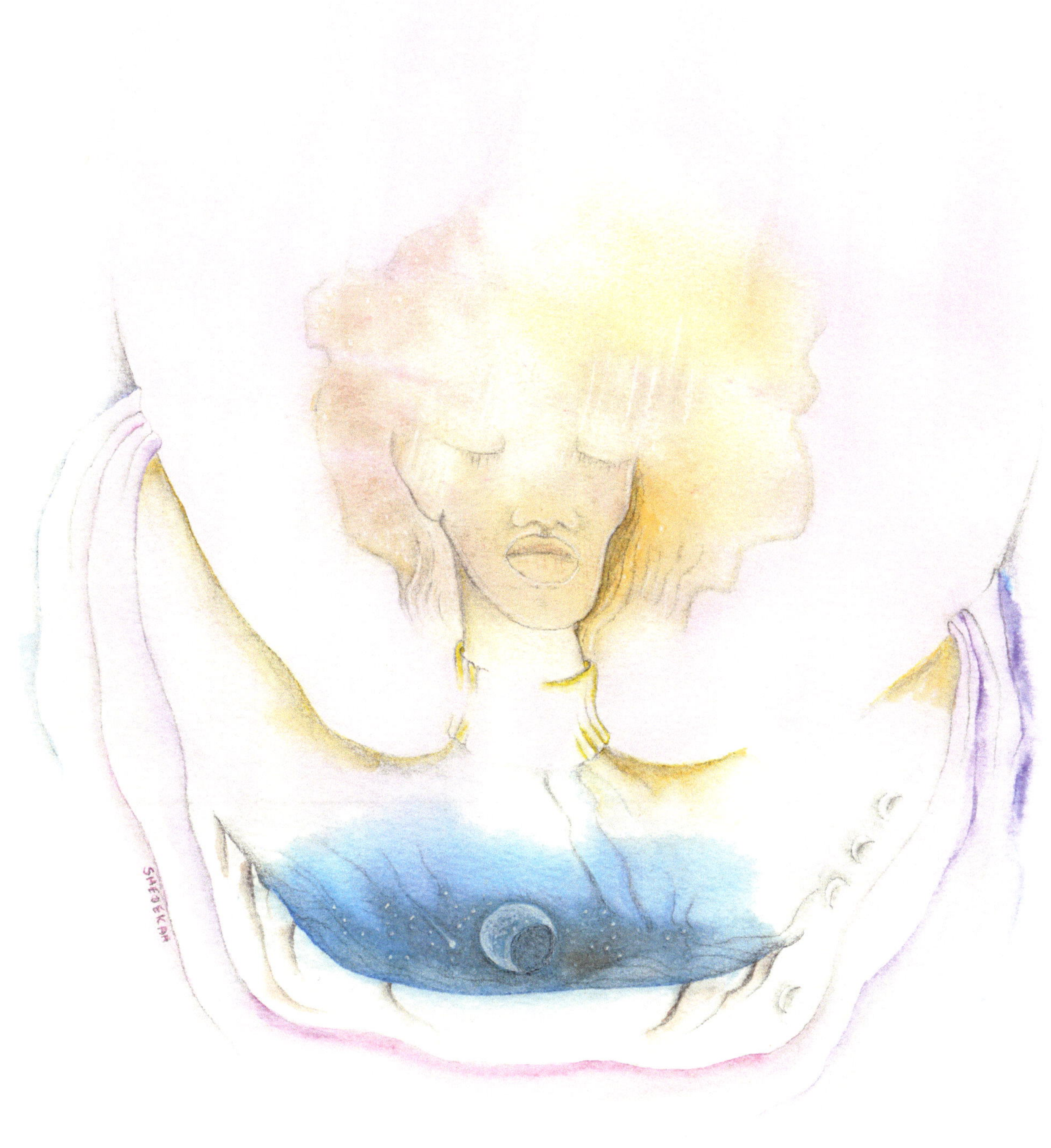

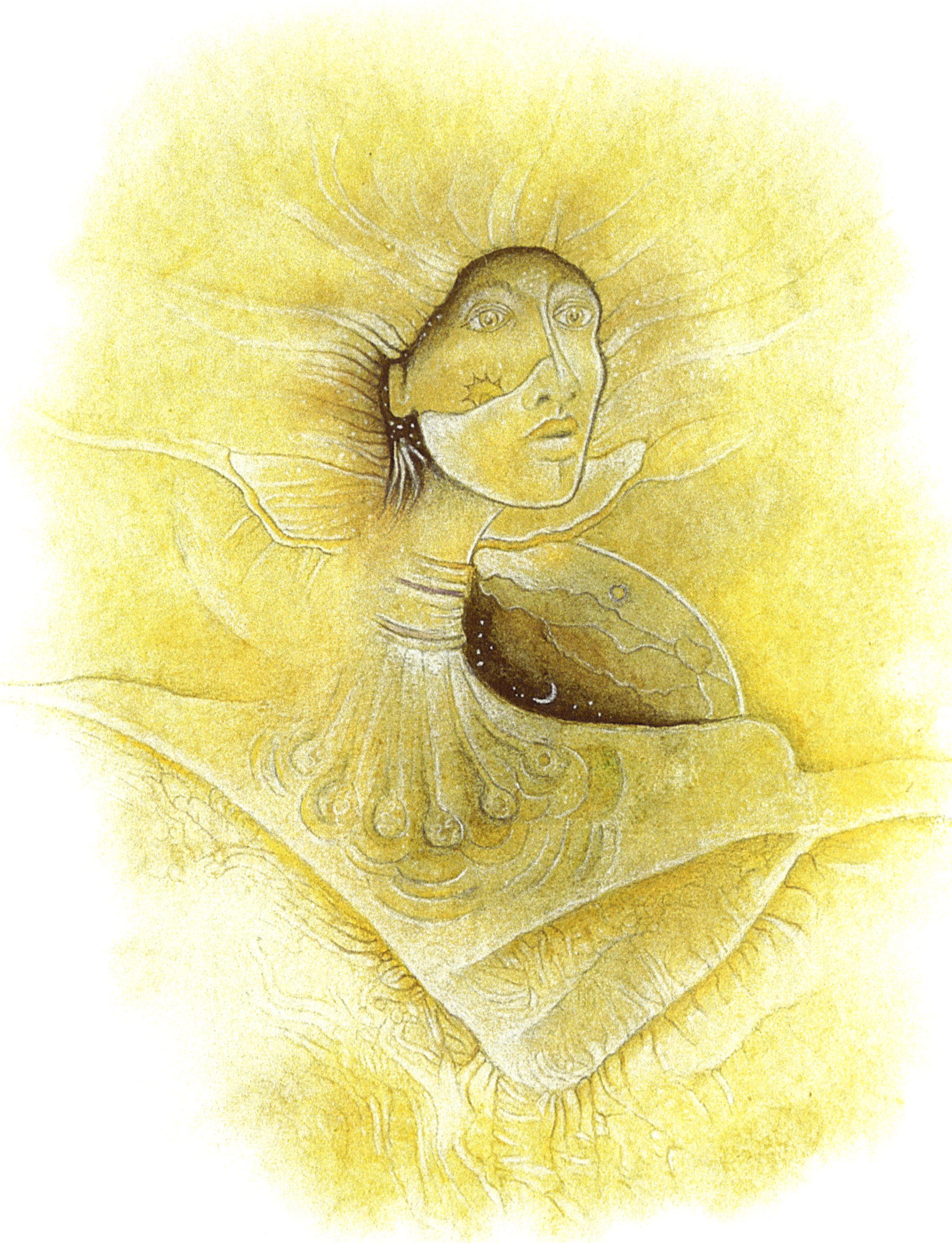

night-SHE adorned for dawn's coming...

night-SHE adorned
for dawn's coming...

open...ever...
to the rising sun...

Seen here is adornment as
symbolic surrender to the
light that IS.

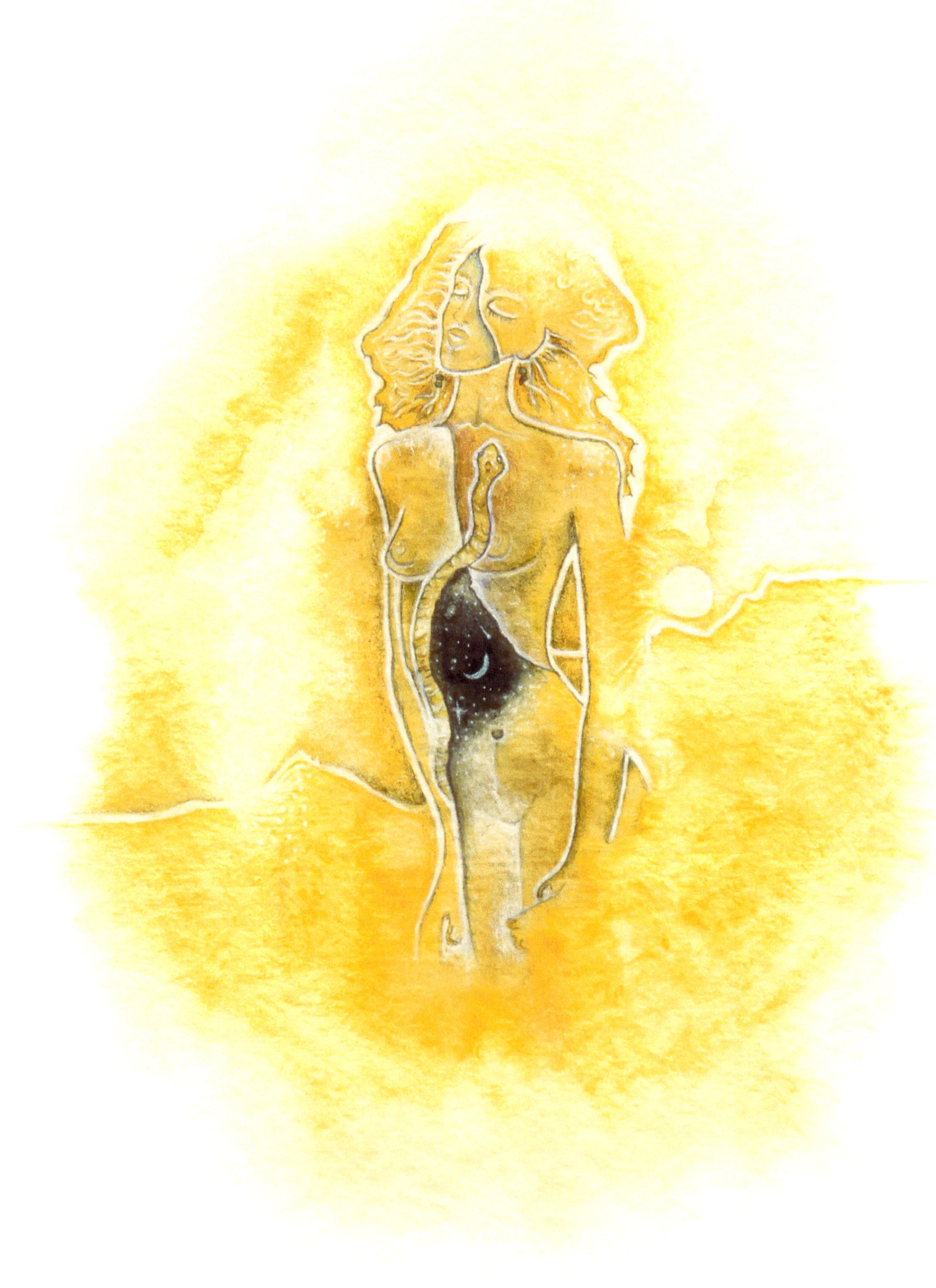

SHE…remembers…
the dance of the Beloved

SHE…remembers…
the dance of the beloved…

SHE dances everywhere….
with everyone…

Here the beloved
does dance
as serpent wisdom.

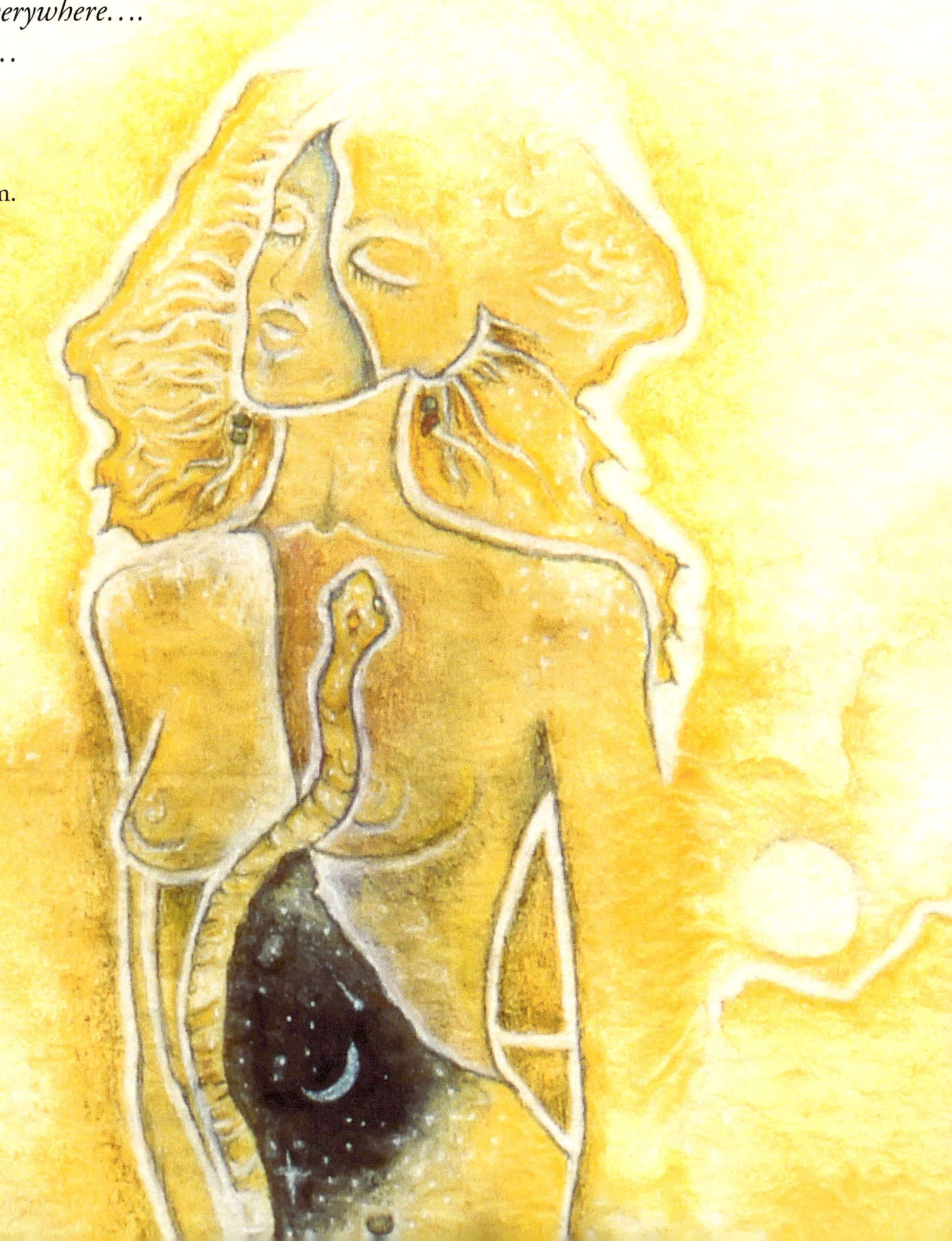

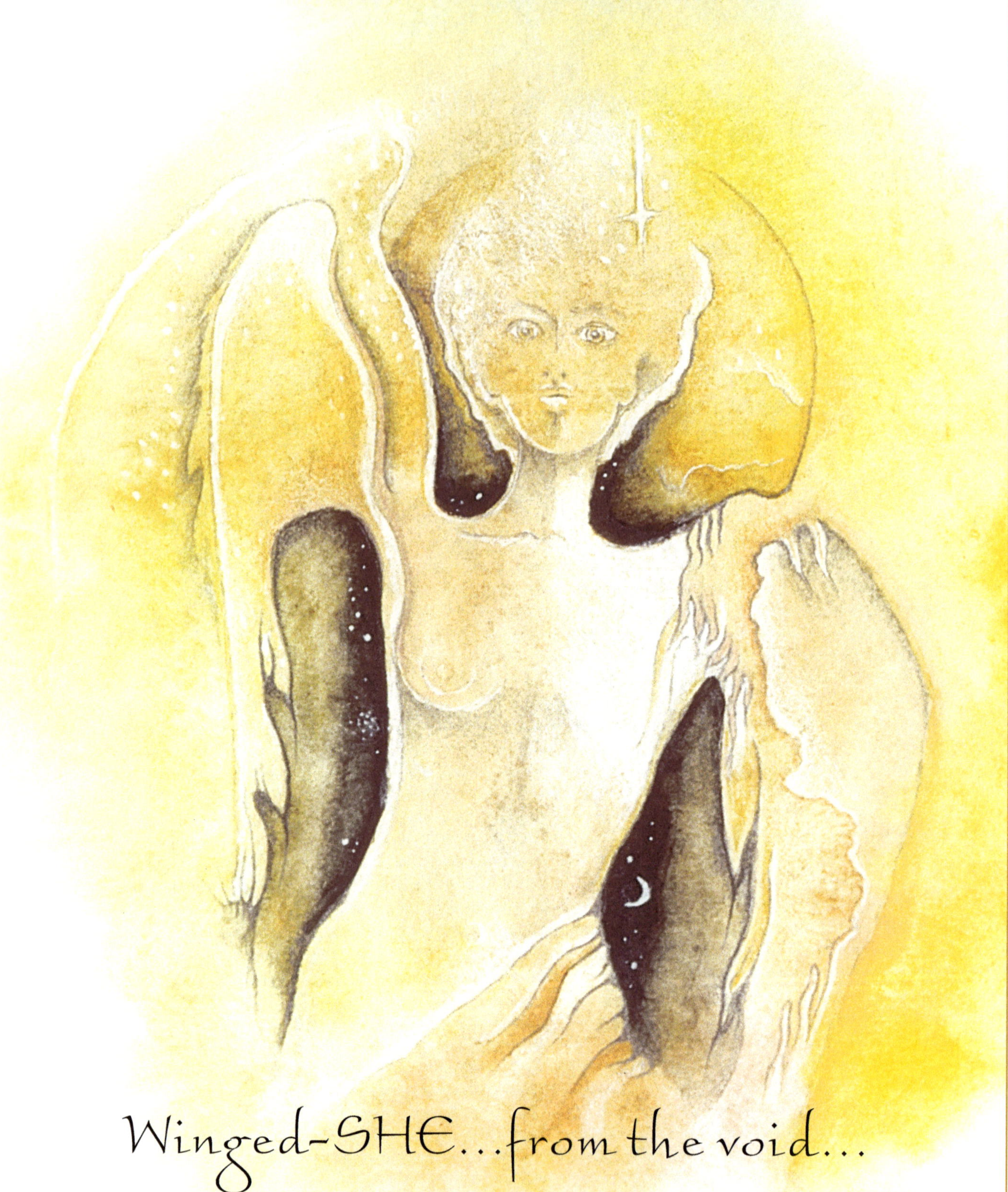

Winged-SHE...from the void...

winged-SHE...appears...
manifest and clad in light...

The feminine in form takes flight from
Unformed regions spreading love.

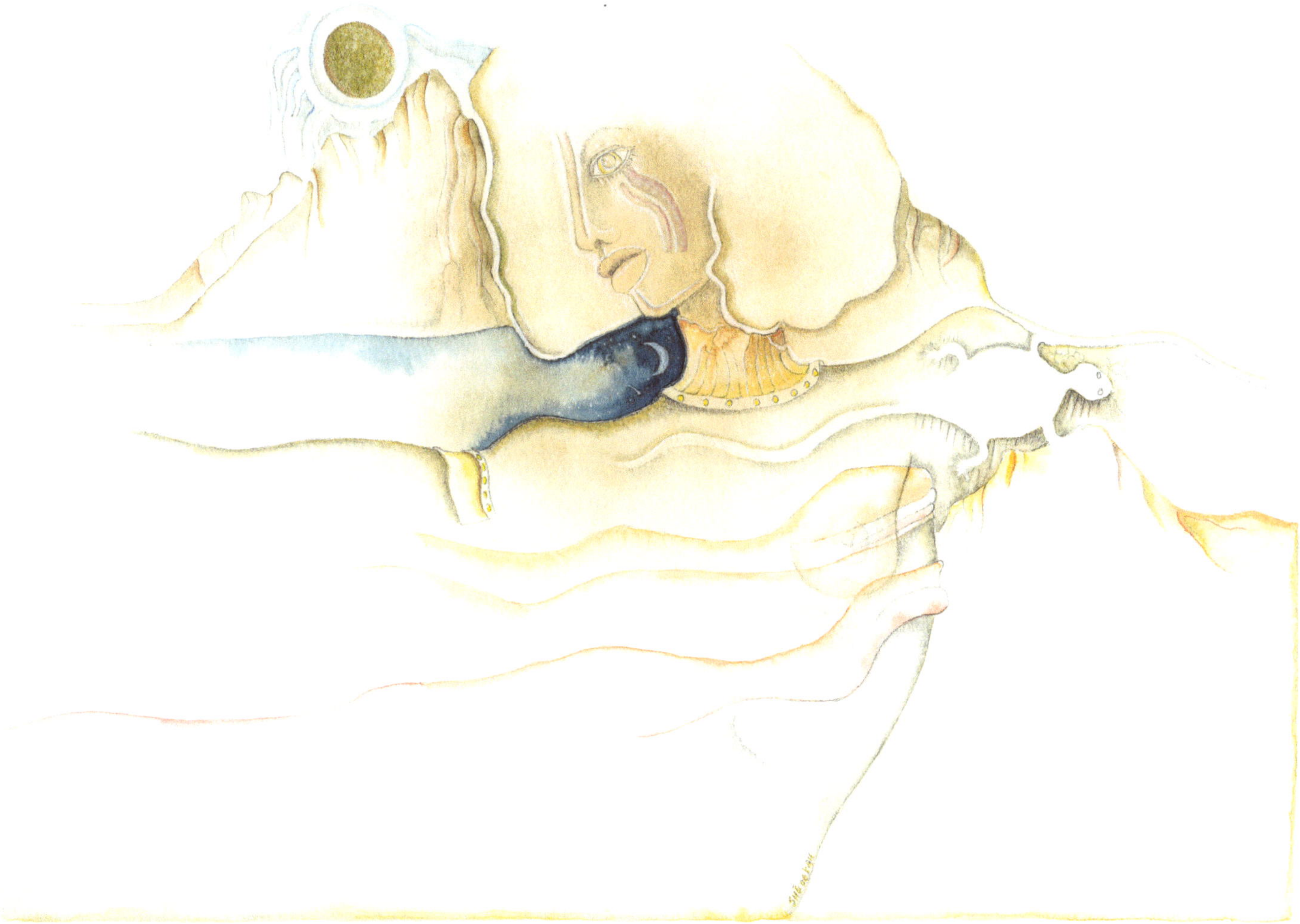

SHE…of the landscape's ancient lore…

SHE…of the…landscape's ancient lore…
revealing there is but One…
mountain, lizard, moon and SHE…

Here is painted the story
of the revelation of Oneness.
There is no other.

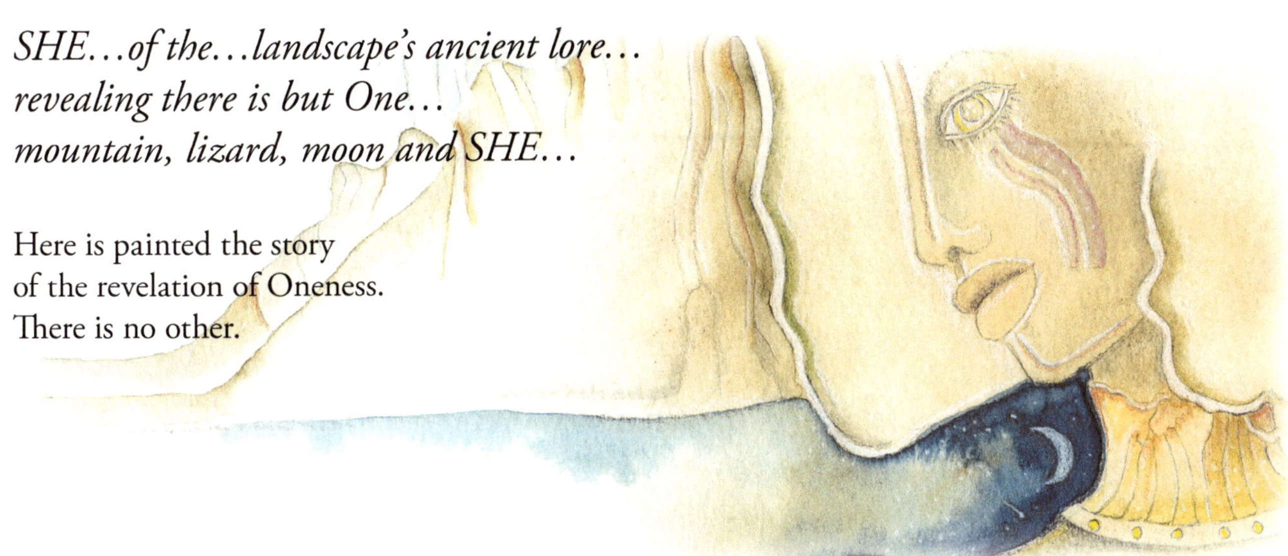

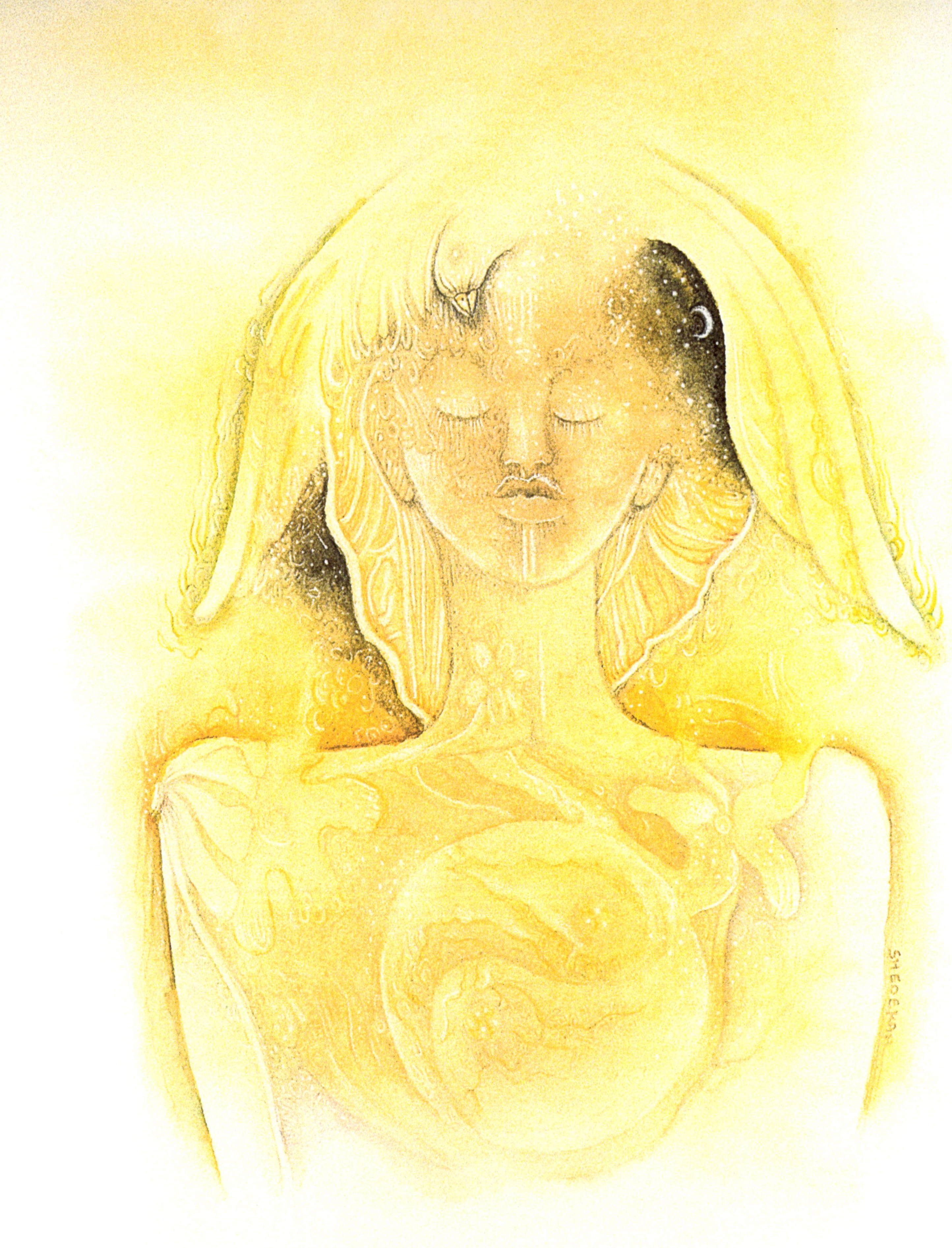

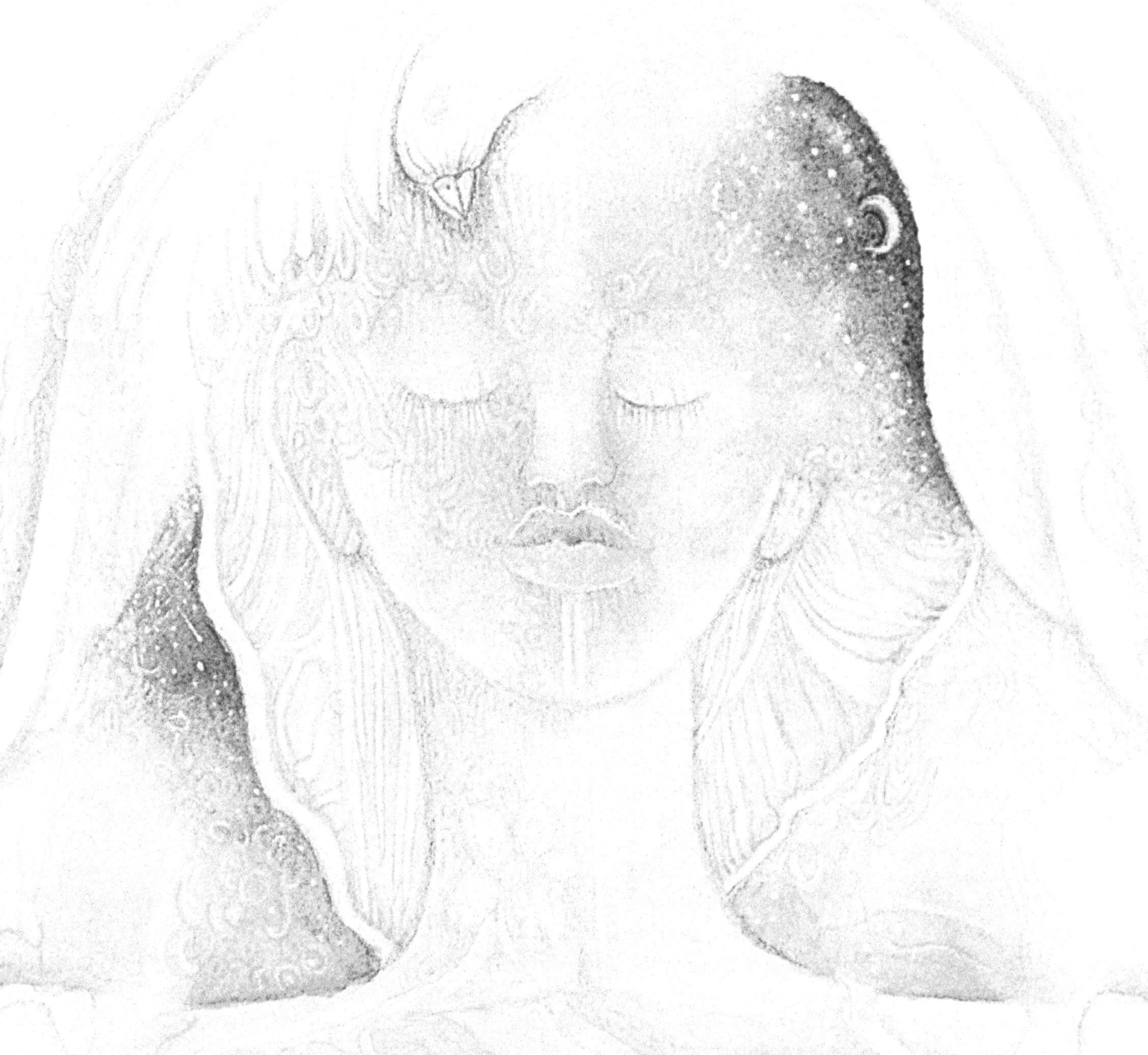

Dreams-SHE...of the Ancient Way

Dreams-SHE...of the Ancient Way...
where purity plays...
where flowers bloom...
where love does light the way...

Awakeness is envisioned and lived.

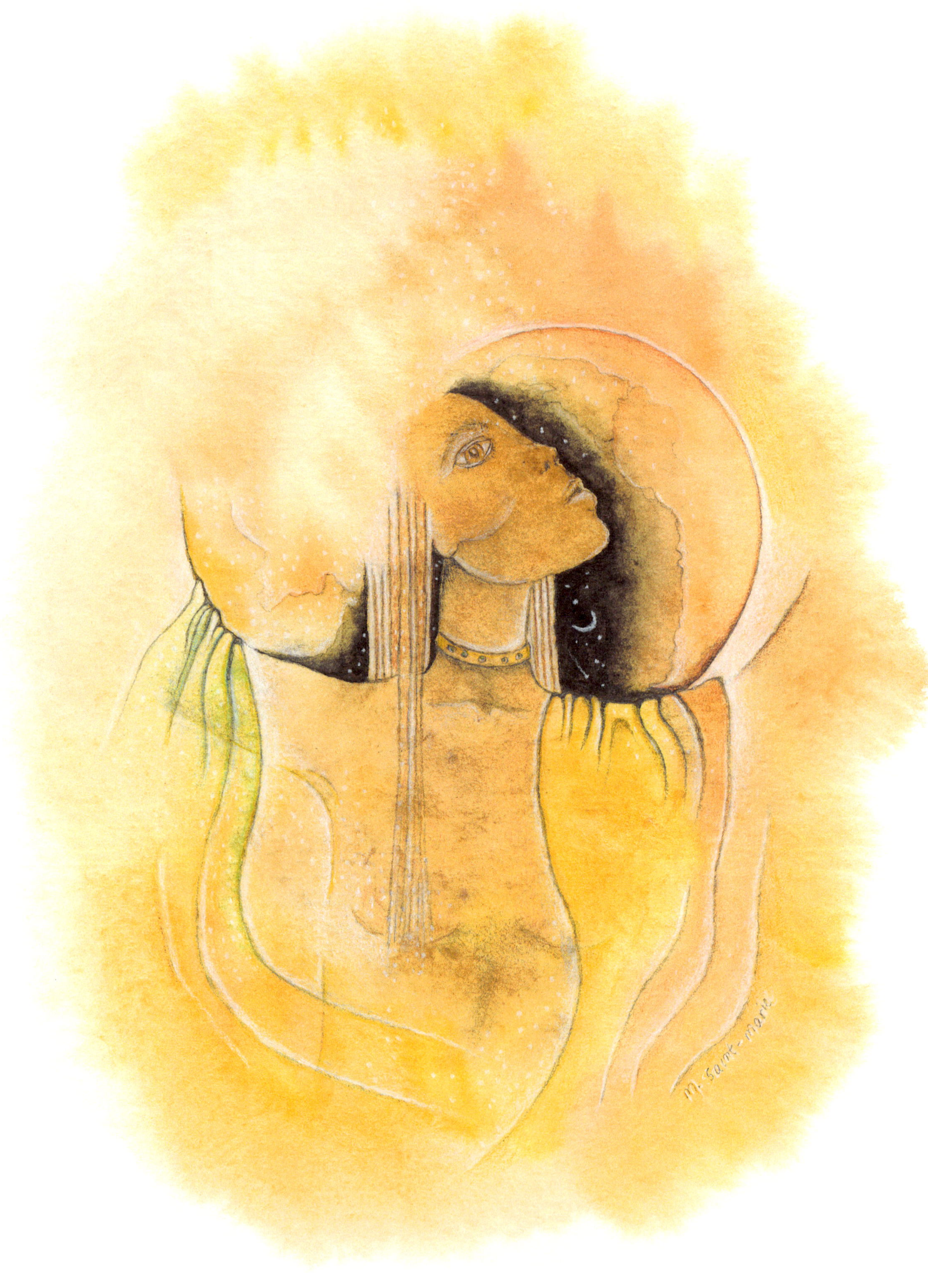
M. Saint-marie

Ancient Passage

upon the waves of light…
exists an ancient passage…

here…joy inexorable does
play the heaven chords…

Sages and wisdom speakers have always pointed to this Ancient Passage which resides ever and always in our very own Consciousness.

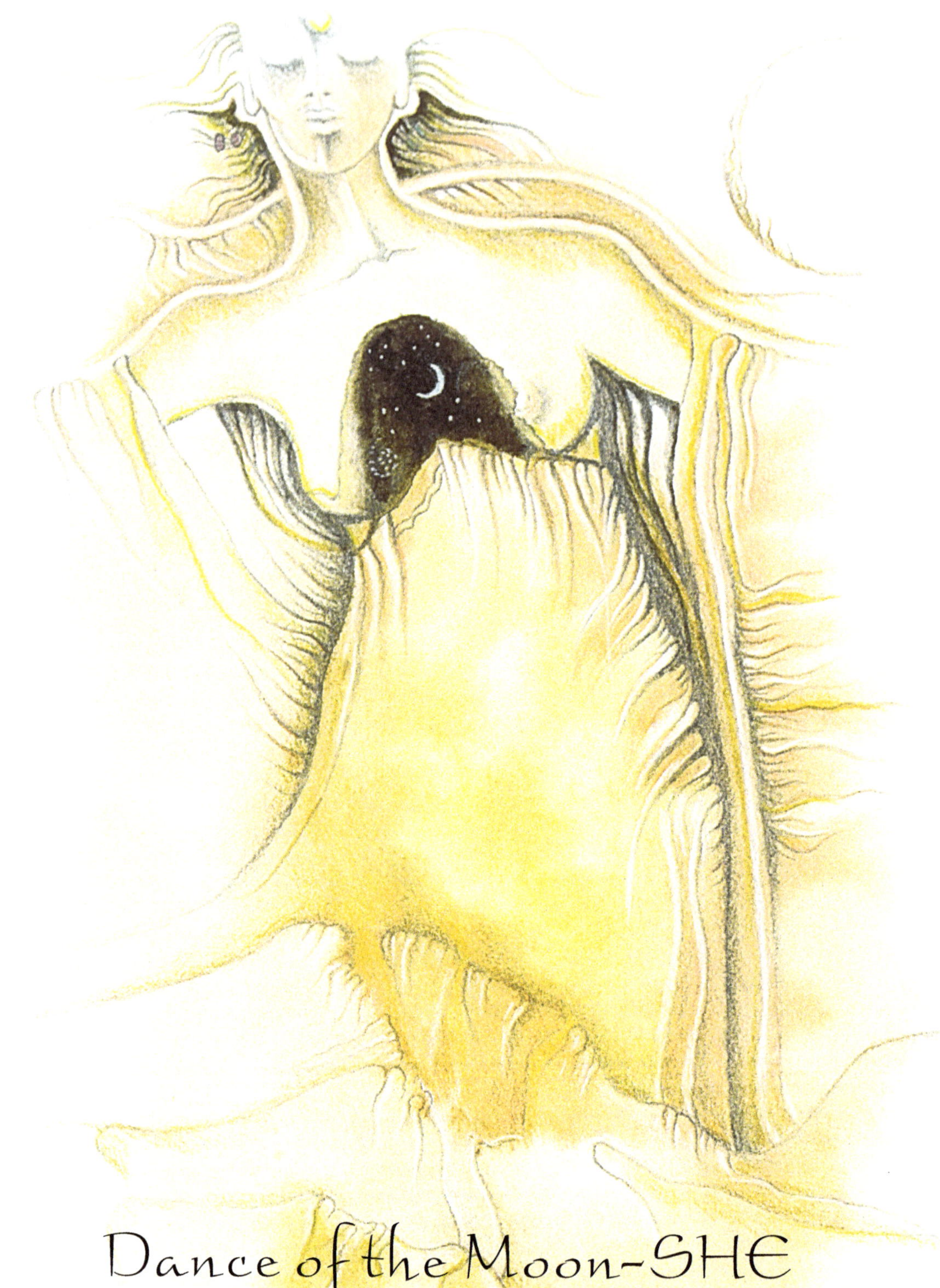

Dance of the Moon-SHE

in her heart does dwell the love…
she listens for its call…

Dance of the Moon-SHE portrays
the feminine values and principles
that exist in the yin/yang world.

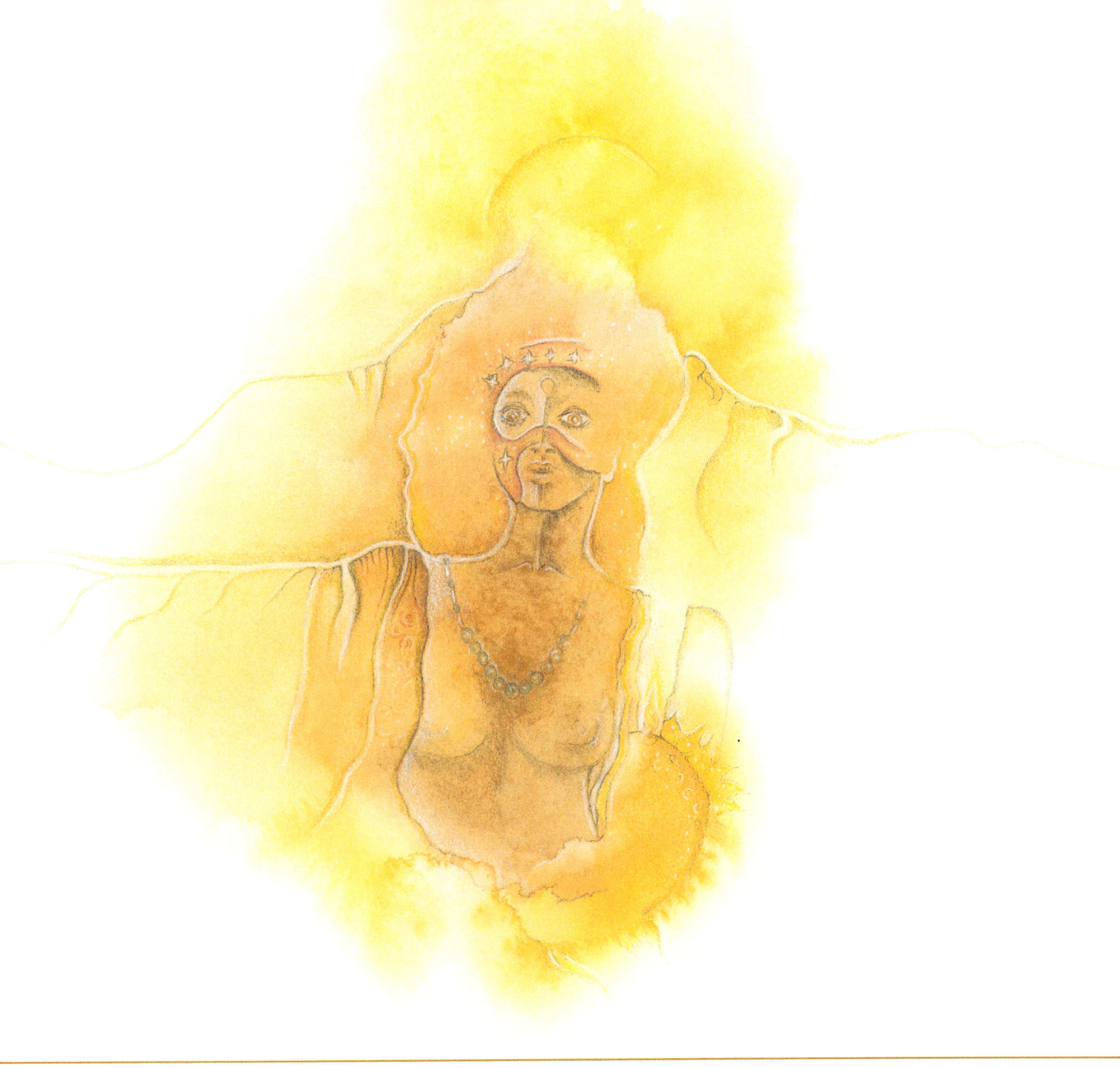

Mask of a Thousand Stars

o breasted one…
wearing now…
mask of a thousand stars…

Woman dons beauty in a mask of stars.

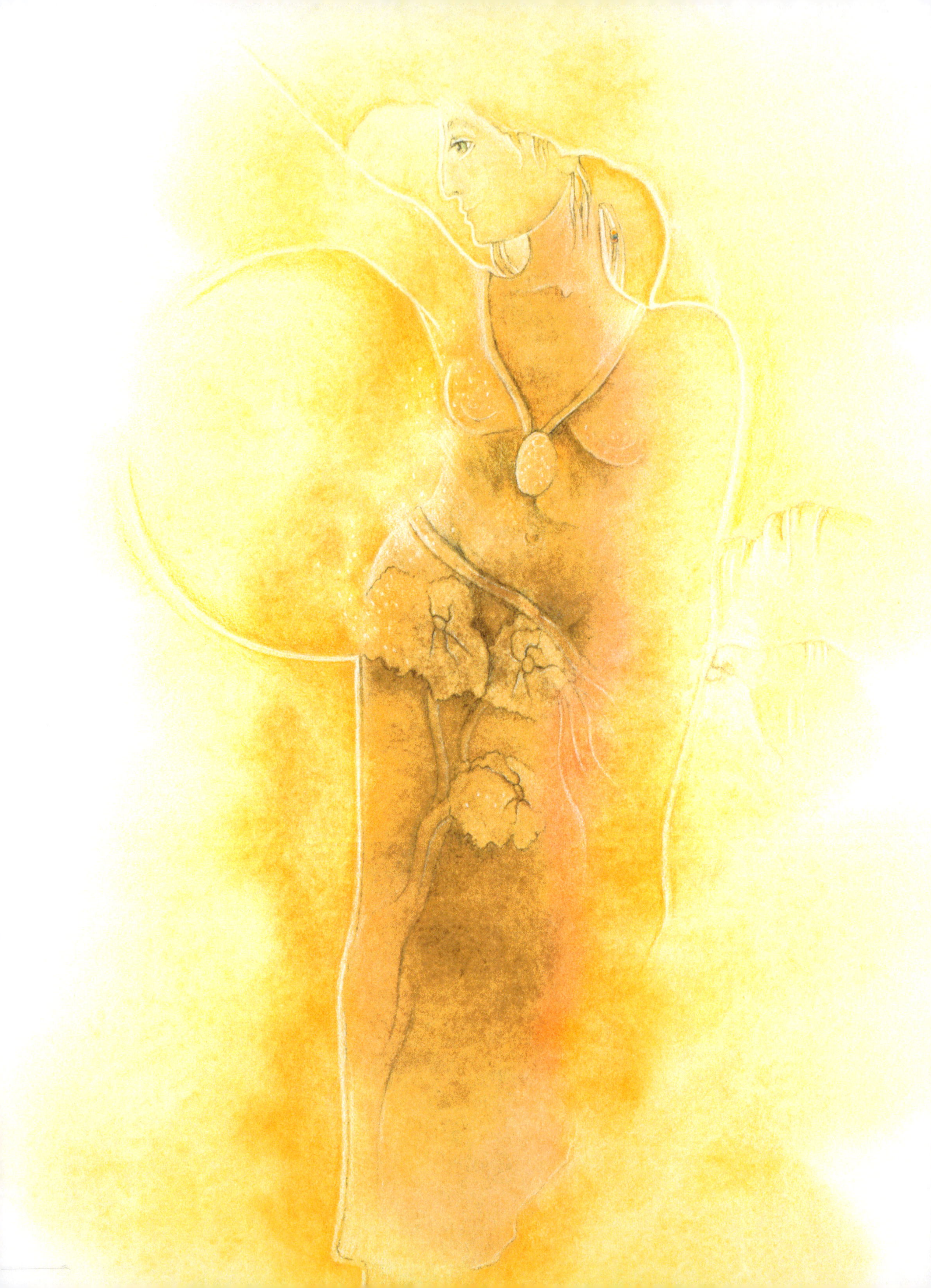

SHE...in ceremony...with the rising sun...

SHE...in ceremony...
with the rising sun...
tells ever...
the story of beauty...

Beauty's essence is voiced in the visual poetry.

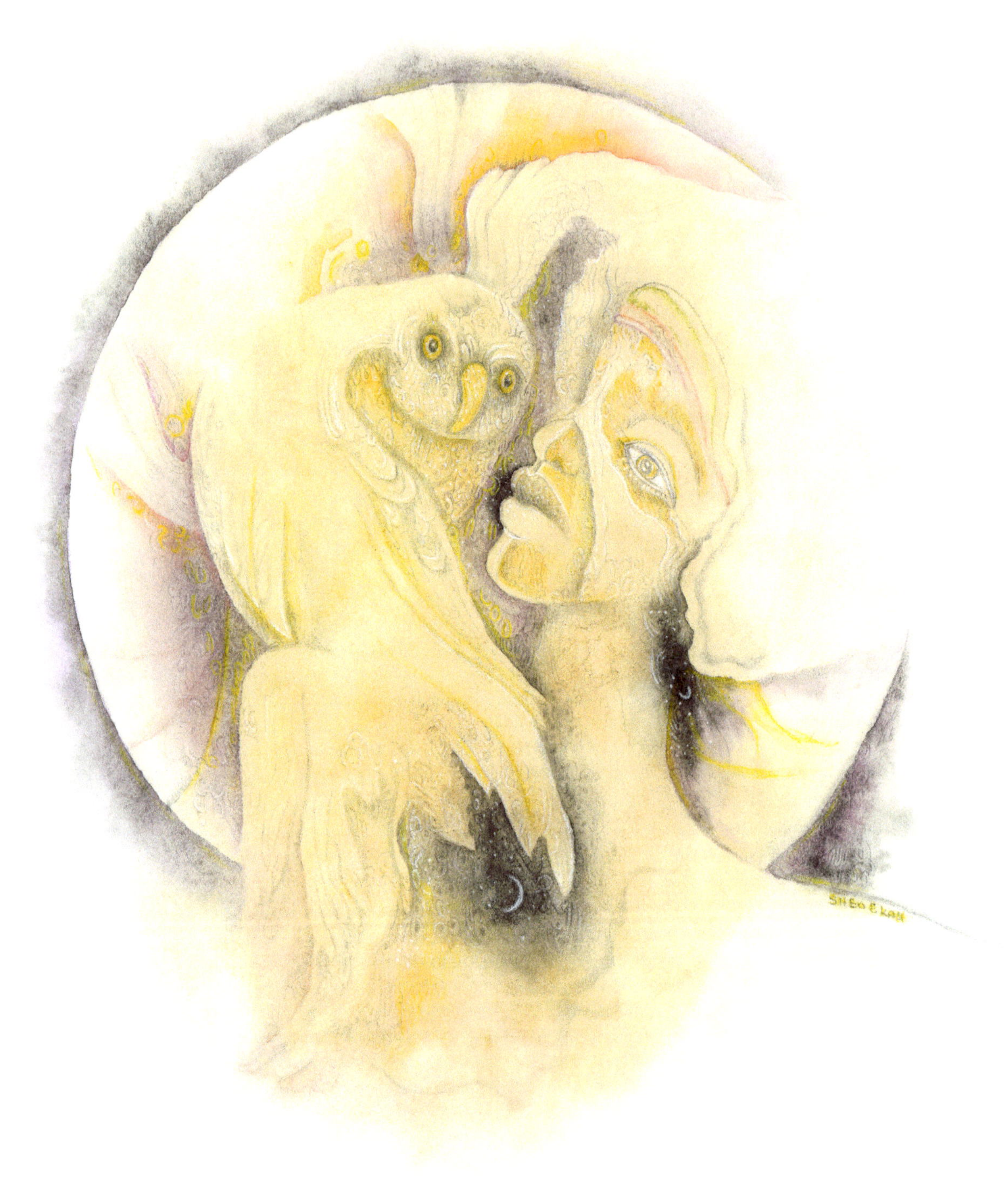
SHEO E KAN

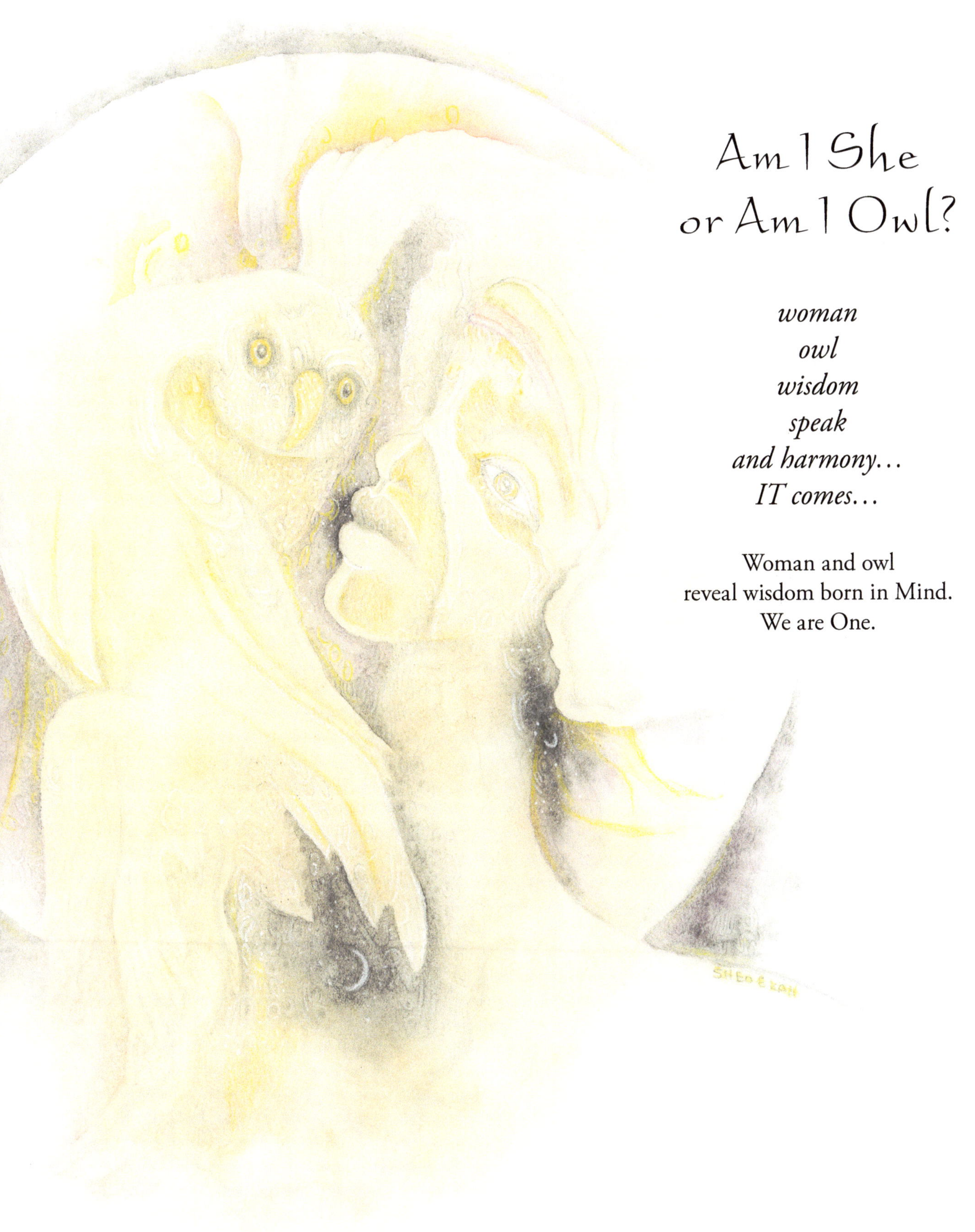

Am I She or Am I Owl?

woman
owl
wisdom
speak
and harmony…
IT comes…

Woman and owl
reveal wisdom born in Mind.
We are One.

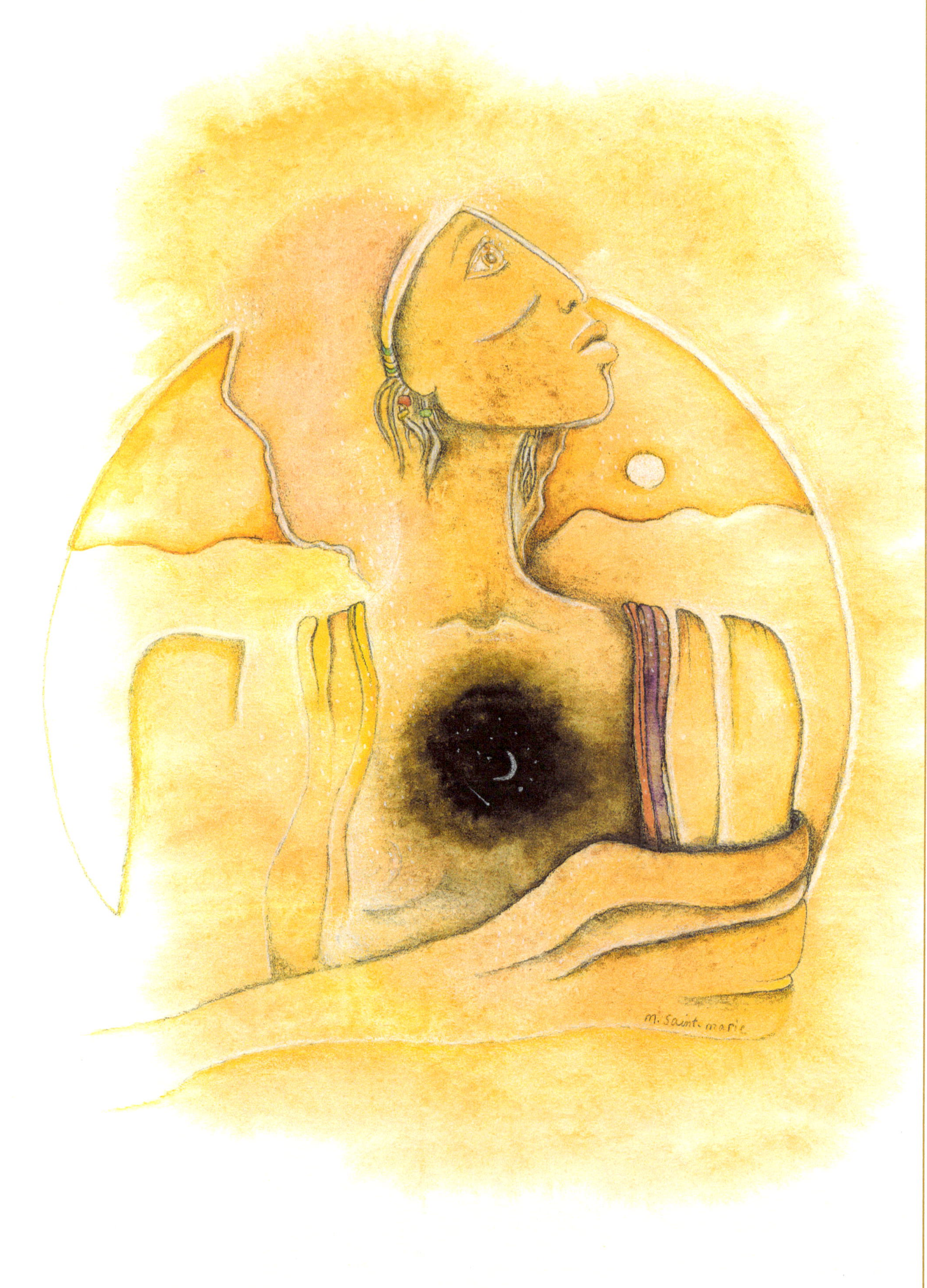
M. Saint-marie

HER-Passage Past the Moon

gazing past the moon…
seeress is born…

passage past the finite…
IT…alone…stands known…

HER-Passage Past the Moon is a visual prayer replete with awareness of the Great Alone… a Silence beyond beliefs.

Wind-SHE…whispers through the stars…

Wind-SHE…whispers through the stars…
silent secrets to the snakes…

The formless appears as formed
giving rise to communion.

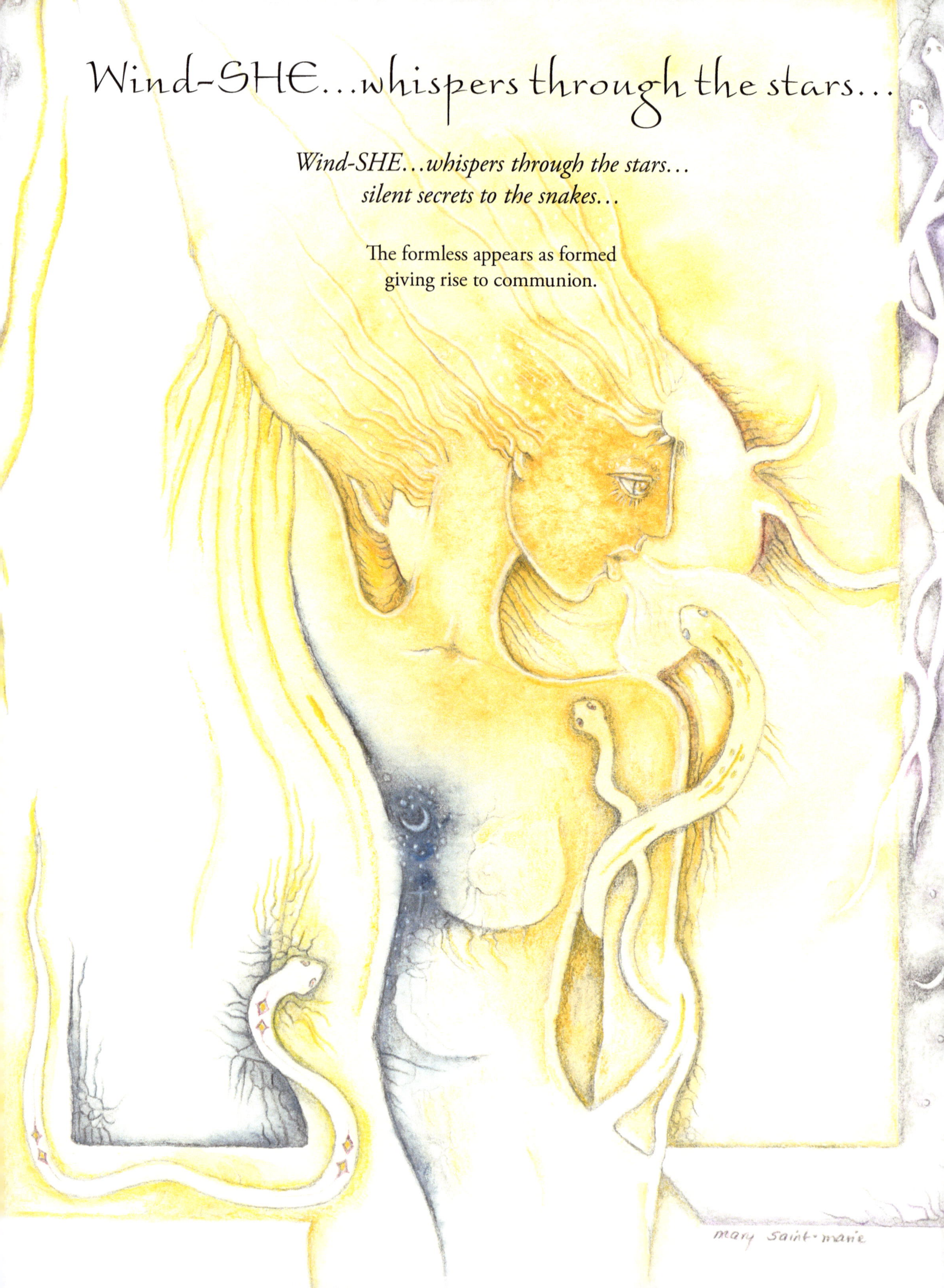

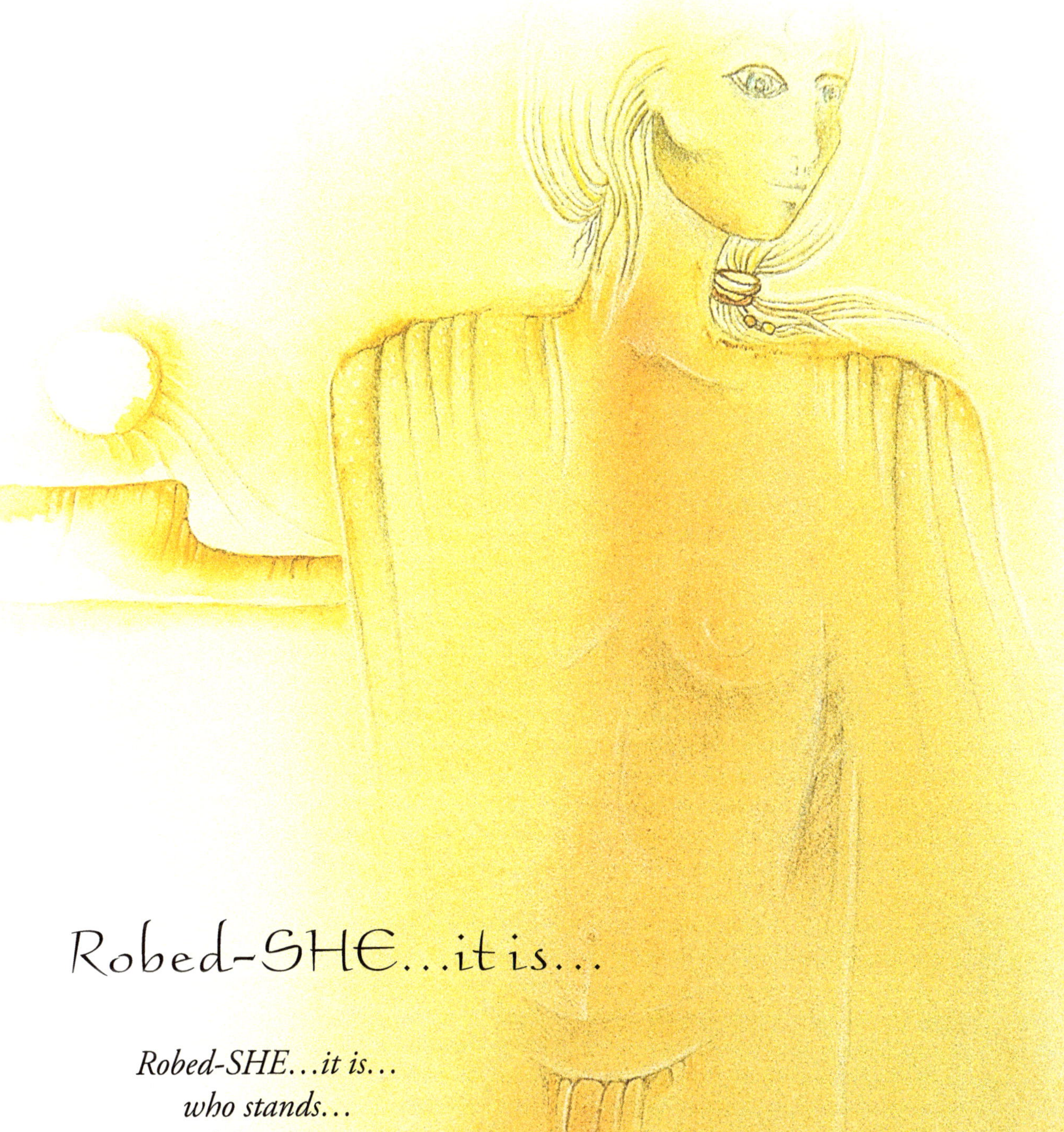

Robed-SHE...it is...

Robed-SHE...it is...
who stands...
as keeper of the Sacred Vision...

Robed-SHE...it is...
who knows...
that Vision guides the way...

This one is robed in gold,
protecting ever
the eternal truths that light the way.

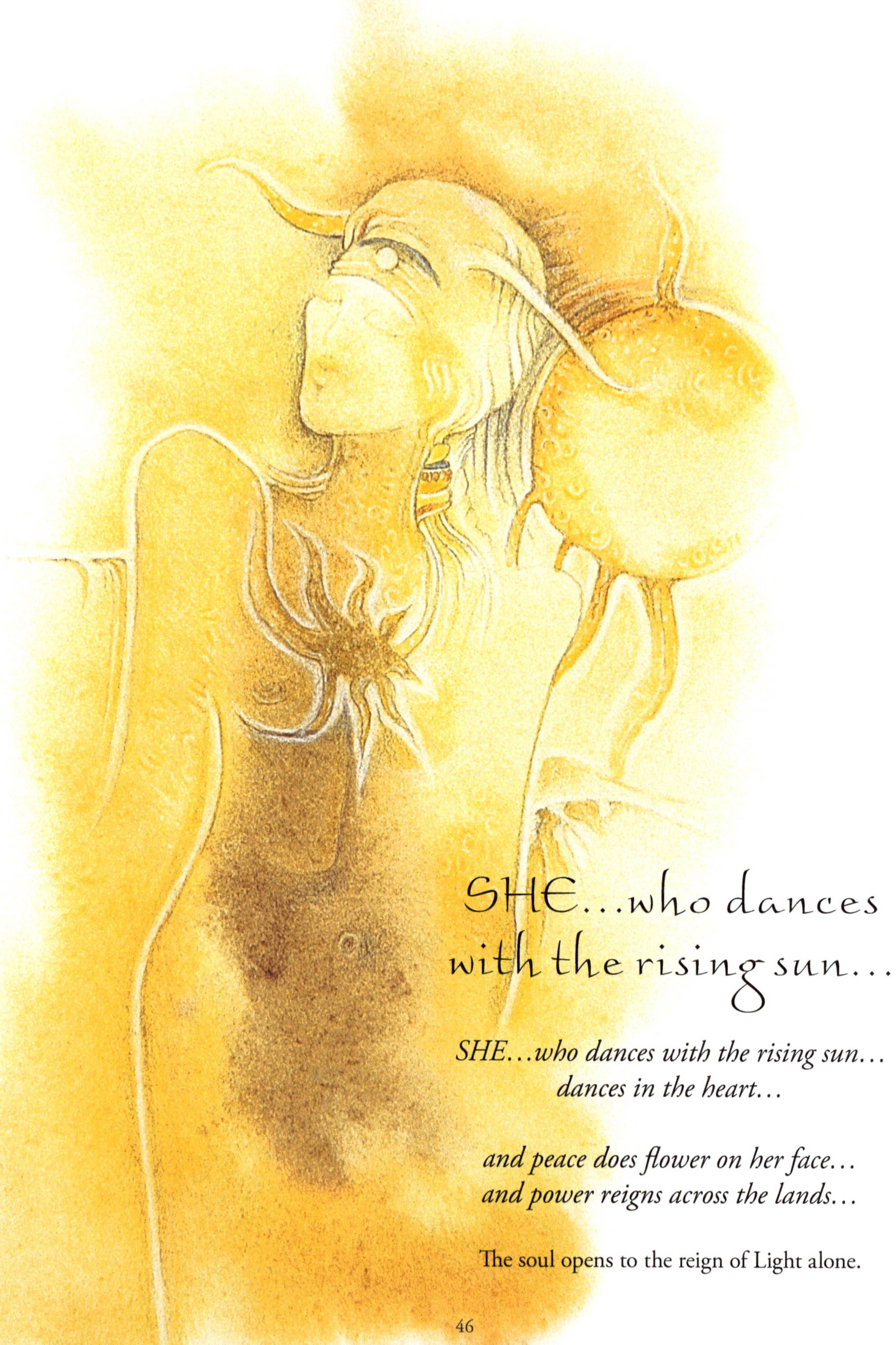

SHE...who dances with the rising sun...

SHE...who dances with the rising sun...
dances in the heart...

and peace does flower on her face...
and power reigns across the lands...

The soul opens to the reign of Light alone.

SHE...who dances with the sun

SHE dances with the sun...
and as a ray of light...

She...clothed as the soil
and robed in flame...does dance...

Woman appears in prayer-dance with
fire element, the fierce purifier.
SHE does dance as the lover of the sun
and of the soil and of the soul.
SHE does dance of purity.

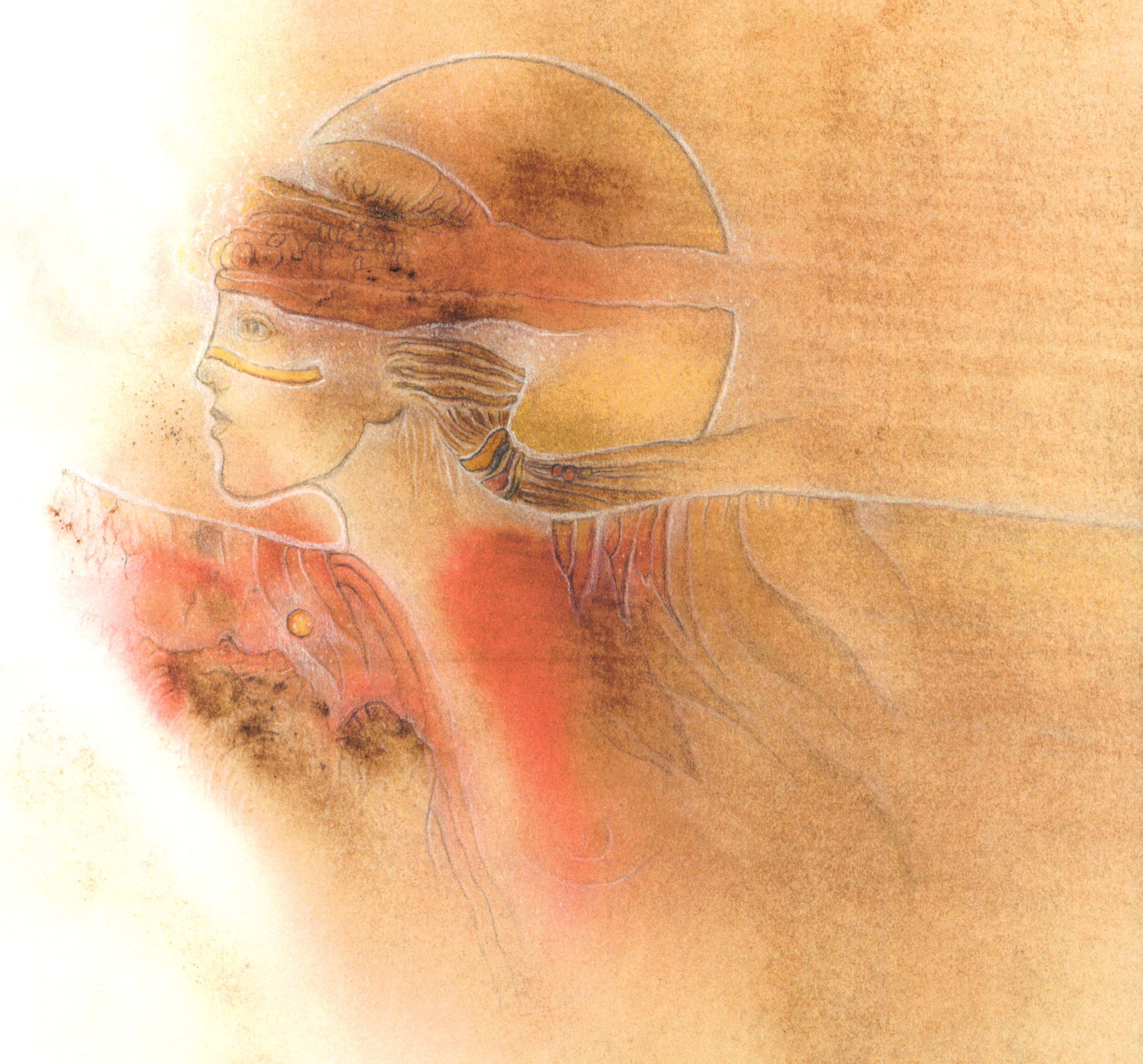

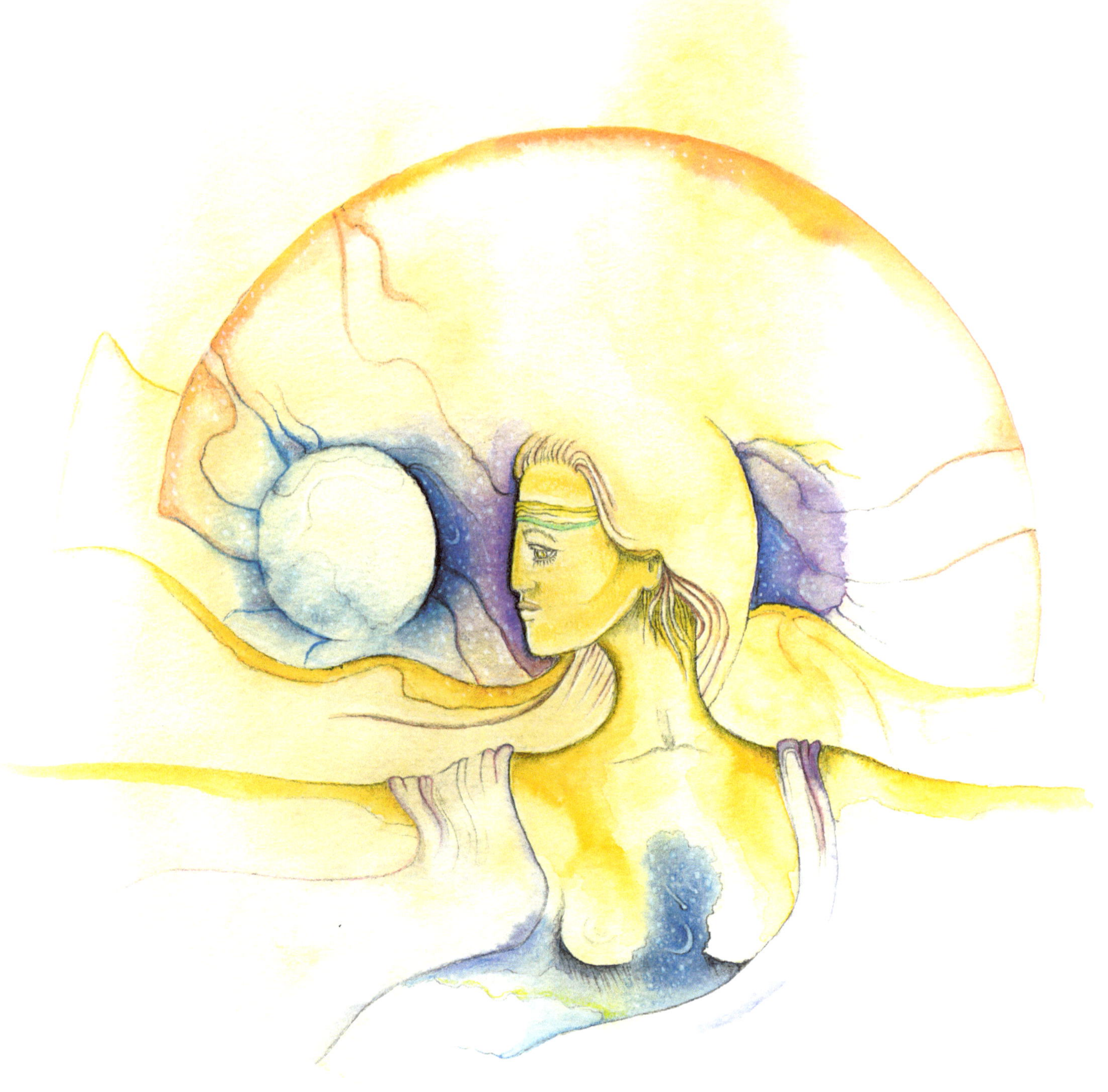

dancing-SHE

dancing-SHE...
at the edge
of many moons...

Called forth from the heart
is the dance beyond time.

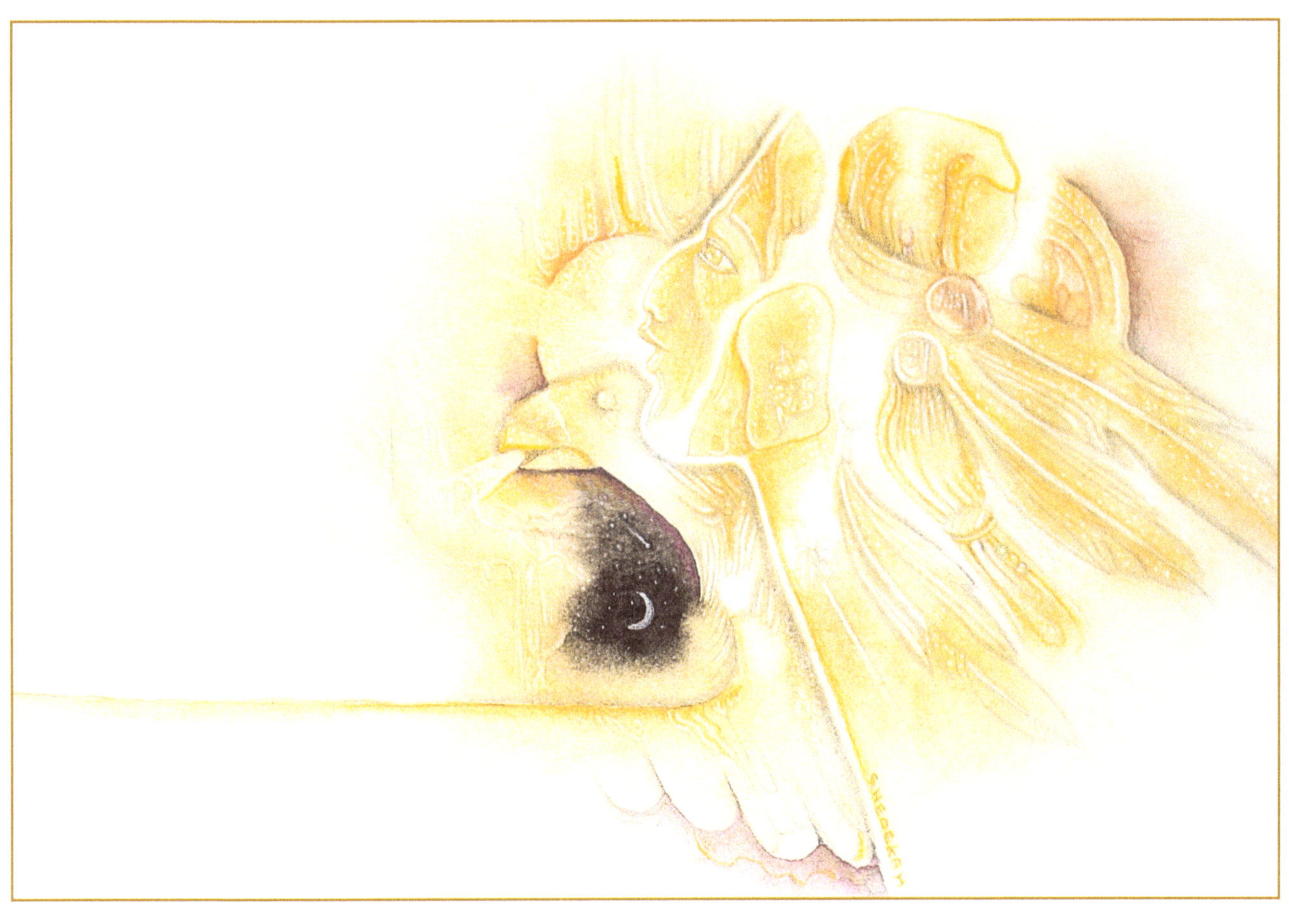

guardian-SHE...of the wilderness...

guardian...SHE...of the wilderness...
...of the world...
...and of the balance...

The Mother of the World alone does prevent
the destruction of the world.
Come...the world does need the Mothers now.

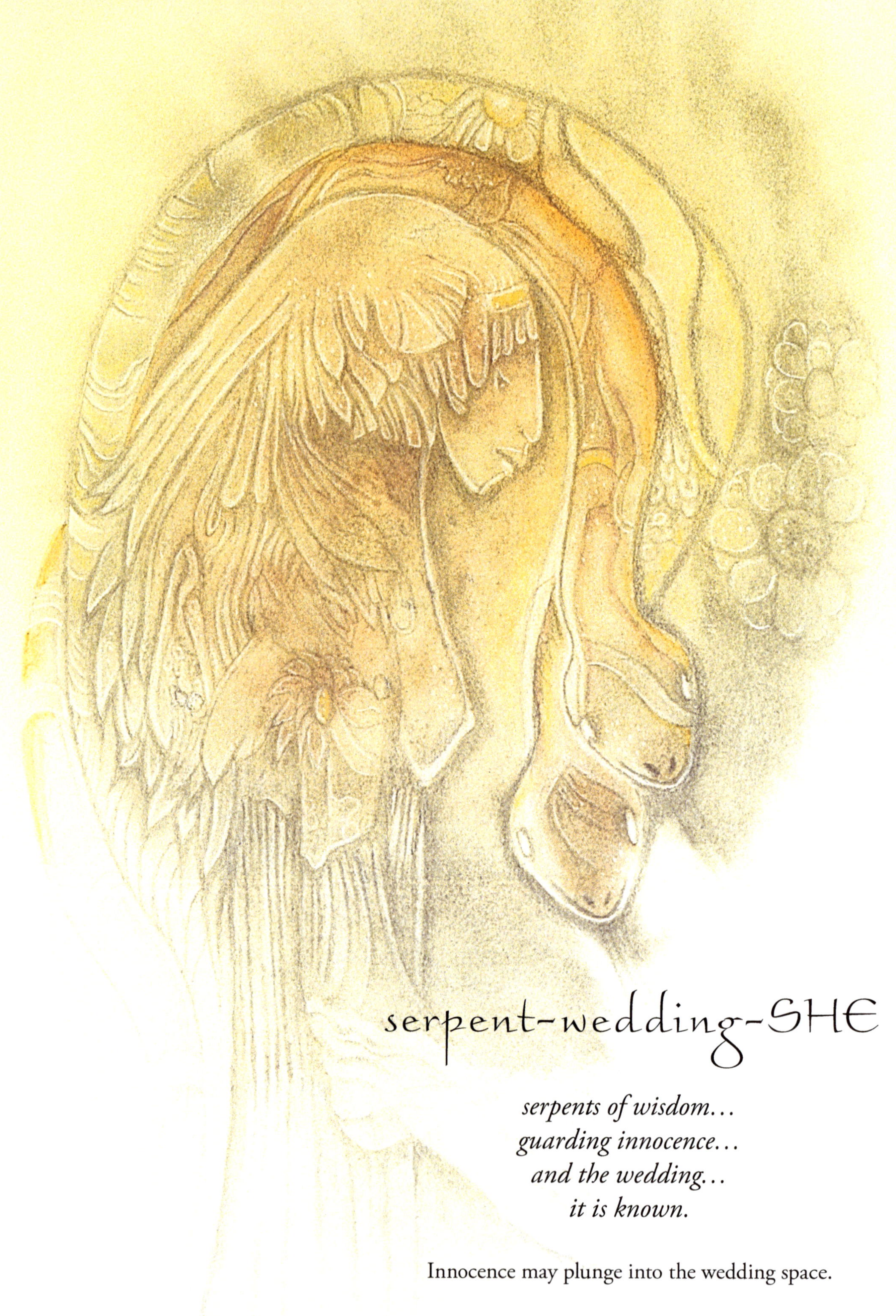

serpent-wedding-SHE

serpents of wisdom…
guarding innocence…
and the wedding…
it is known.

Innocence may plunge into the wedding space.

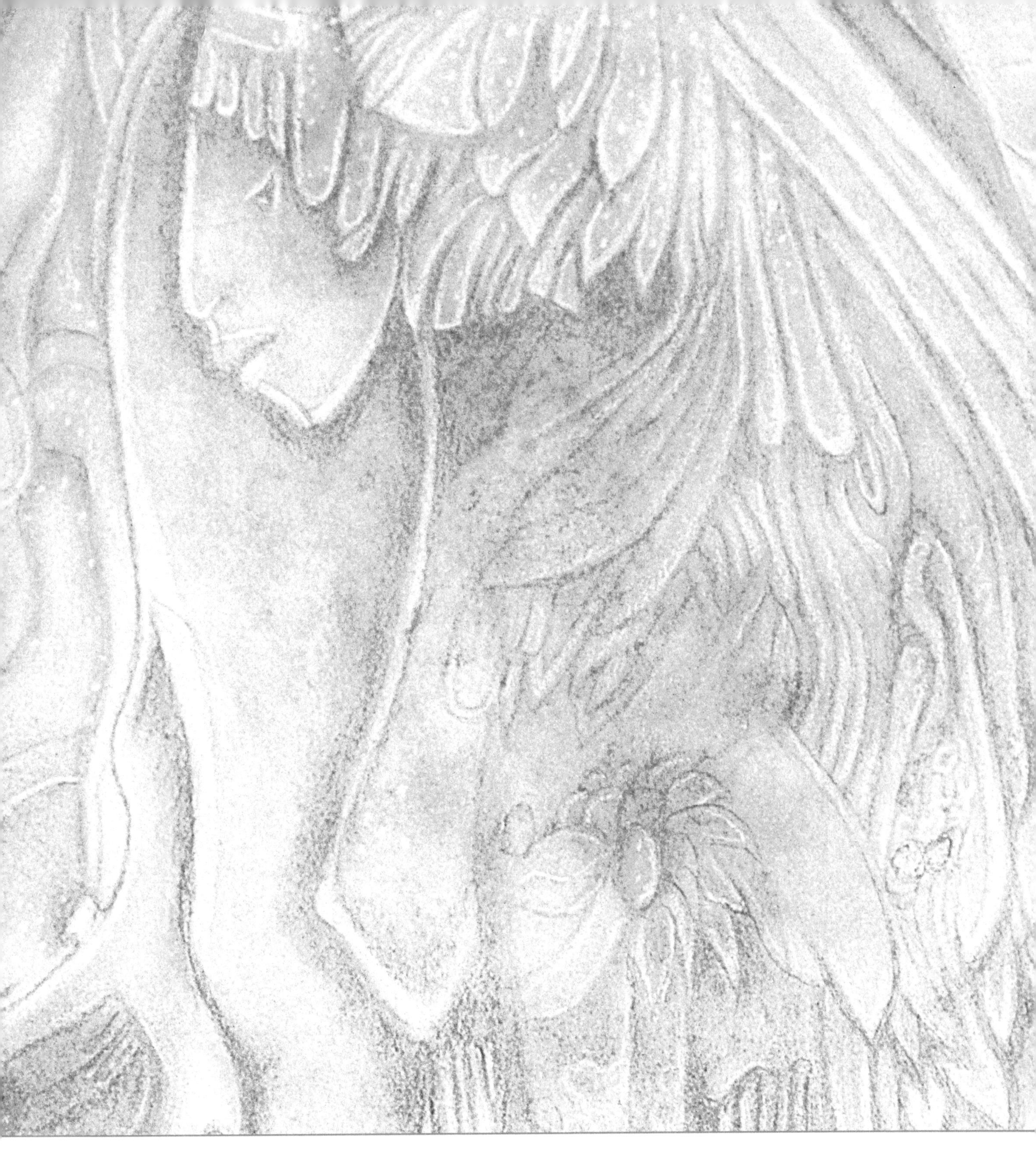

guarding innocence…

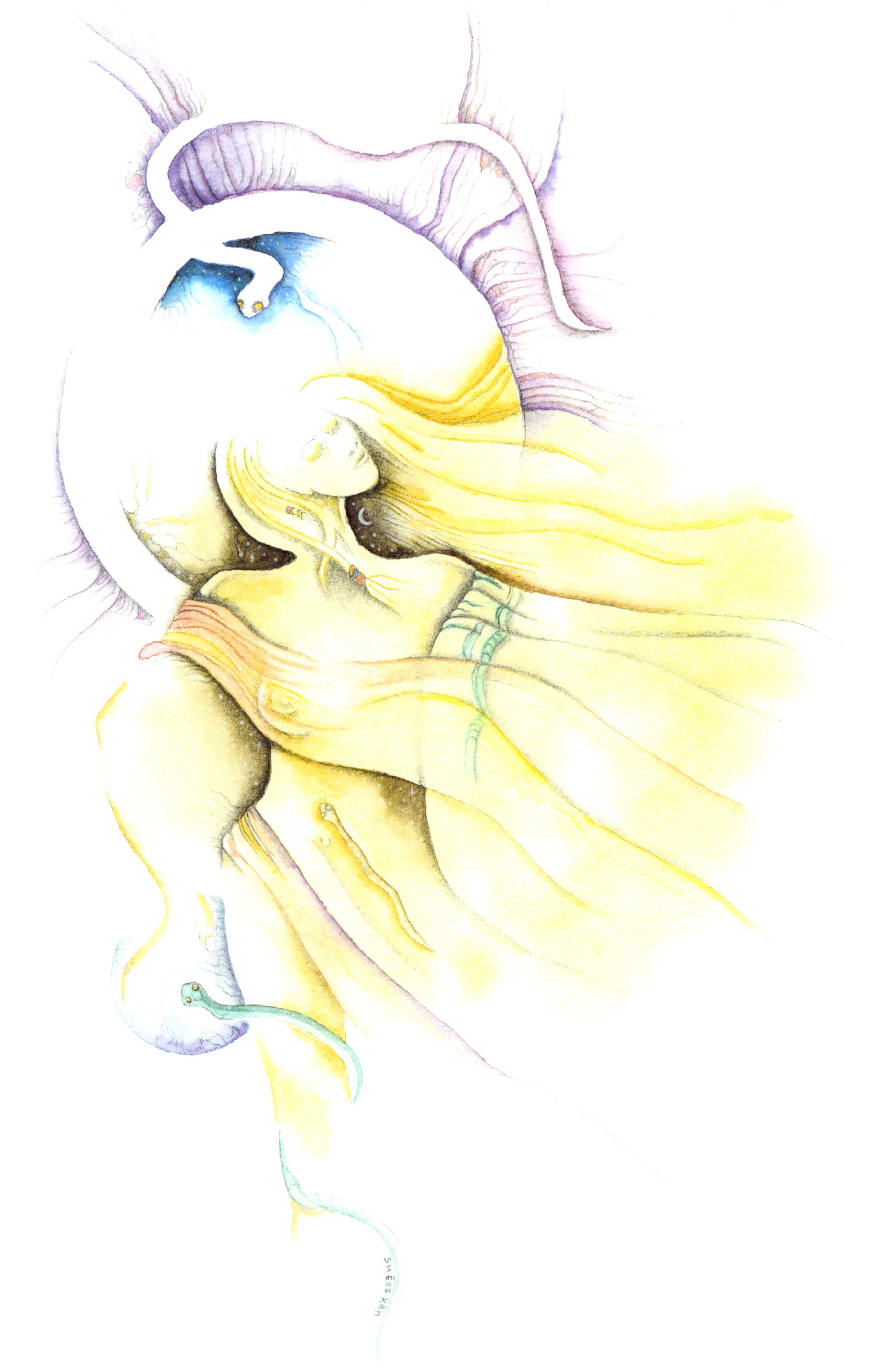

wind-SHE...dances with the snakes...

wind-SHE...
dances with the snakes...
and with the stars...
form known as formless...
invisible visible in endless space...

Wind joins with form and moves as One.

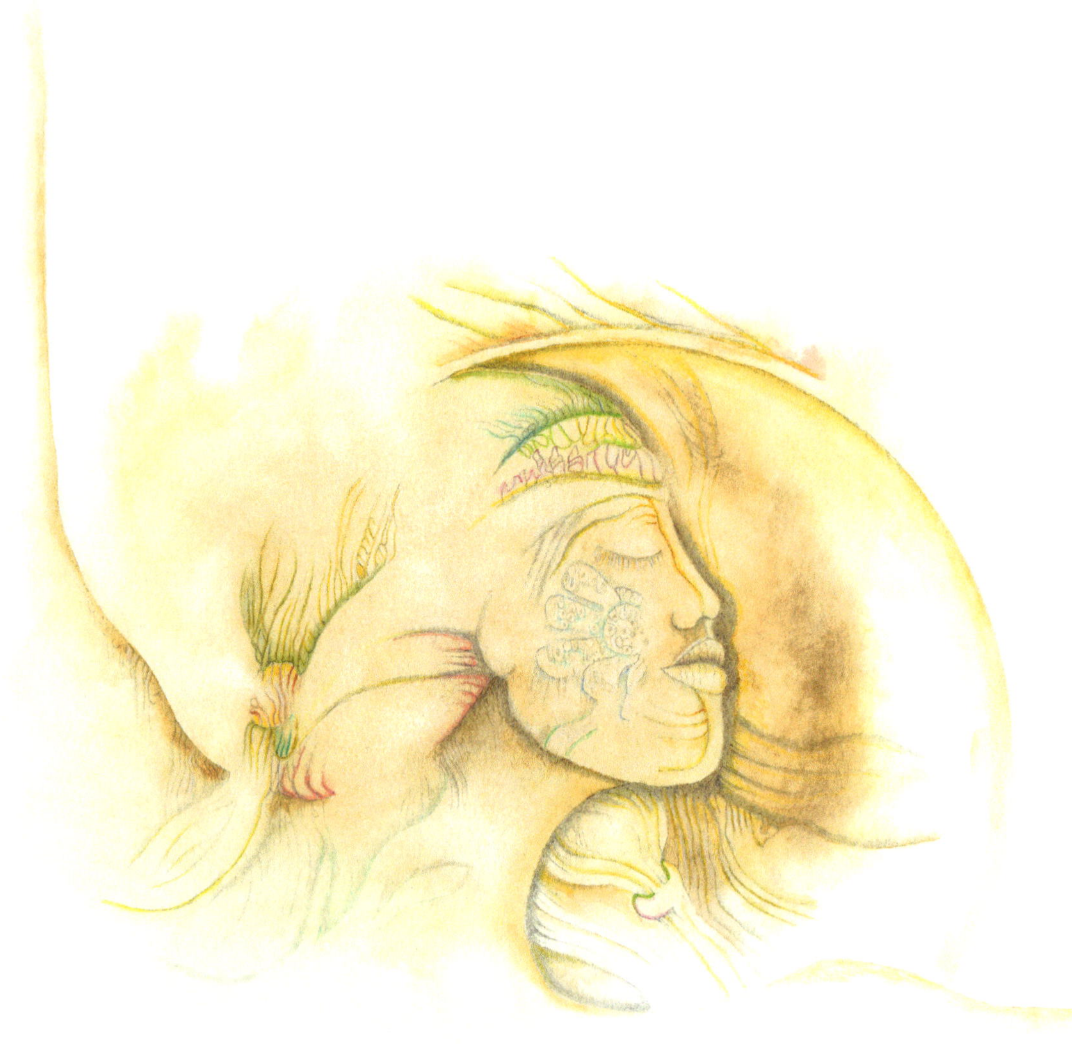

Ceremony of the flower-SHE

Emptiness opens…and comes…
ceremony of the flower-SHE…

The simple story of our Oneness with the flowers of the fields is told. We are but One. Never were we two.

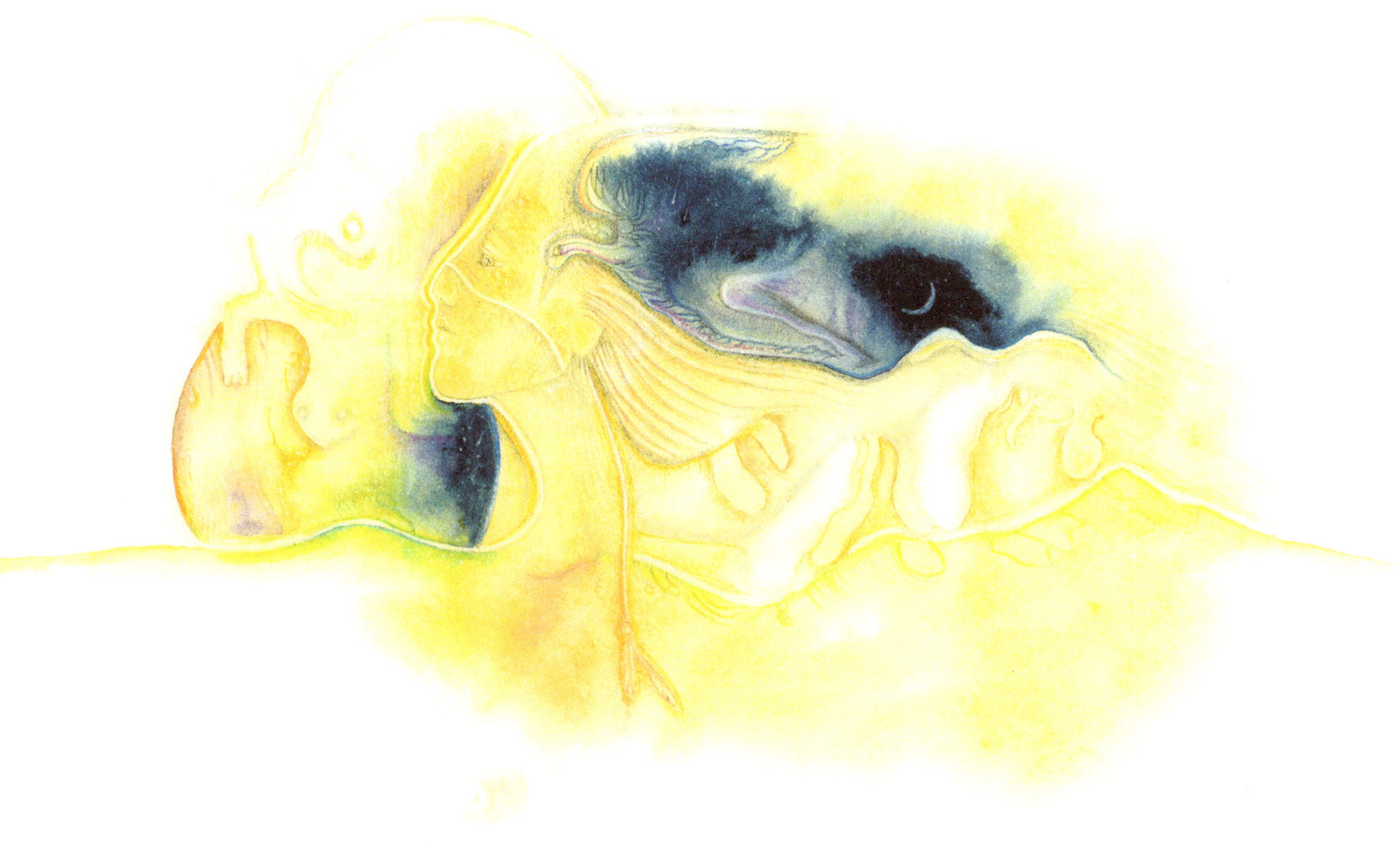

dream-dance of Oneness

SHE does realize her Self…
as the mountain…
the lizard…
and the vastness that ever IS…

Imaged is a dream-dance of
the Oneness of Creation.

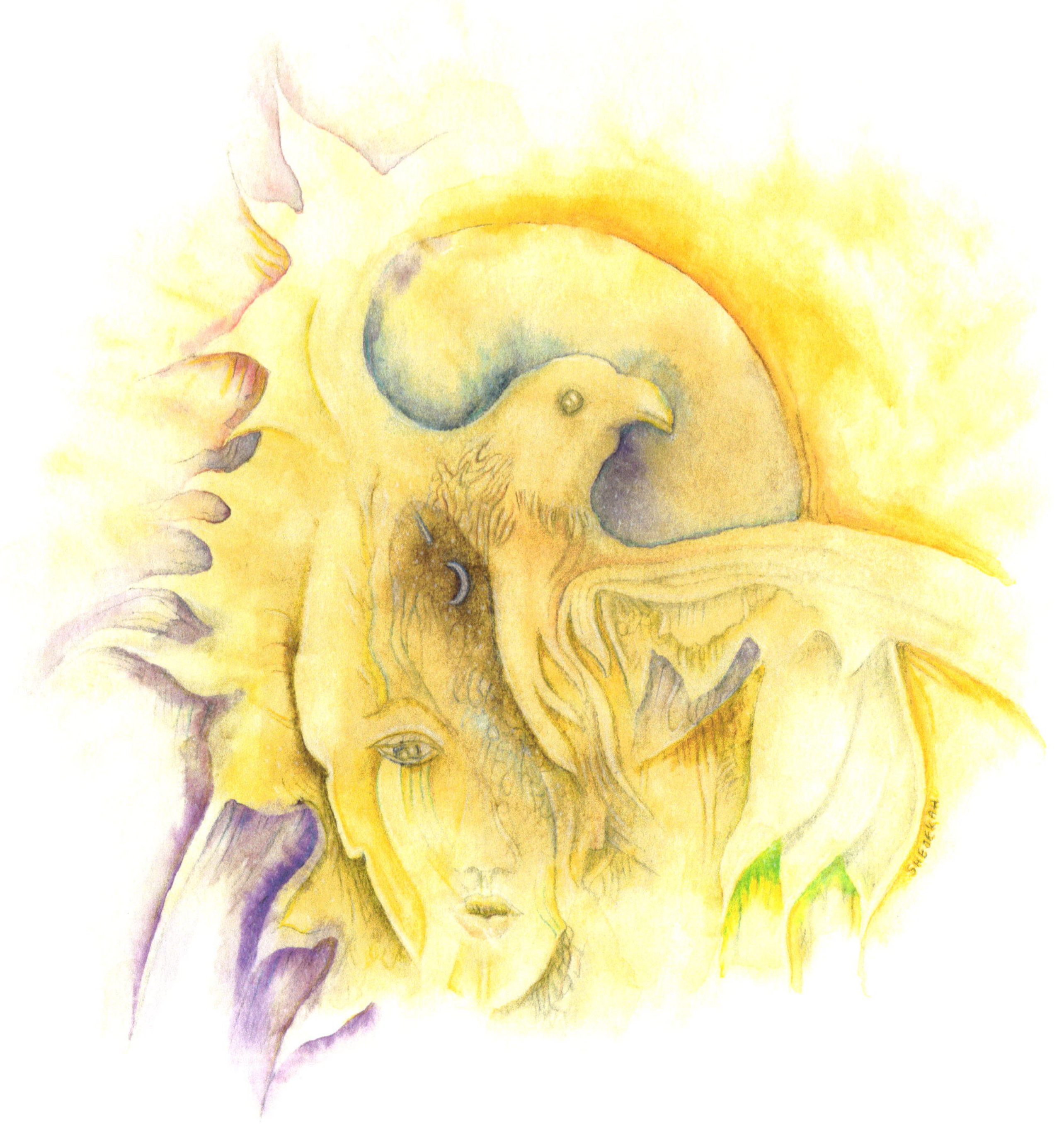

Flight of the Soul

ever does the soul…
inhabit infinity…

Consciousness takes form
as a winged one.

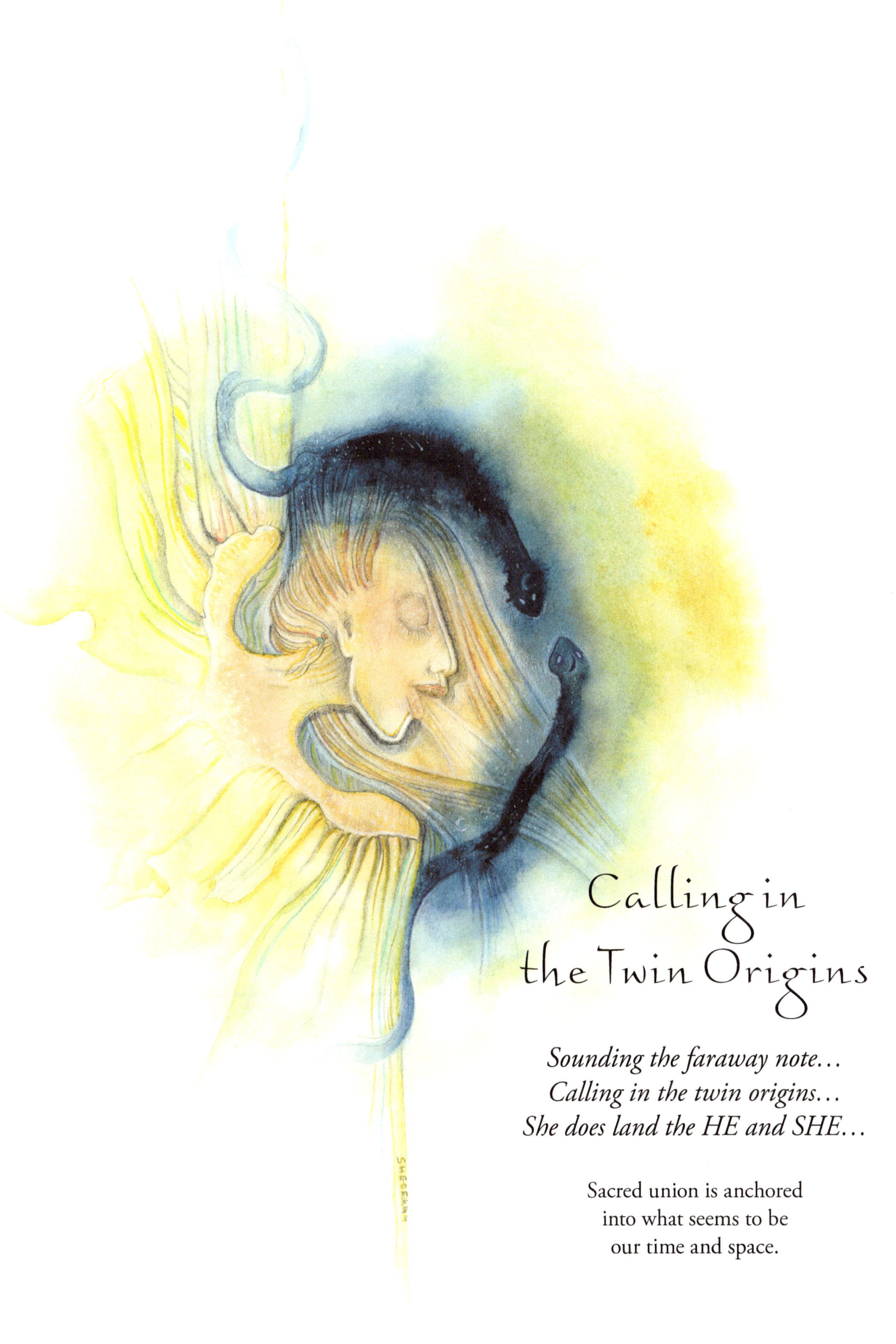

Calling in the Twin Origins

Sounding the faraway note…
Calling in the twin origins…
She does land the HE and SHE…

Sacred union is anchored
into what seems to be
our time and space.

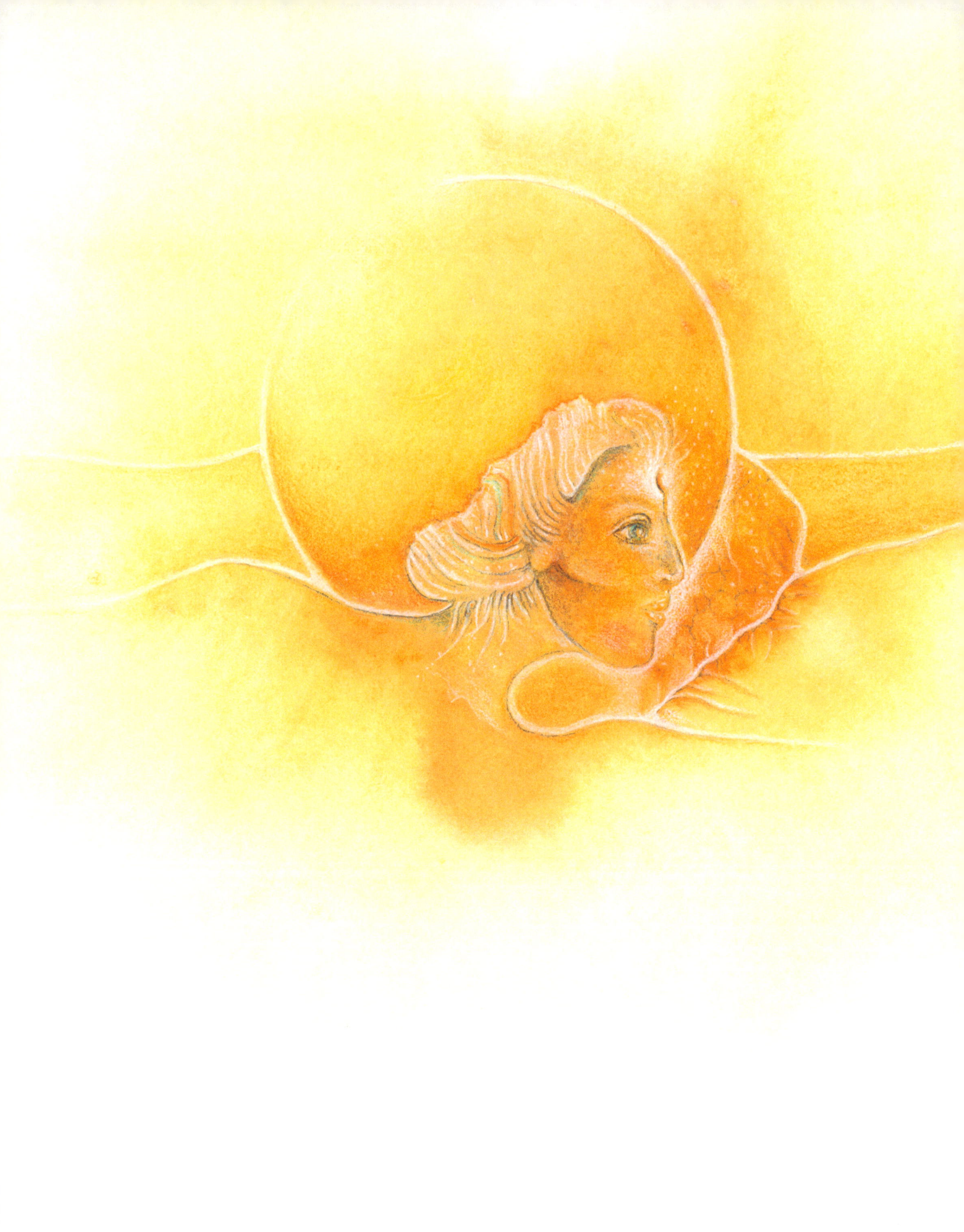

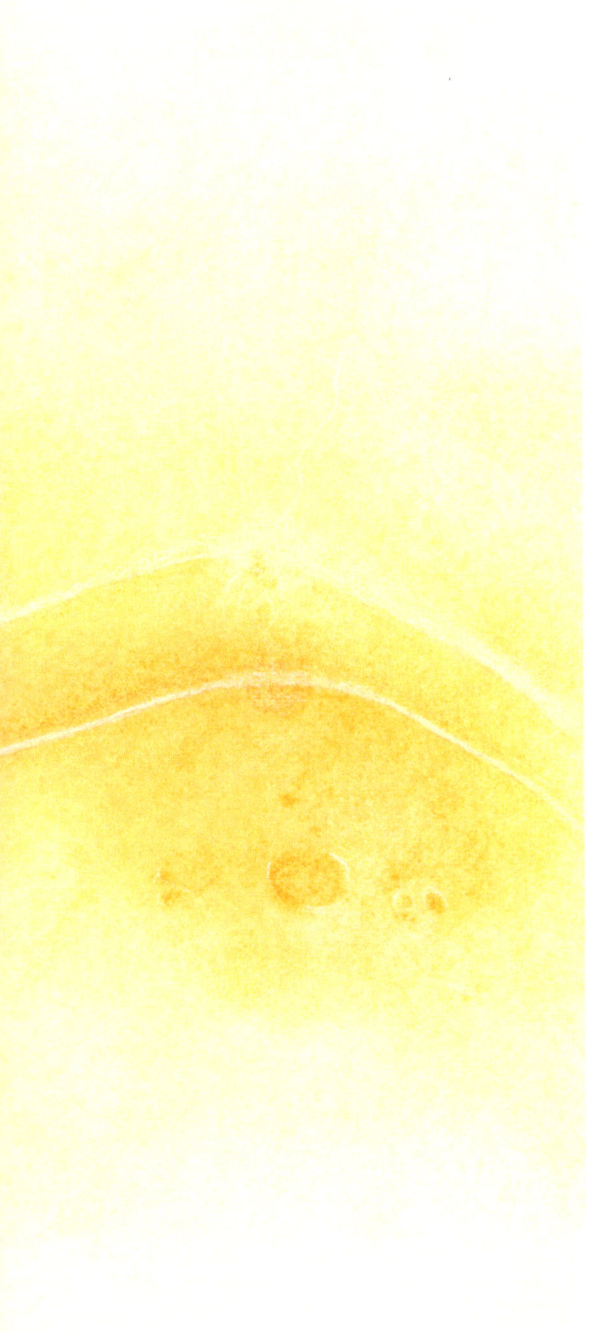

Keeper of the Desert Vision-SHE

Keeper of the Desert Vision-SHE
abandons vision to find Vision…
and joy does come…

Here human images and ideas
are discerned from
Vision borne of Spirit.

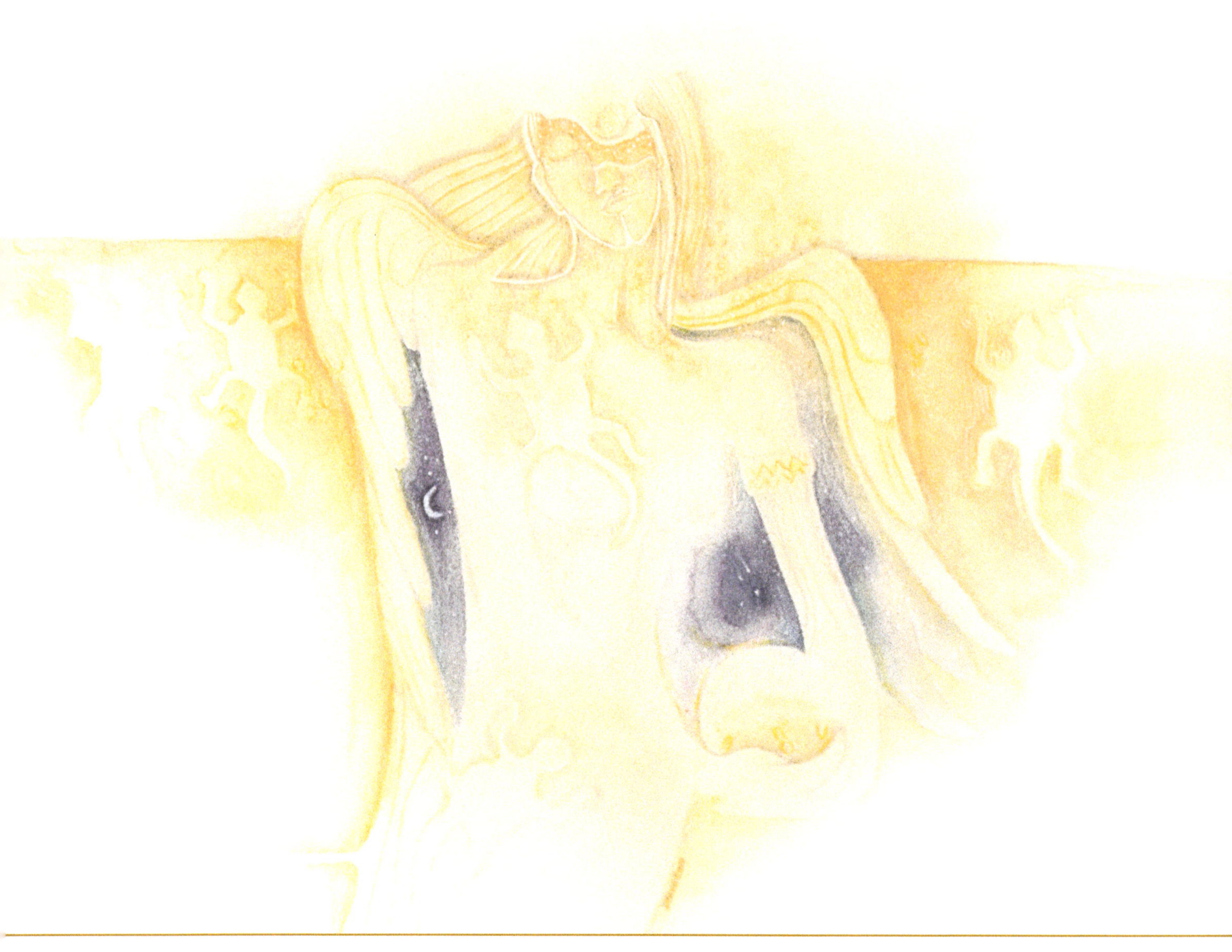

Angel of the Path

the stars…the stones…
do meet this day…
a sphere of love is borne…

Angel of the Path
represents our very being
as the vehicle of love
come upon this earthly home.

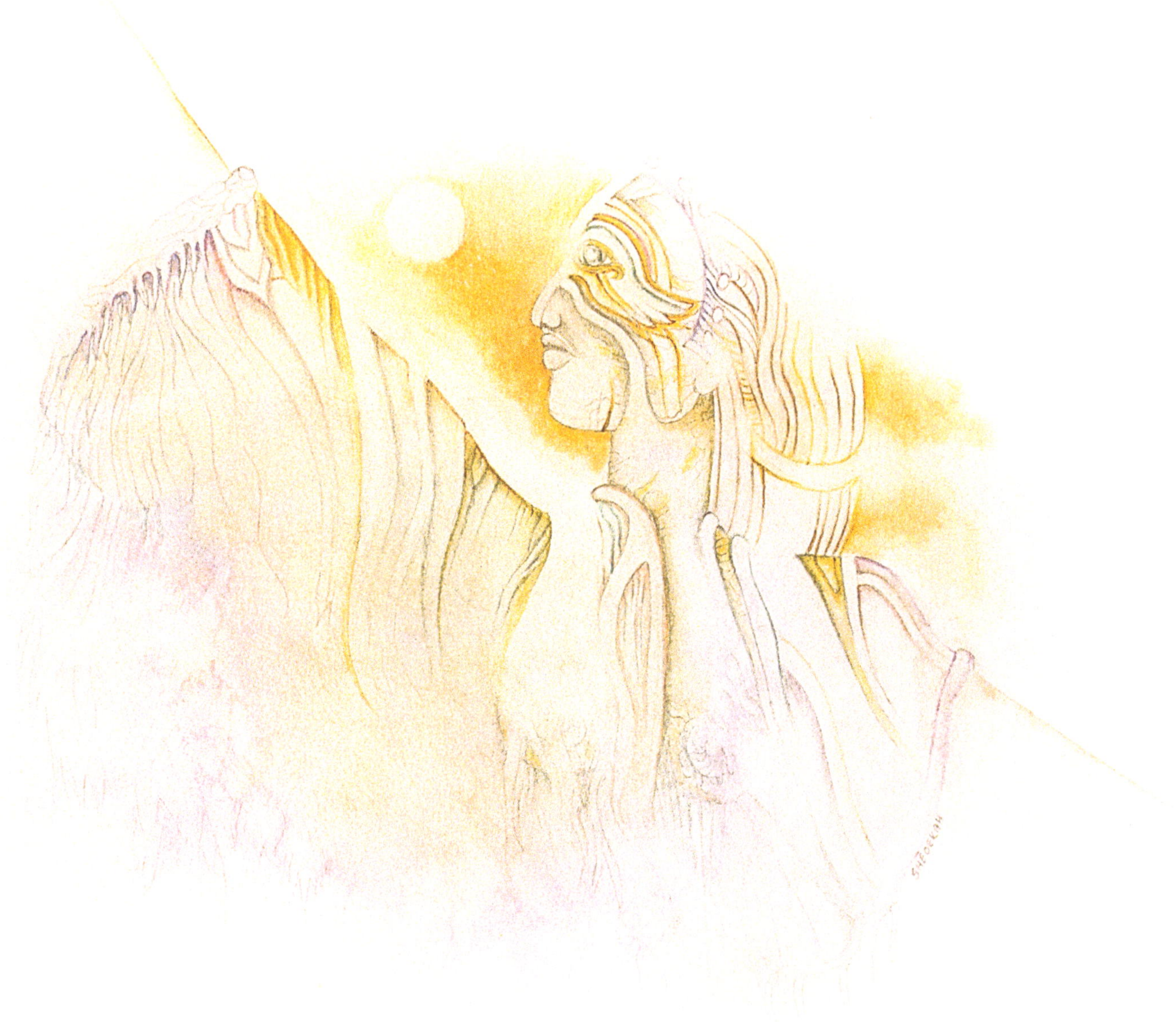

Rainbow Woman of the Circle

Rainbow Woman of the Circle...
bringer of the joy...
bringer of the calm...
bringer of humanity's shift...

Rainbow Woman of the Circle is
an announcement of a change and
a pronouncement of a radiant world.

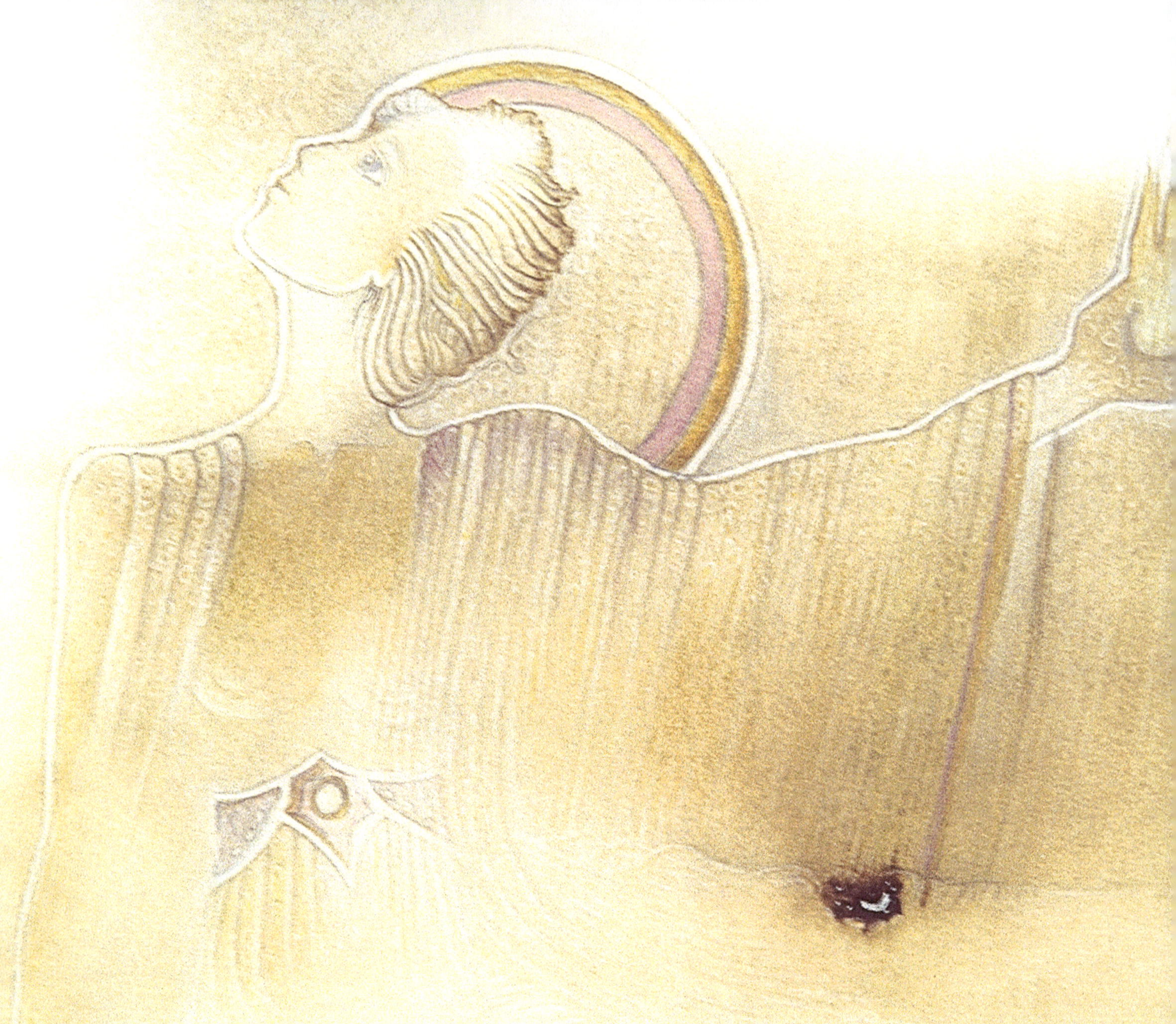

SHE…who gathers in the light…
…to give her gift…

SHE…who gathers in the light…
…to give her gift…

SHE…who gathers in the light…
…to feed the hungry souls…

The light is understood to be manna.

Rainbow Mother of the Fiery Worlds

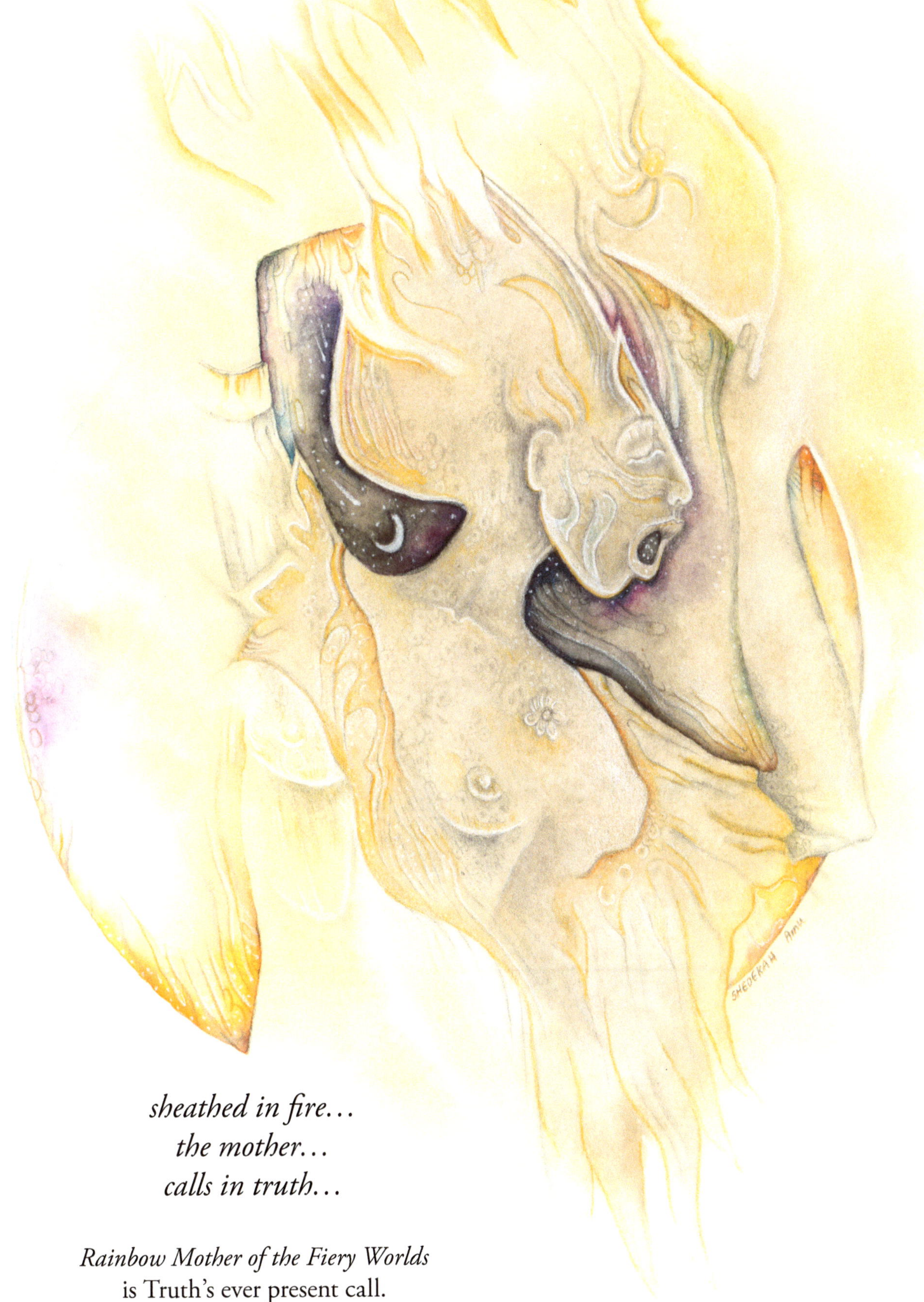

sheathed in fire…
the mother…
calls in truth…

Rainbow Mother of the Fiery Worlds
is Truth's ever present call.

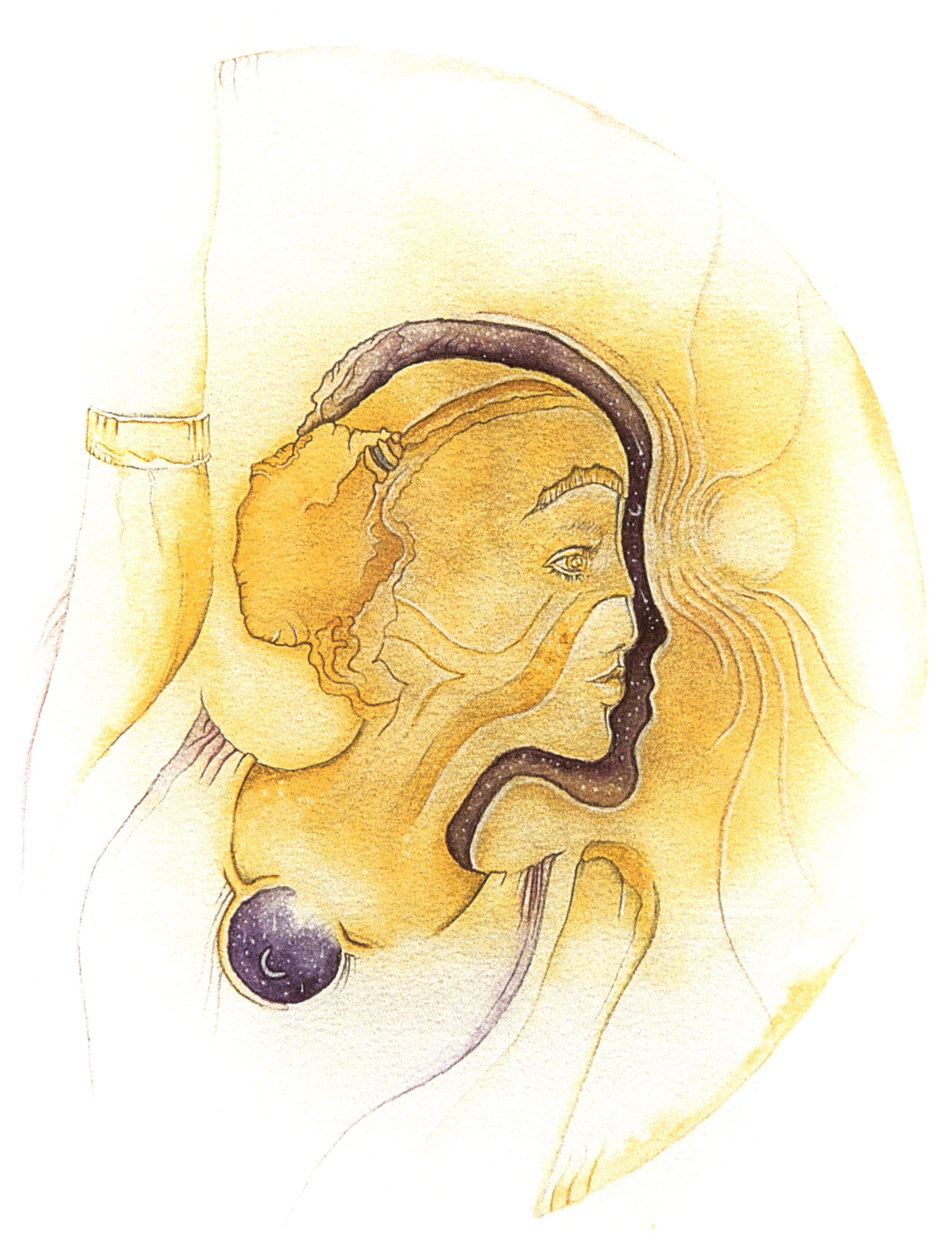

SHE…it is…
who wears the muses' mask
and dances with the moon…

SHE…it is…
who wears the muses' mask
and dances with the moon…

SHE…it is…
who wears the muse's mask
and dances as the very moon…

That we are Consciousness….alone…
is this visual story.

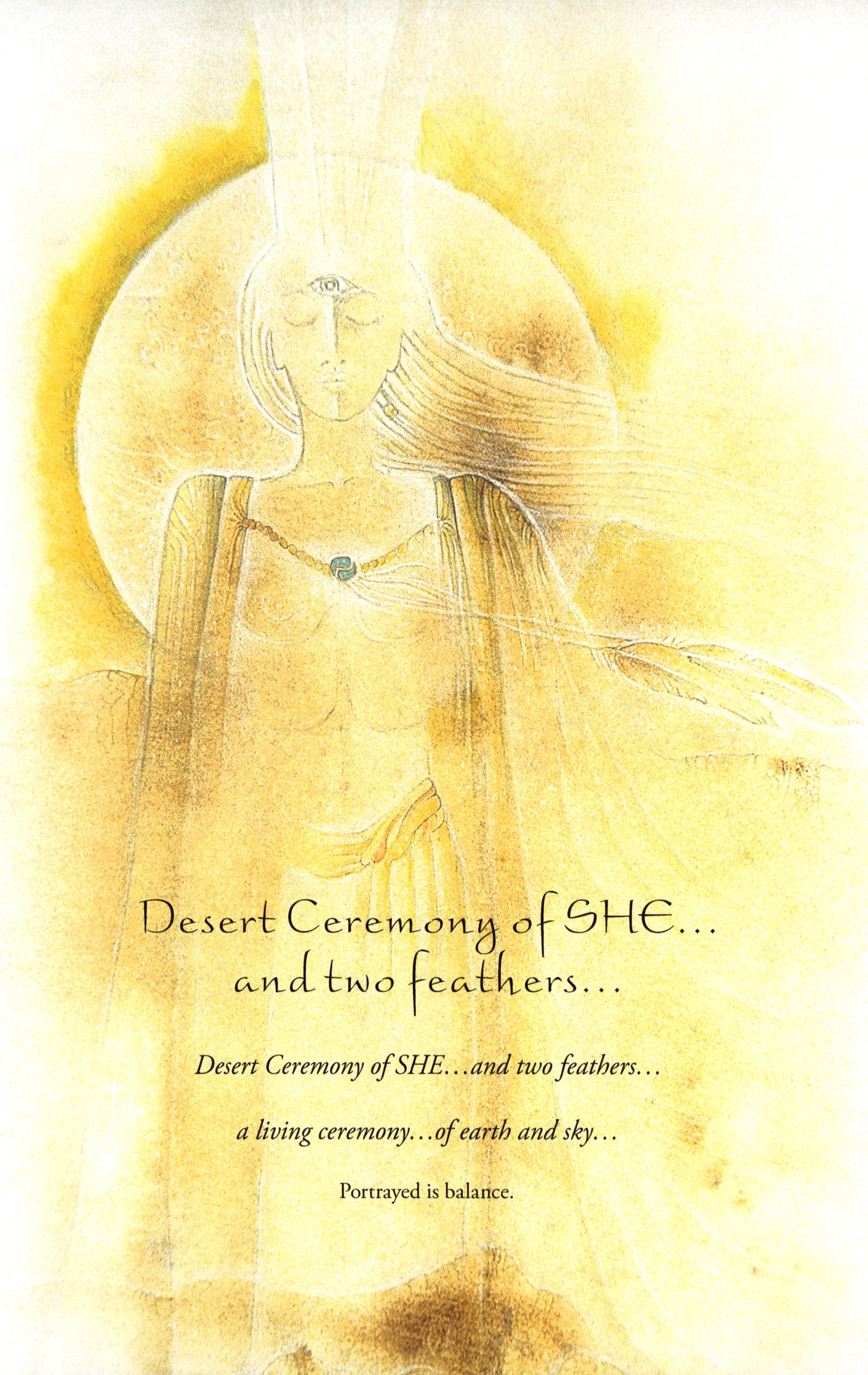

Desert Ceremony of SHE...
and two feathers...

Desert Ceremony of SHE...and two feathers...

a living ceremony...of earth and sky...

Portrayed is balance.

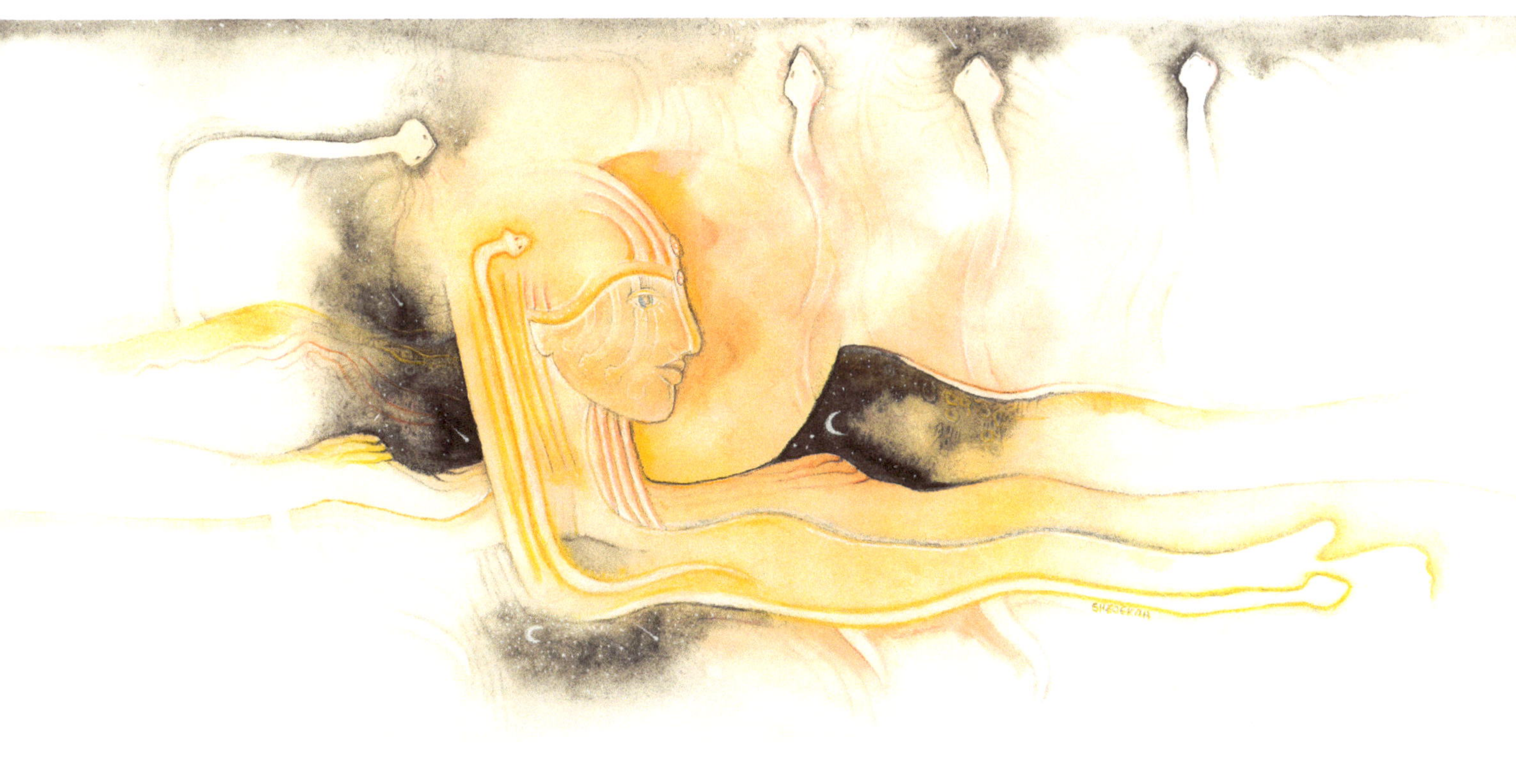

from the stars does she come…
and dances with the snakes…

from the stars does she come…
and dances with the snakes…

unveiling nature…
unveiling the One…
unveiling the veiled…

The images serve as symbols
to tell a bigger story.

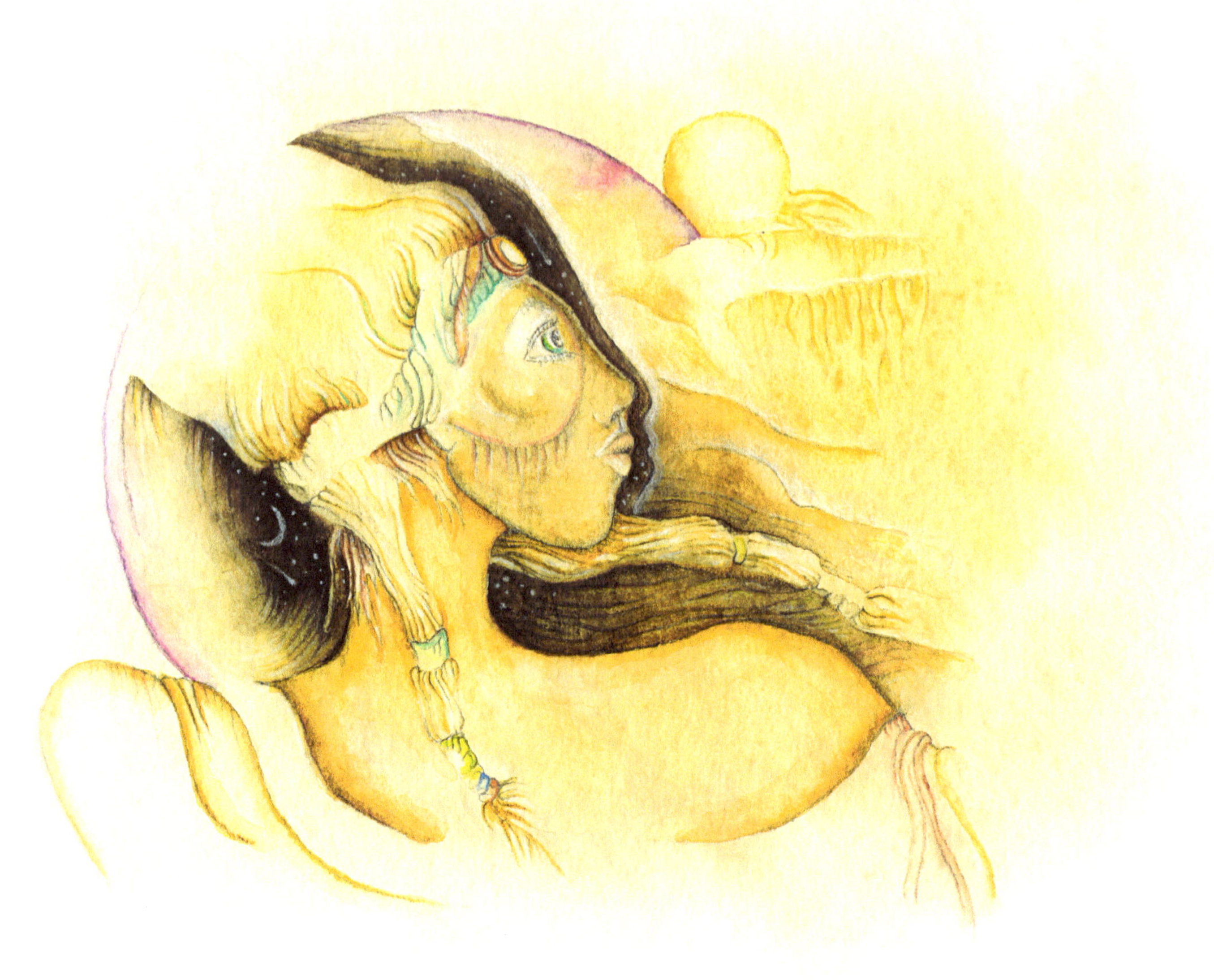

HER-Ceremony...past the stars...

past the stars...
past the moon...
beyond her death...

Captured here is the perceived
journey home. It is now.

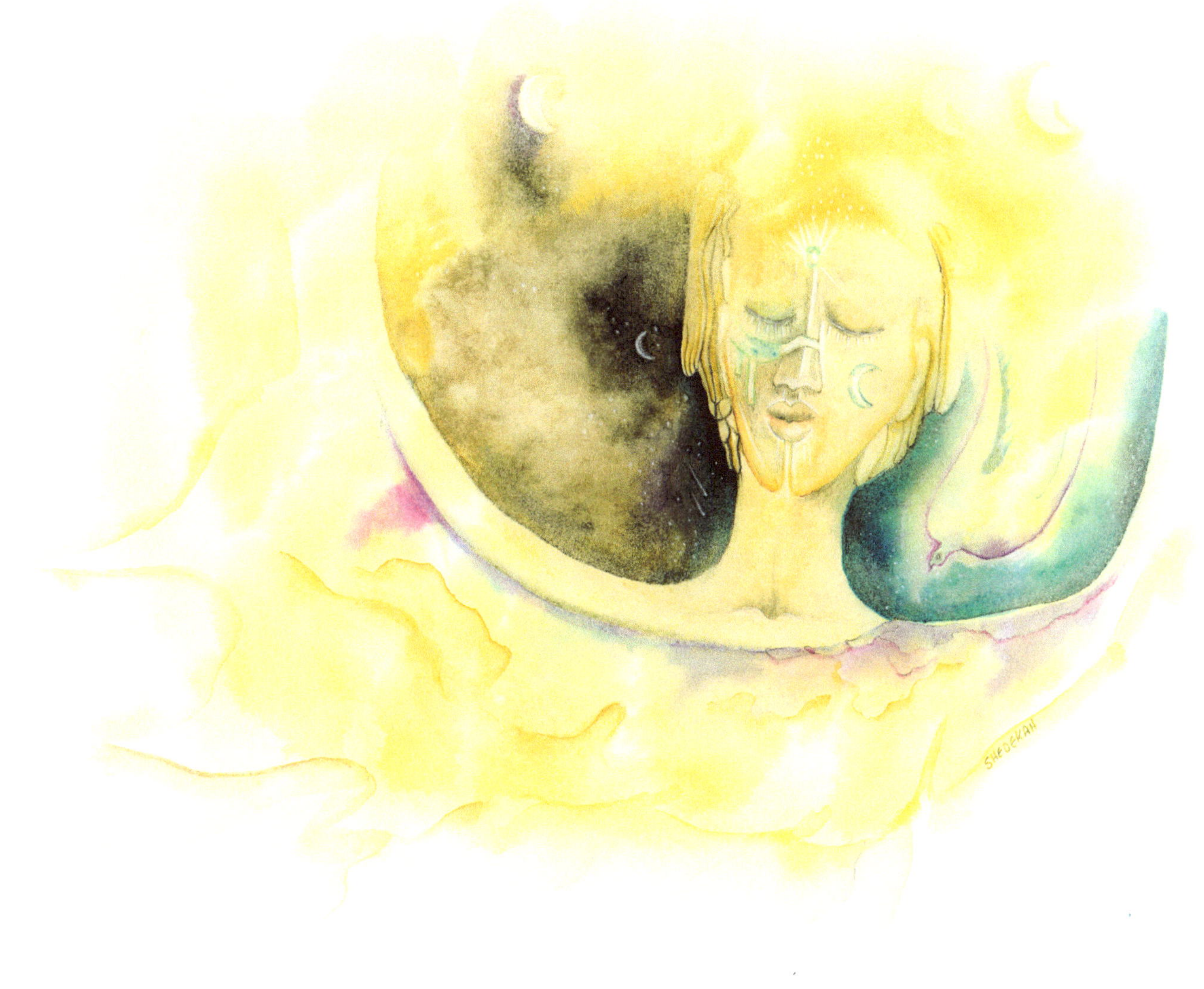

SHE…who celebrates… the marriage of earth and sky…

SHE…who celebrates…
the marriage of earth and sky…
is SHE…who celebrates unity…

A celebration of the Oneness is revealed.

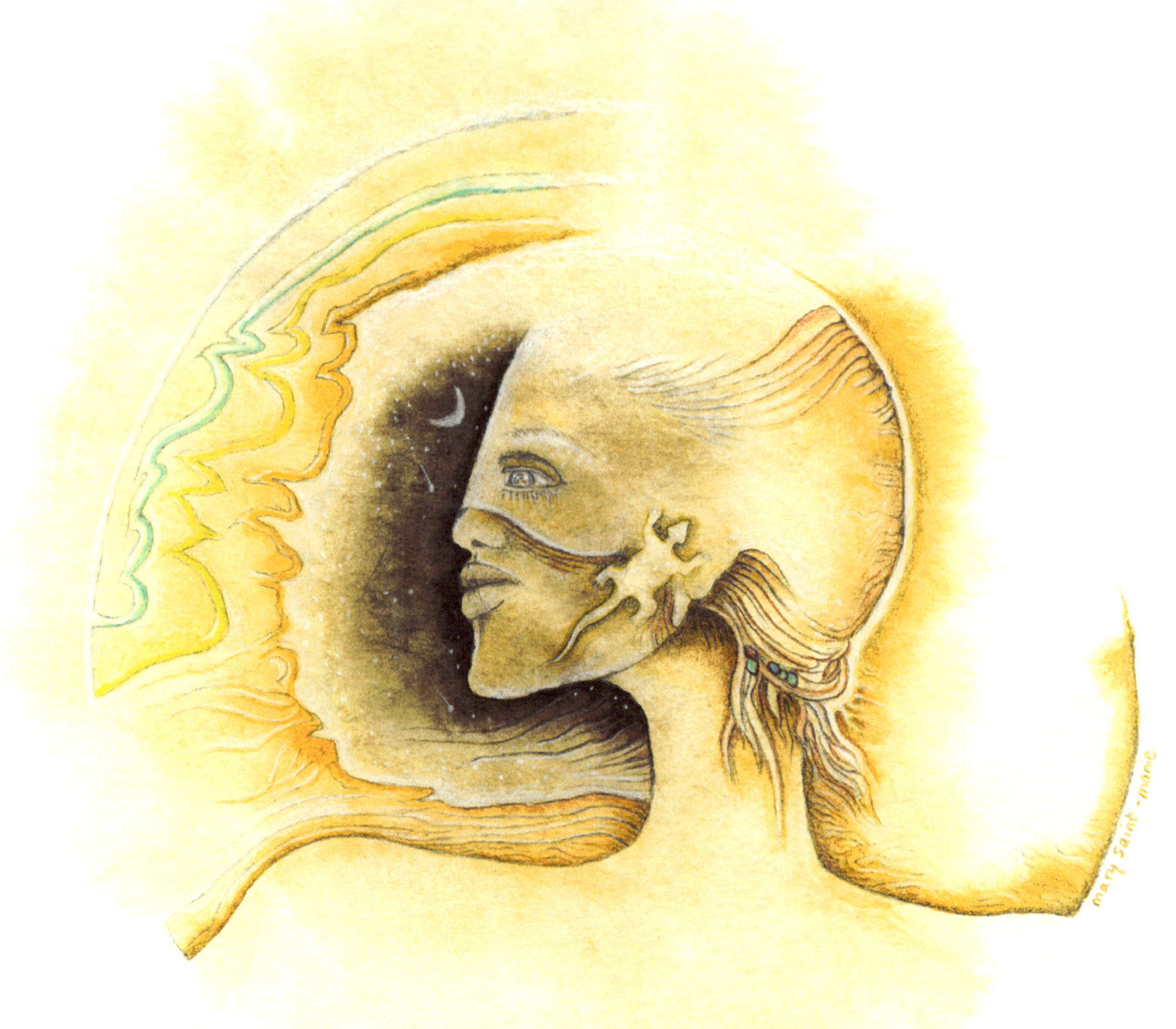

HER-story

HER-story…
as the lizard…
and the farthest star…

HER-story…
as the landscape that dwells…
where distance travels not…

Portrayed is the awareness of
a Consciousness that escapes time.

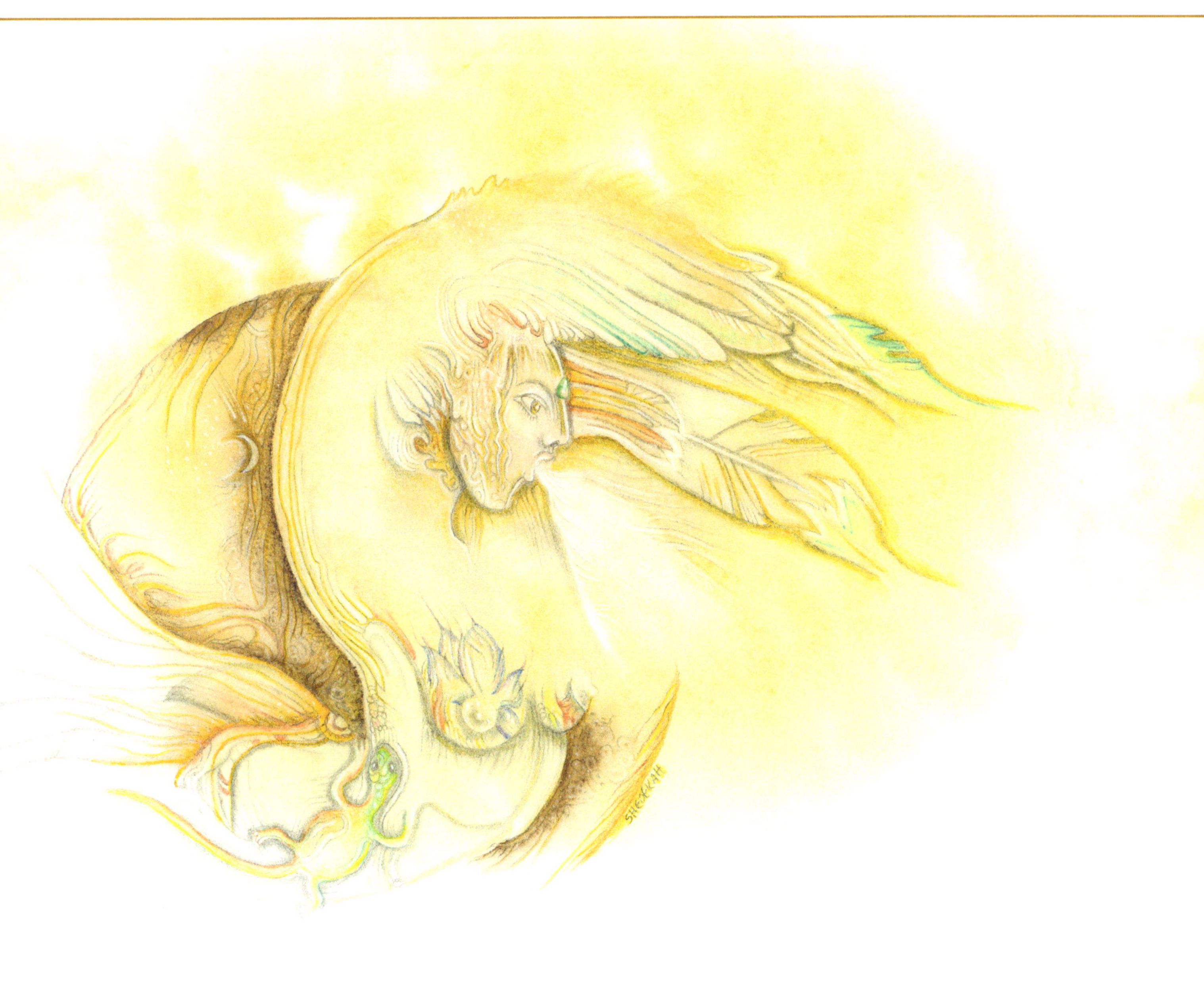

shaman-angel-SHE

shaman-angel-SHE…
sounding note of guardian…
flowers…lizards…all our Self…

Protectress of the world
voicing the law of love.

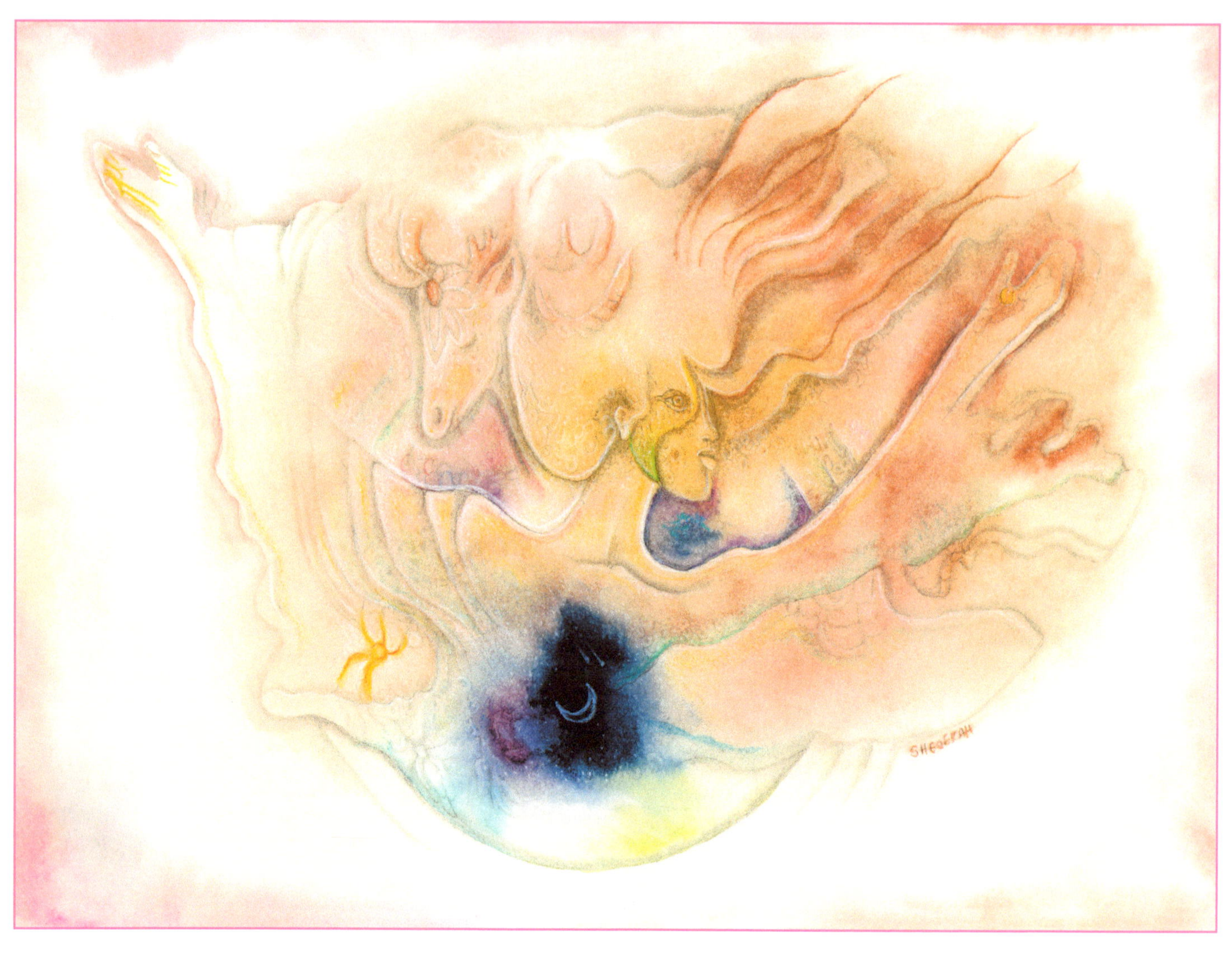

SHE…who guards wilderness…

SHE…who guards wilderness…
wears a heart embracing all…

This is a visual prayer
of the protectress in us all.

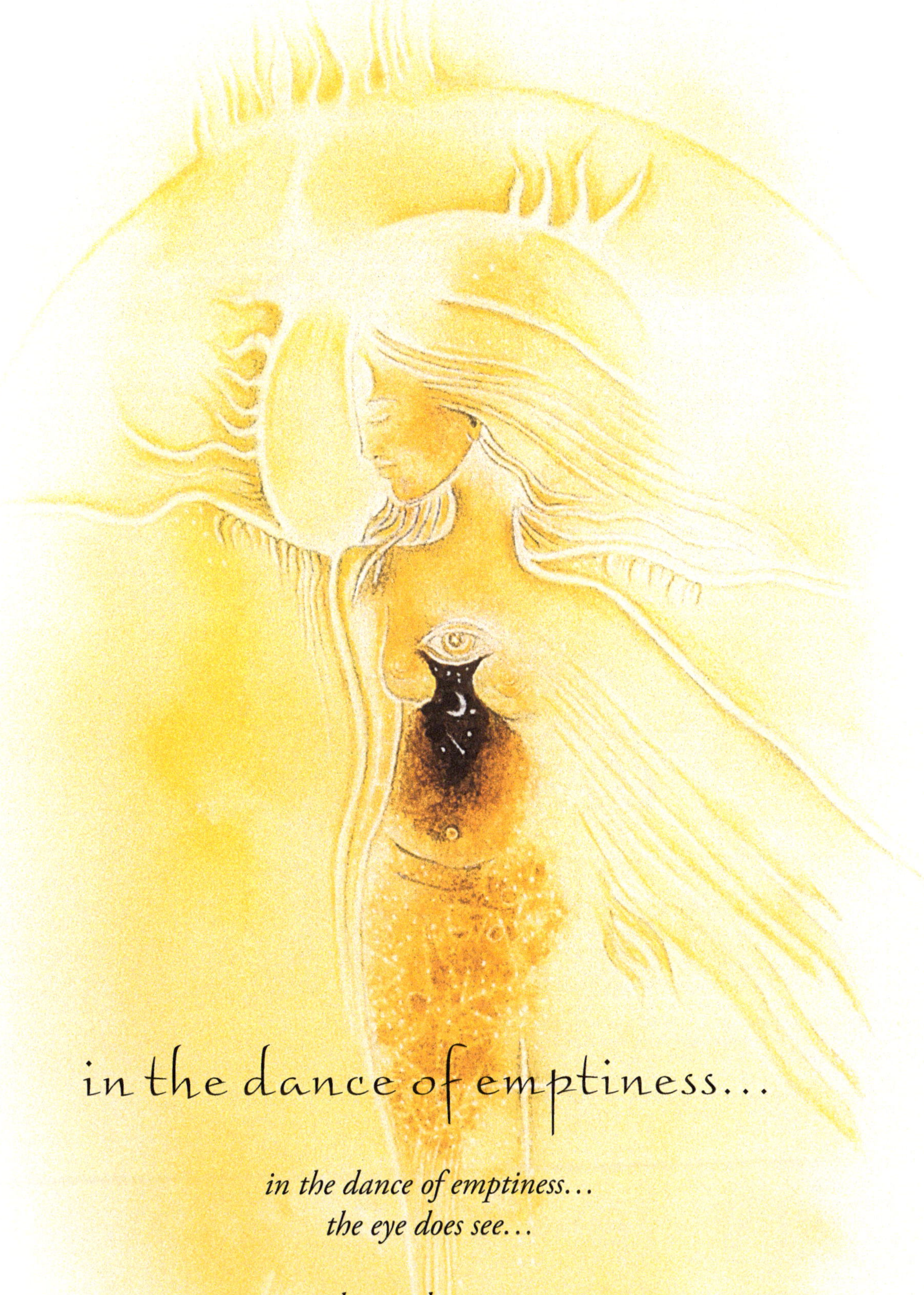

in the dance of emptiness...

in the dance of emptiness...
the eye does see...

the eye does see...
the heart does know...
the universe does smile...

This image depicts the single eye of the heart.

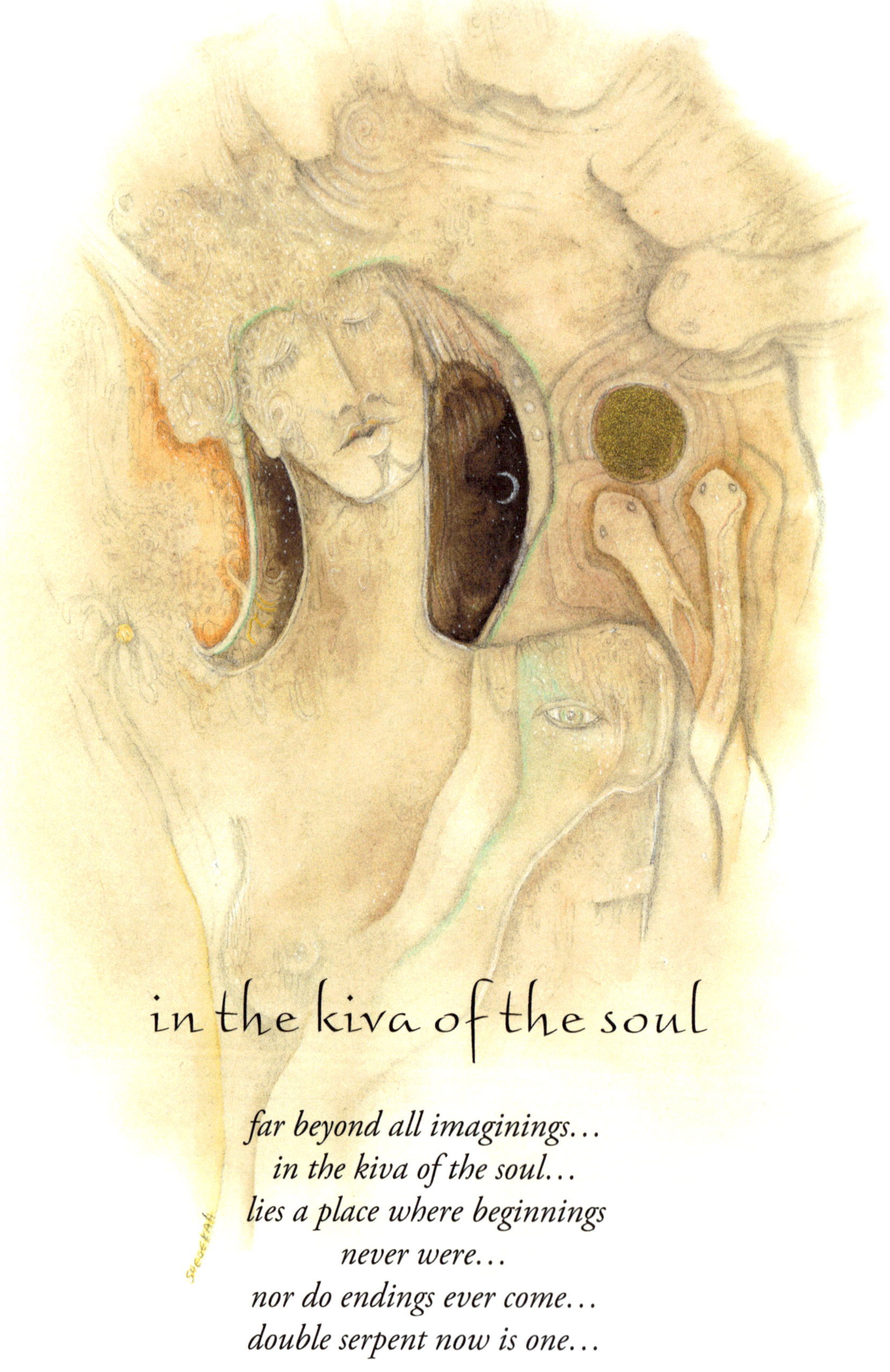

in the kiva of the soul

far beyond all imaginings…
in the kiva of the soul…
lies a place where beginnings
never were…
nor do endings ever come…
double serpent now is one…

Woman retreats into the inner kiva womb. Unfathomable splendor invisible to the double eye is known.

Winged-SHE…from Infinity's Space…

winged-SHE…from Infinity's space…

emerges ever…as dancer of the heart…

A visual impartation
of Infinity's space,
the Vastness.

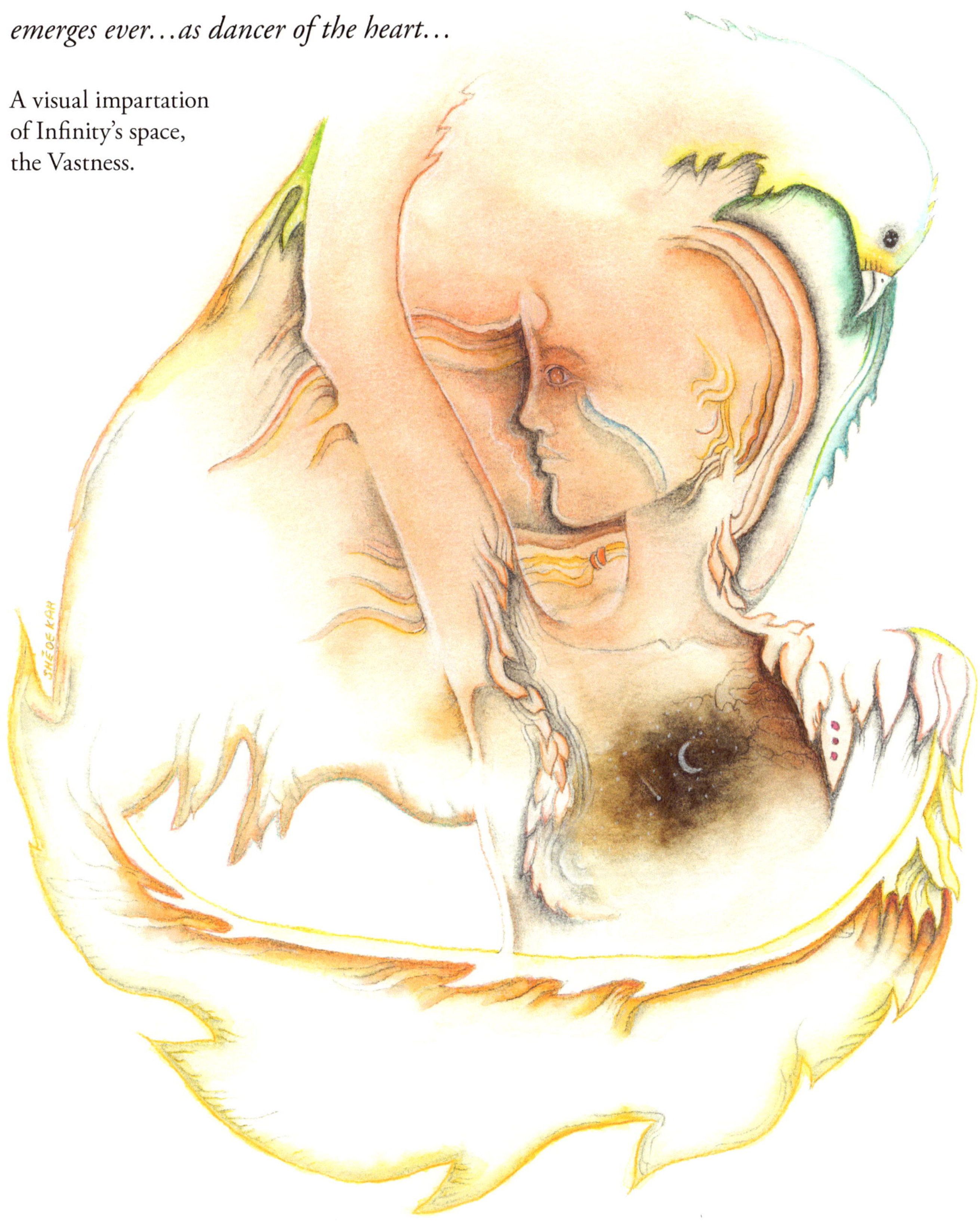

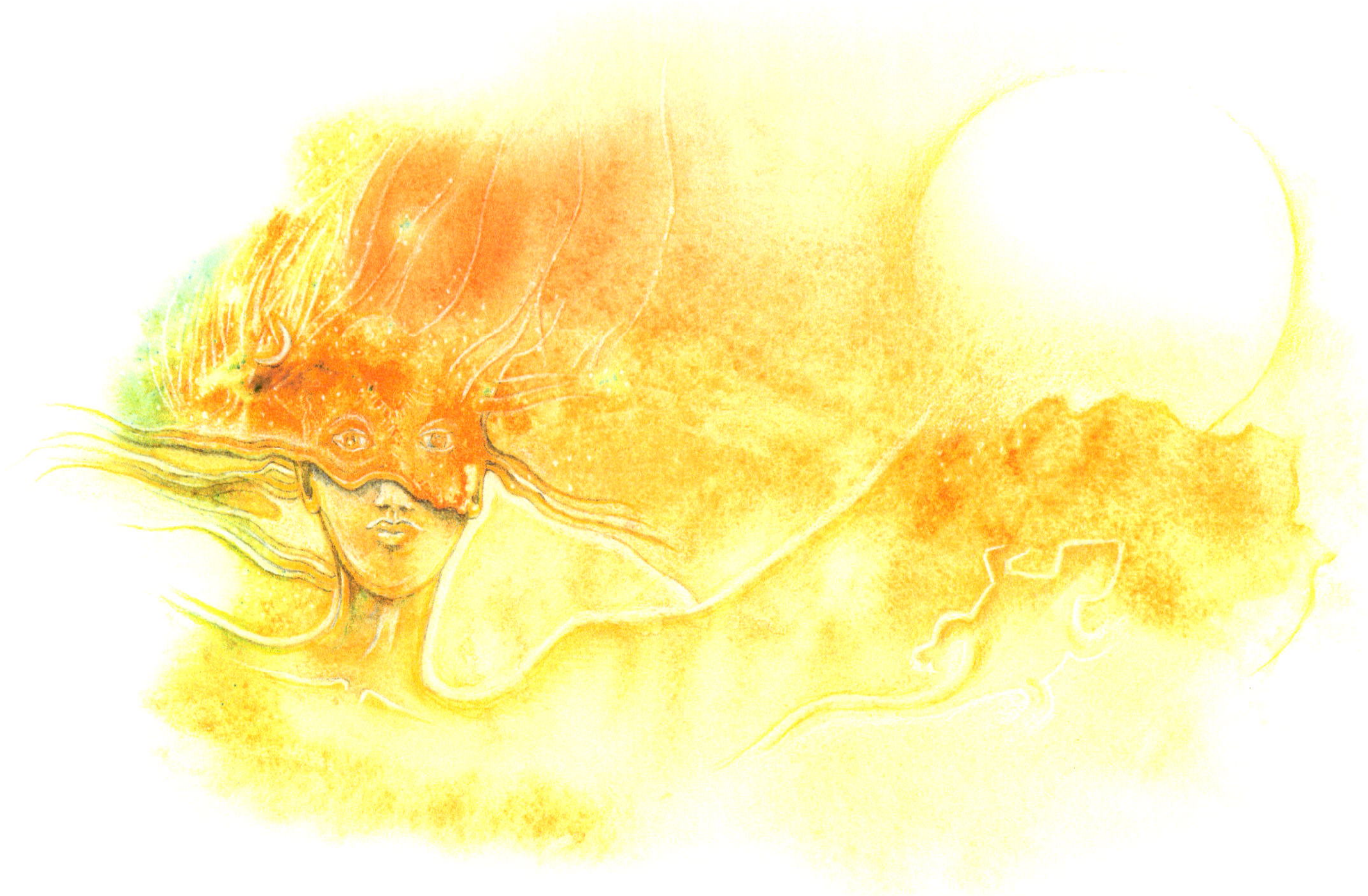

desert-dance...
in the rising sun...

desert-dance...
in the rising sun...

donned in nature...
masked as mountain...

Portrayed is the dance of Oneness.

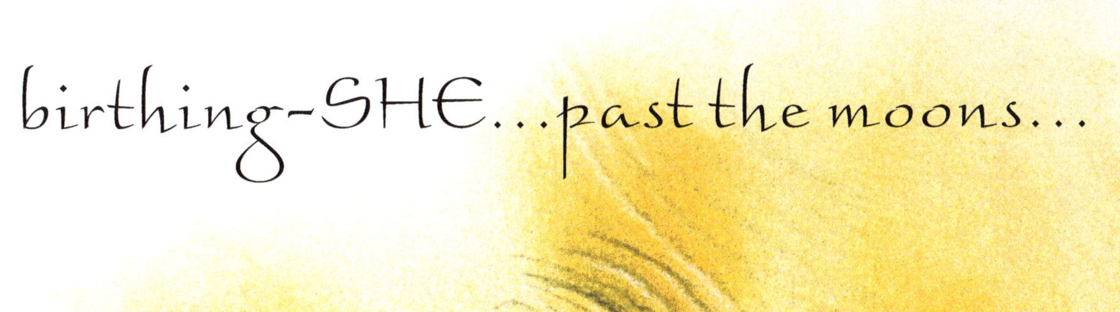

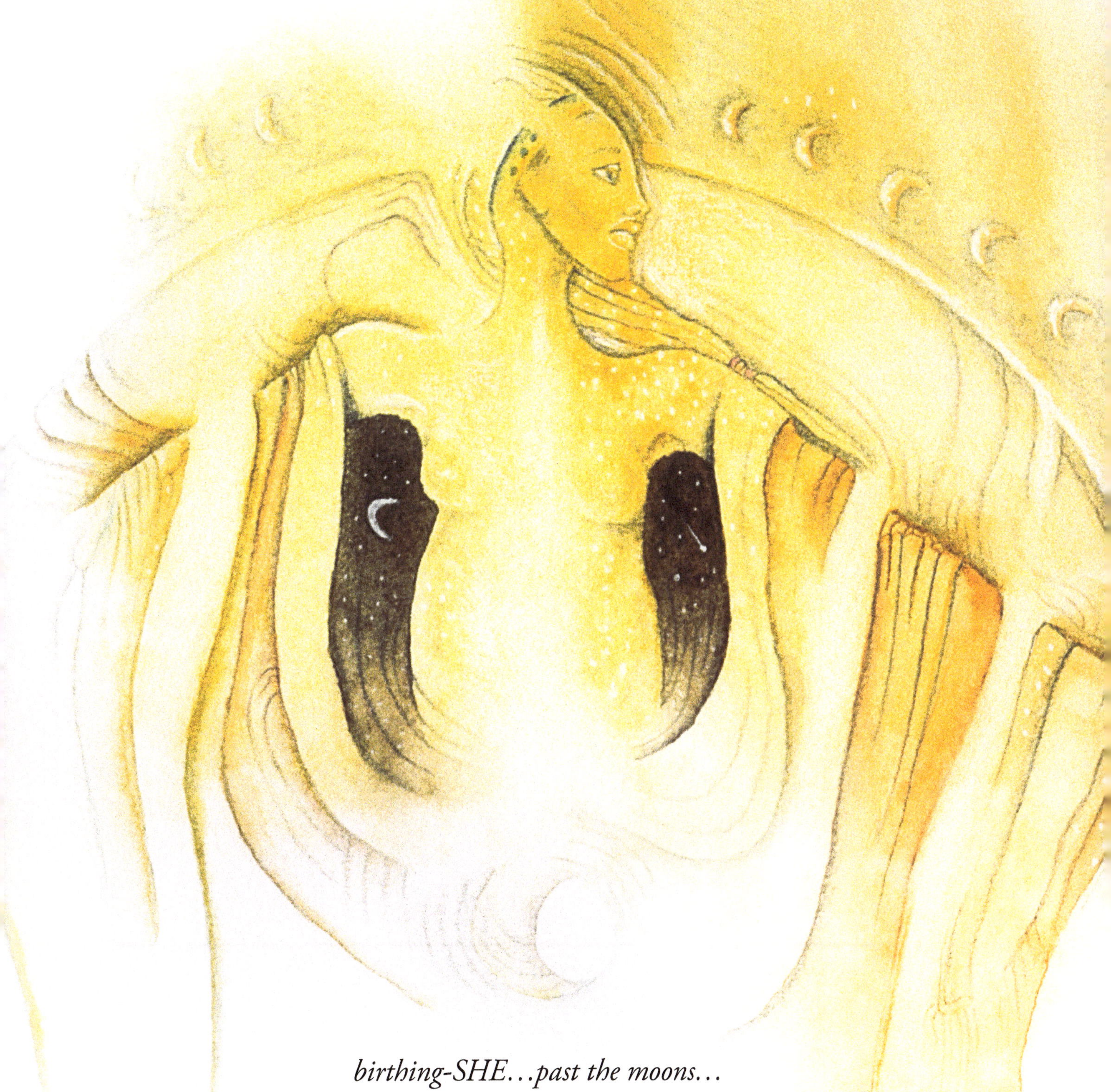

birthing-SHE…past the moons…

birthing-SHE…beyond the forms…

The invitation here is to
the formless realms…
the infinite invisible…

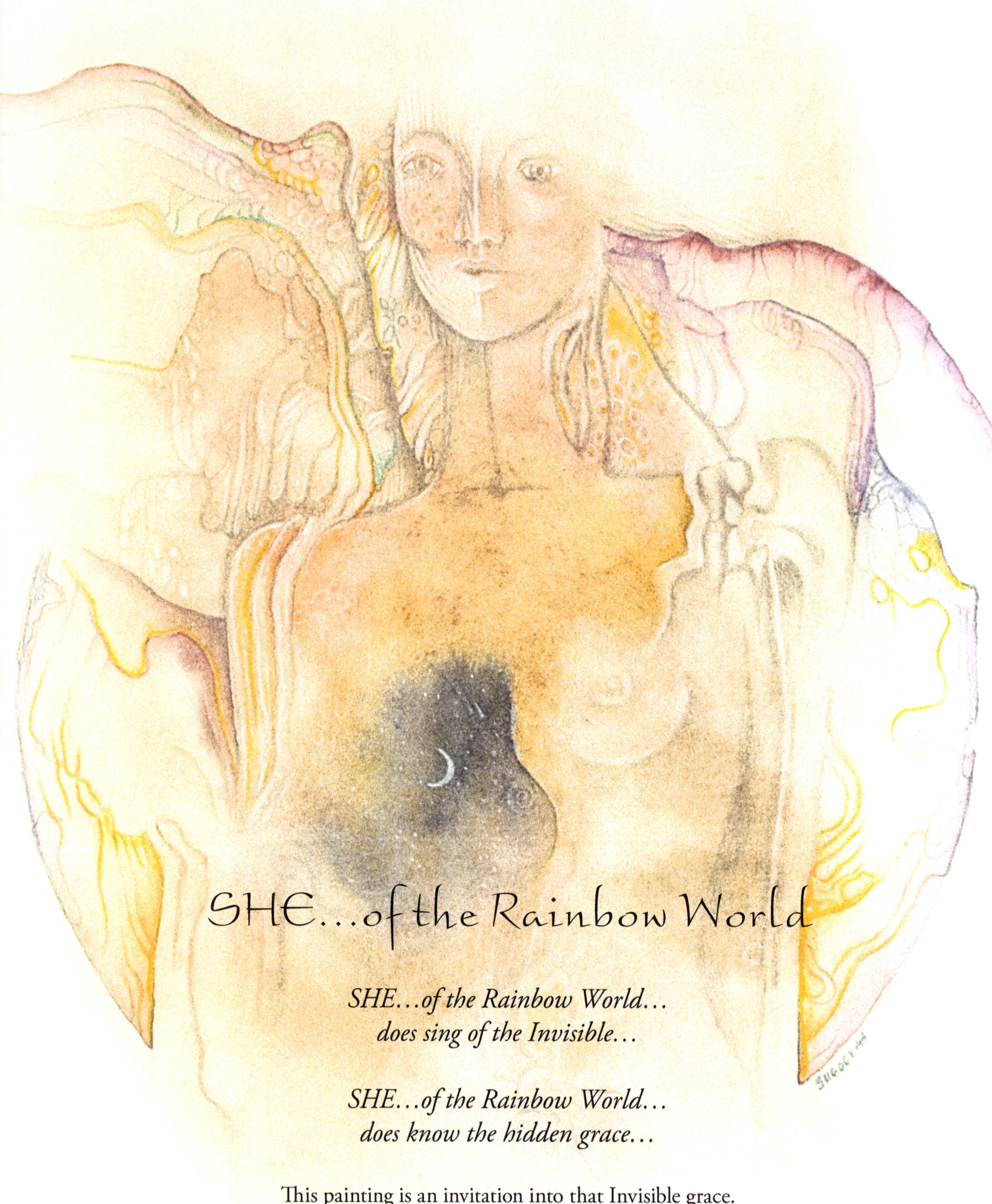

SHE…of the Rainbow World

SHE…of the Rainbow World…
does sing of the Invisible…

SHE…of the Rainbow World…
does know the hidden grace…

This painting is an invitation into that Invisible grace.
To feel…to know…to realize…

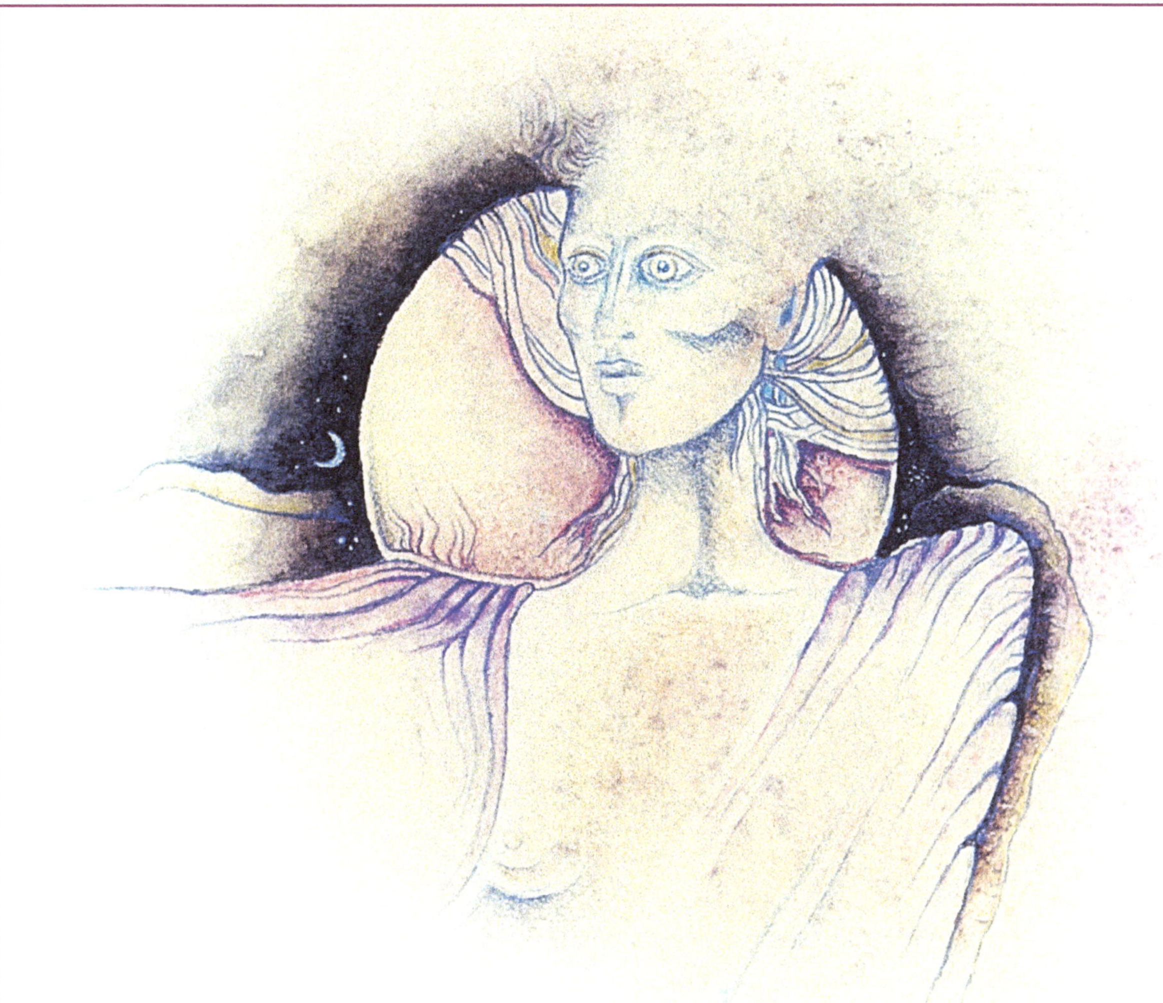

SHE...walks through the door...
beyond beginnings...

SHE...walks through the door...beyond beginnings...

SHE...walks through the door...beyond form...

The Formless does speak and informs the formed.

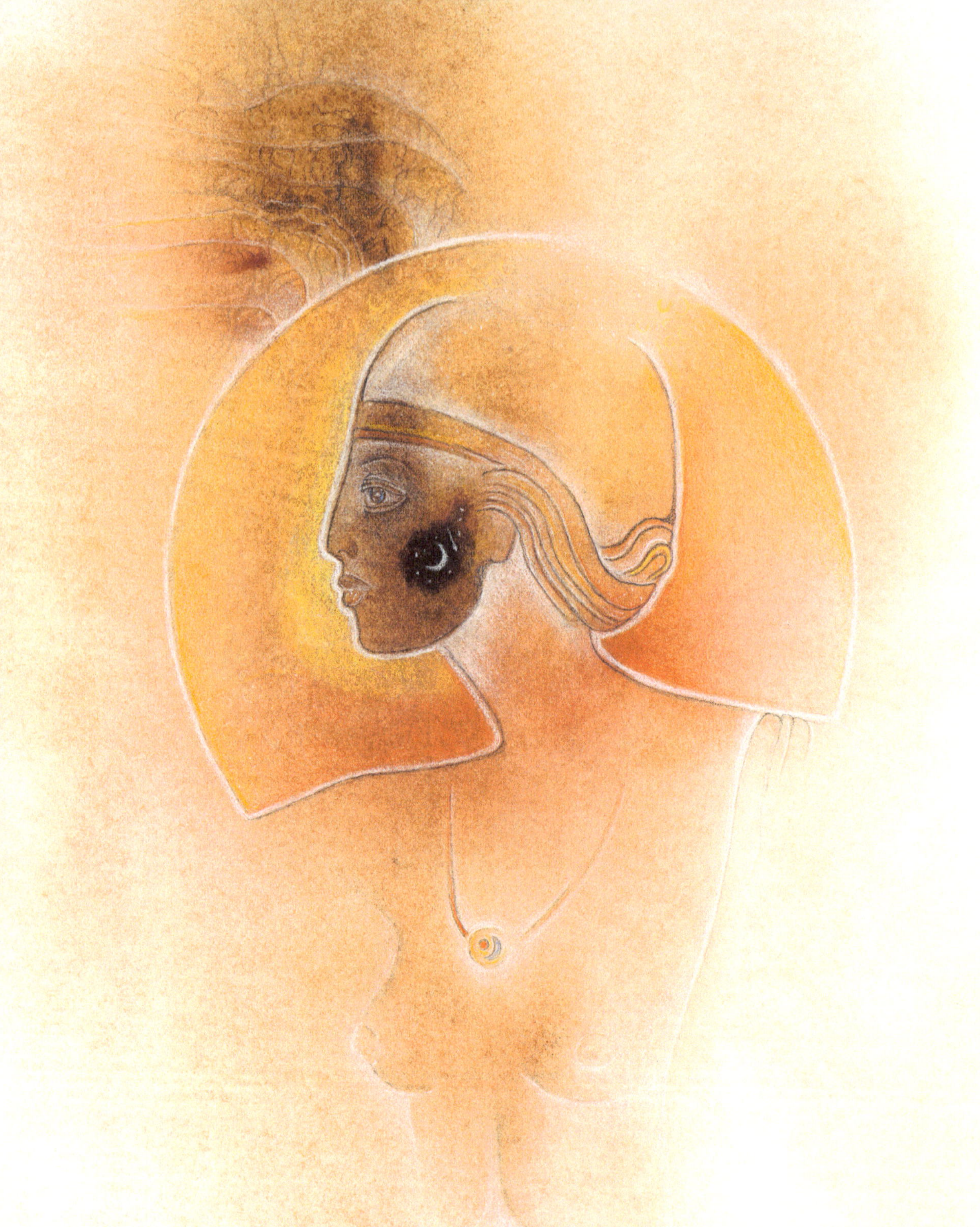

adorned-SHE...as Infinity's desert dance

adorned-SHE...as Infinity's desert dance...
comes a flame of knowing...
that beauty lights the way...

Adornment stands forth as Beauty's path into the world.

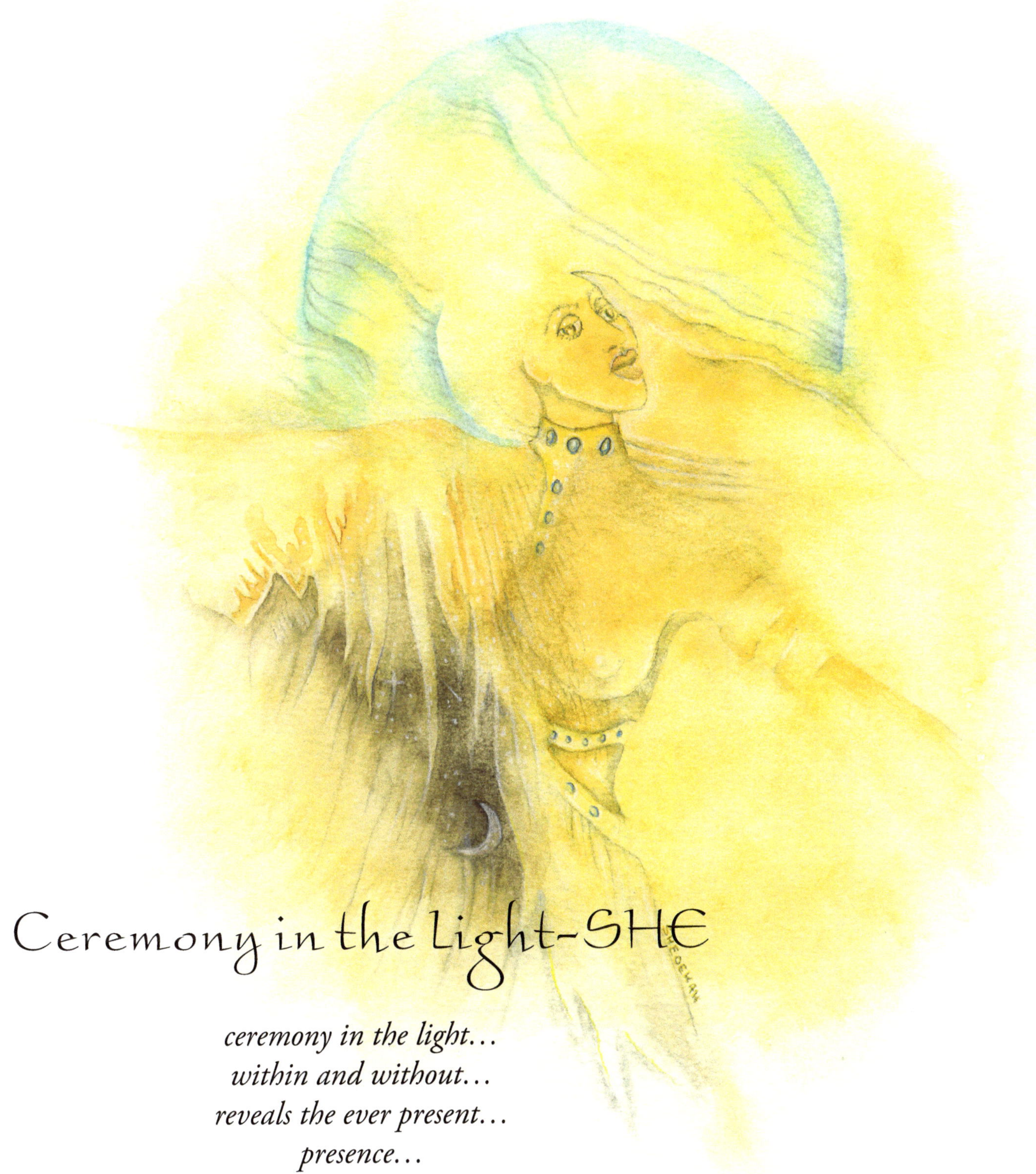

Ceremony in the Light-SHE

ceremony in the light...
within and without...
reveals the ever present...
presence...

Omnipresence reveals herSelf.

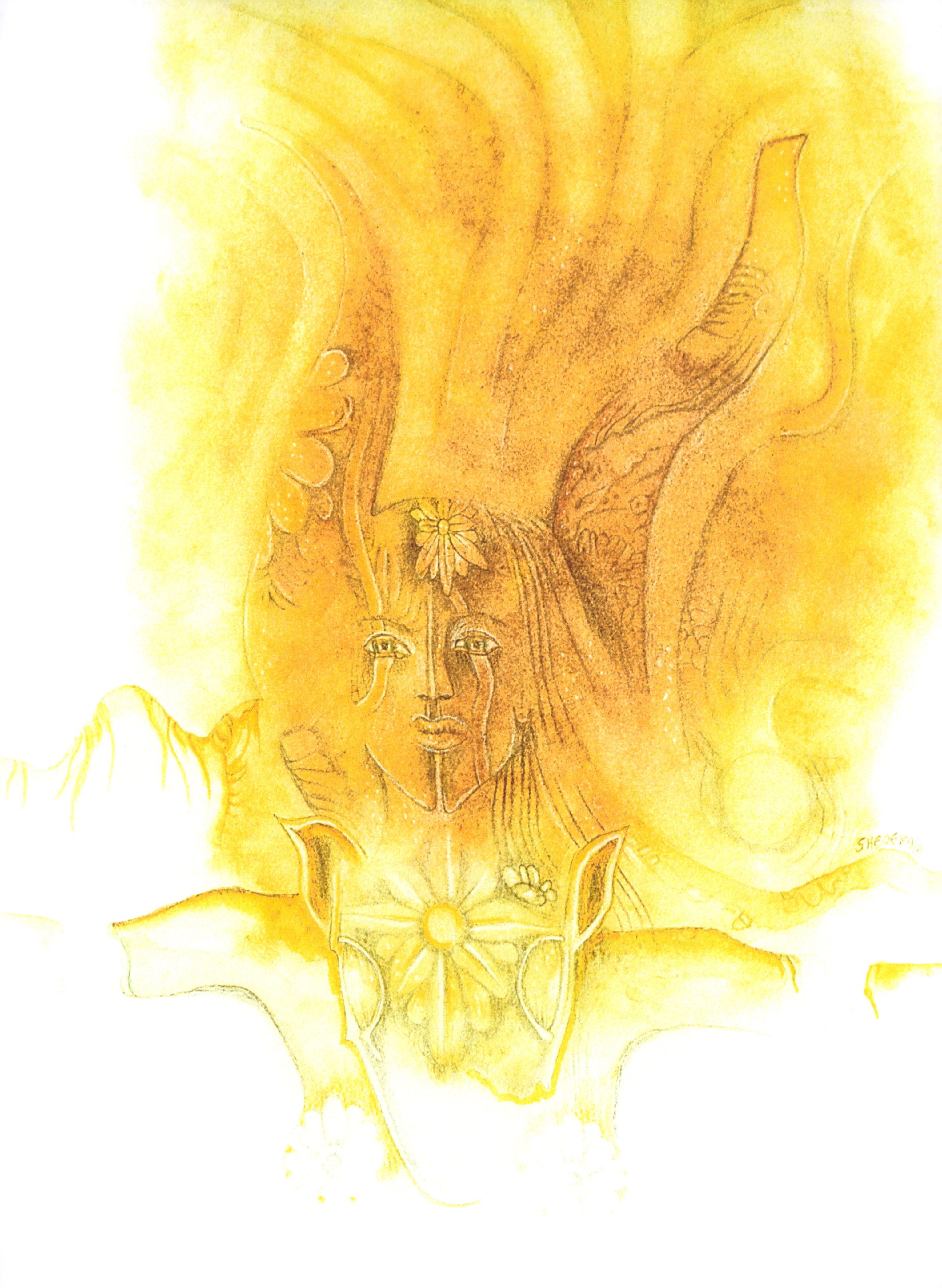

Flower of Life-SHE

SHE stands quiet…
as the formed and formless…

The formed and formless are revealed as one.

Ancient Knowing-SHE

SHE carries sight far beyond the winged one…

SHE carries knowing of the One…

The divine feminine has never lost the knowing.
Unveiled is Awareness as the Self.

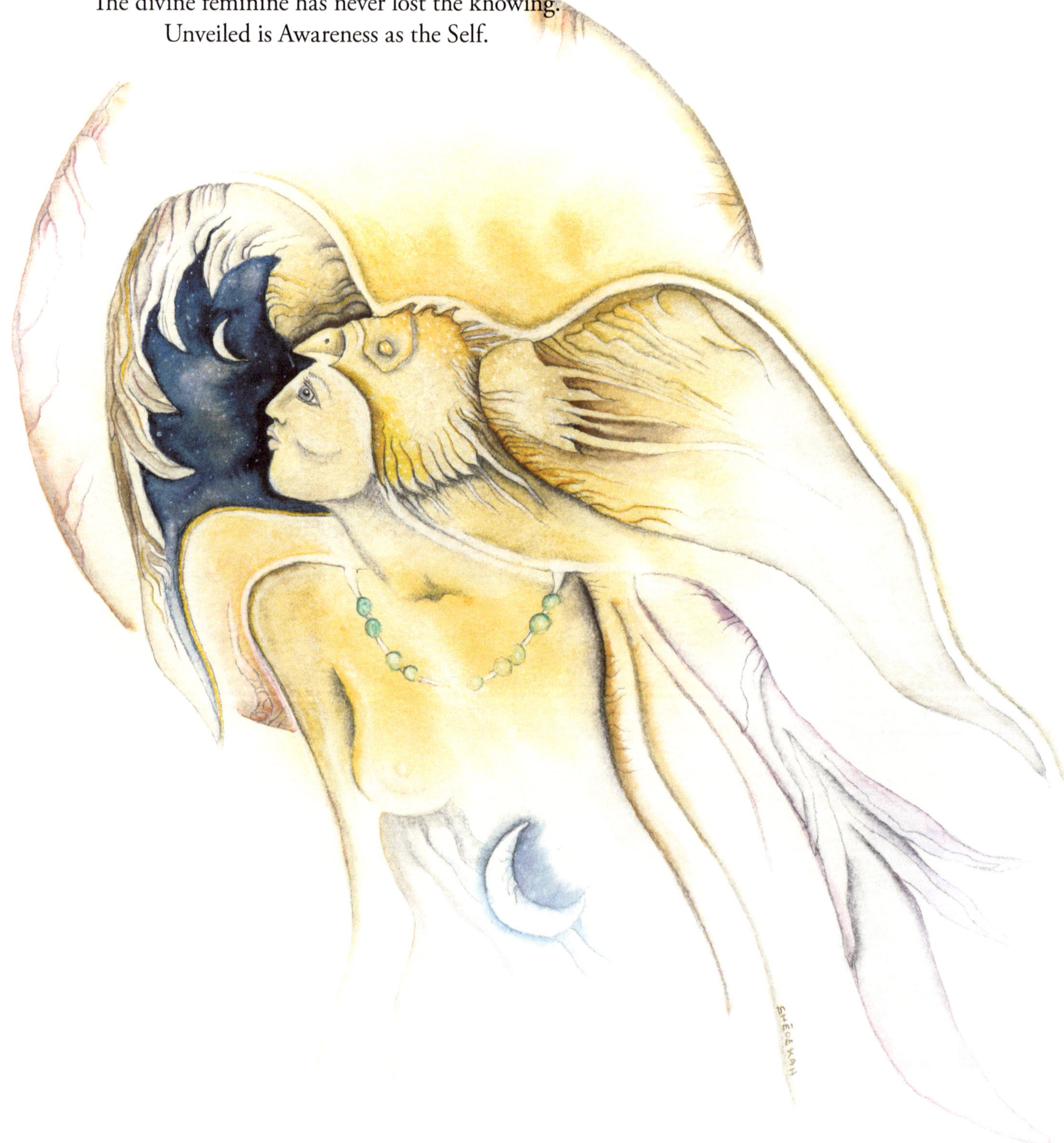

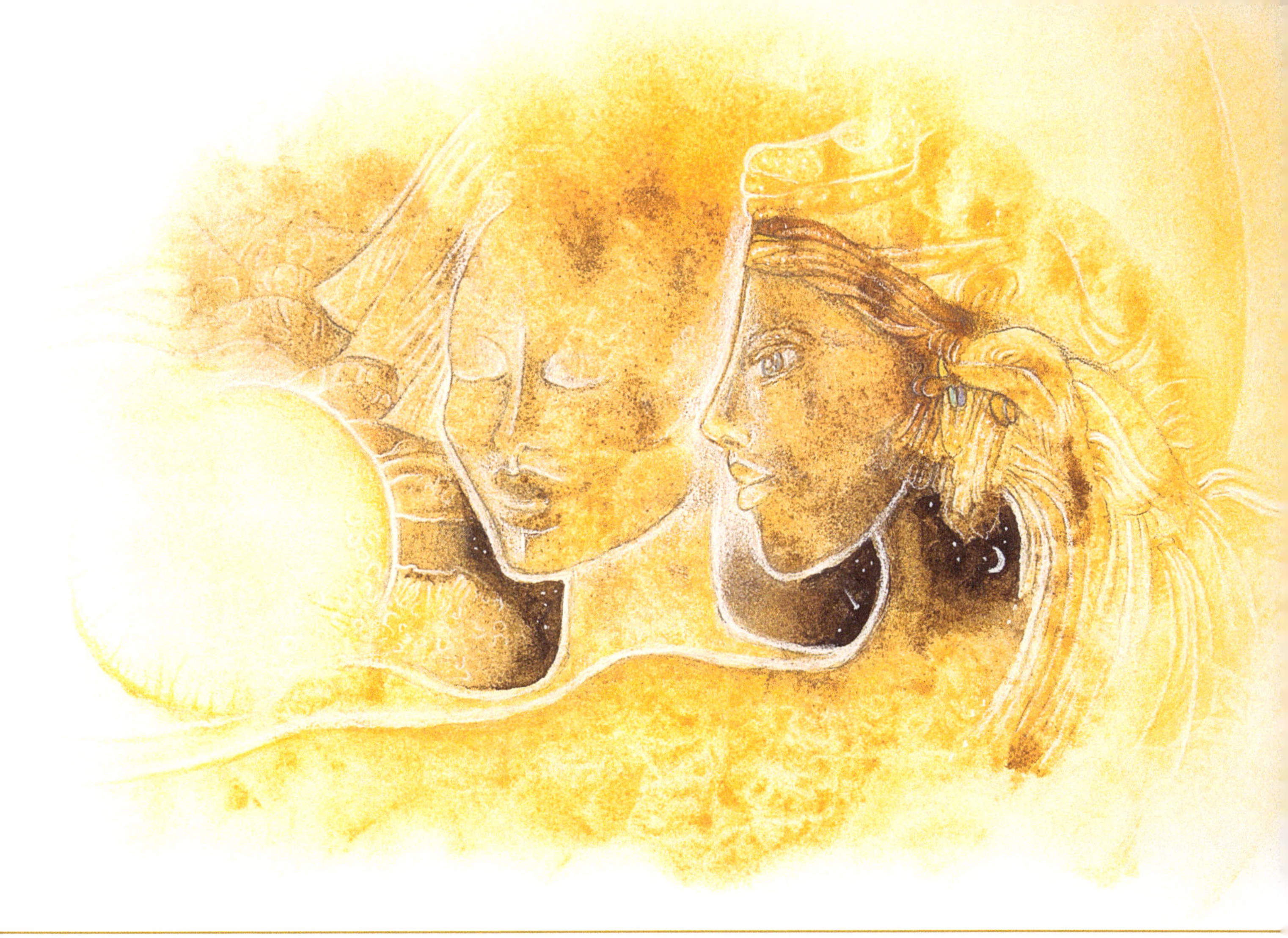

Sisters of the moon...
in ceremony with the sun...

the sun...
the moon...
the he and she...
the undivided one...

The sisters of the moon point
ever to the One.

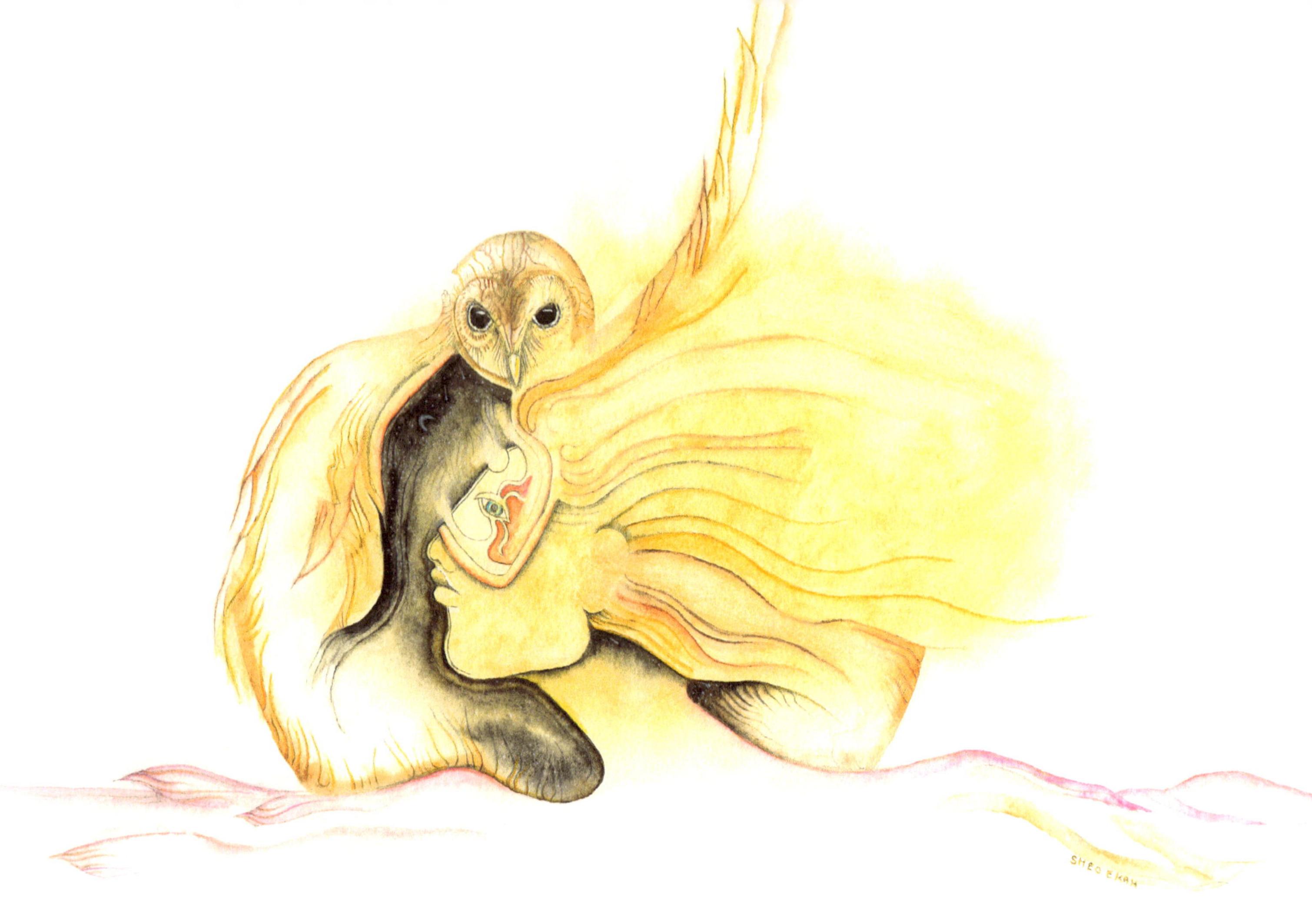

Woman-SHE...of the Circle... hears...the message of the owl...

woman-SHE...of the circle...
hears...the message of the owl...

woman...hear...
hear the wisdom of the night...

The yin of the feminine reflects
the wisdom of the night.

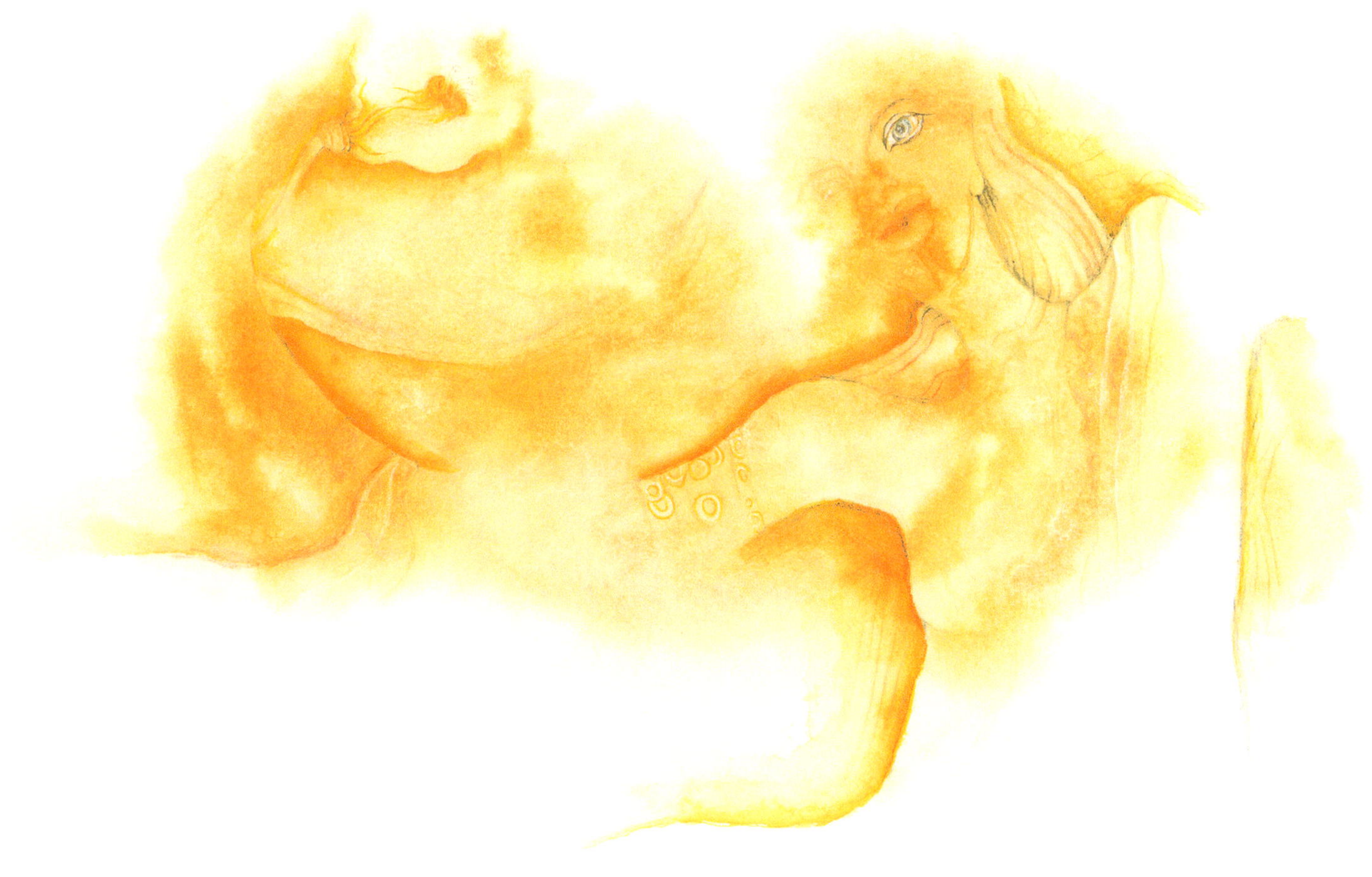

Beloved...I dance for you...

I dance for you in the wind...
I dance for you as the flower...
ever...
ever...do I dance for you...

Here self does disappear and Self is known.
Gossamer is the realization.

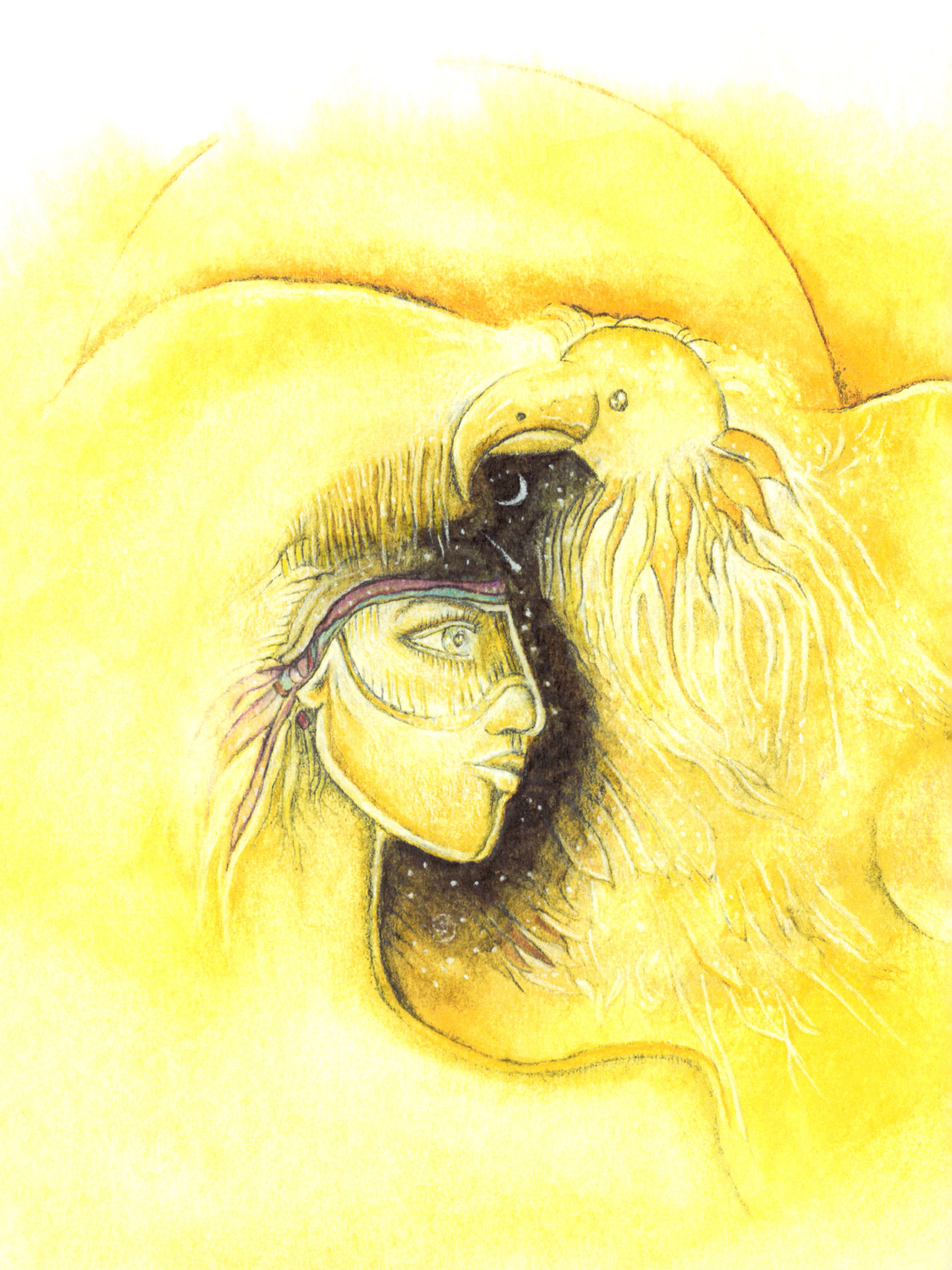

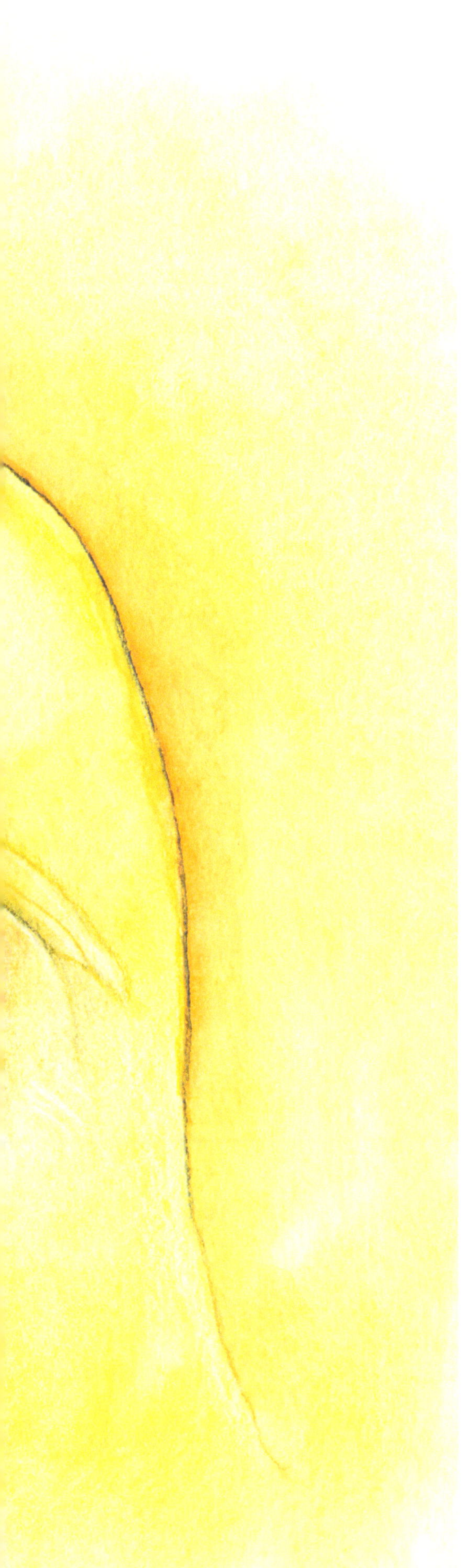

Message from the Sky...

...vulture does come...
speaking messages of decay...
speaking messages of passing world...
speaking of rebirth...

Divine mind as manifestation does fill our days.
Would we listen to the messages?

...message from the sky...
imparts awareness of transcendence.

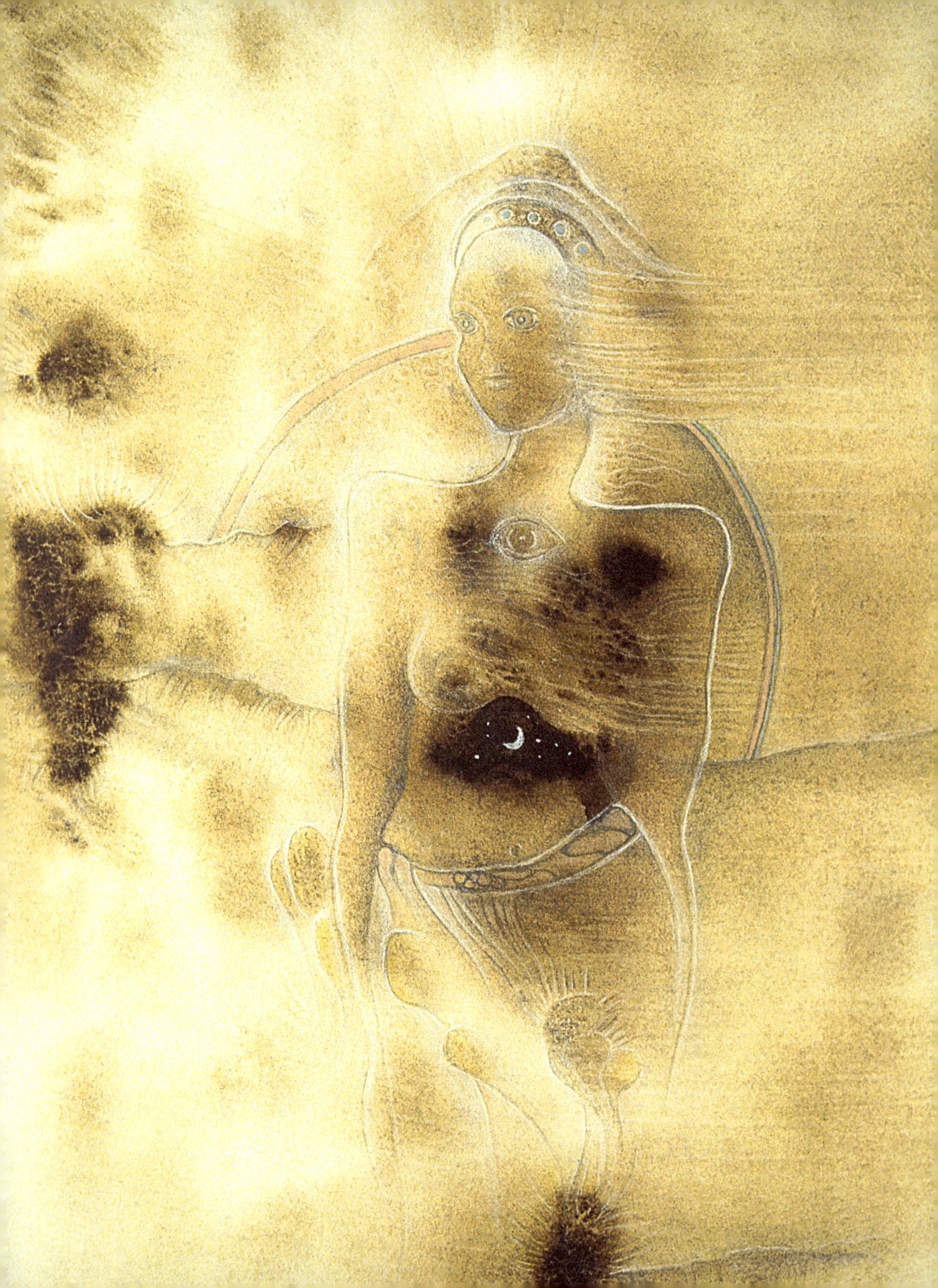

SHE...it is...who stands naked

SHE…it is…who stands naked…
in the medicine shield of the light…

SHE…it is…who stands bare…
radiating stars and moons and suns…

The feminine force is an energy the world does welcome. It heralds life out of time.

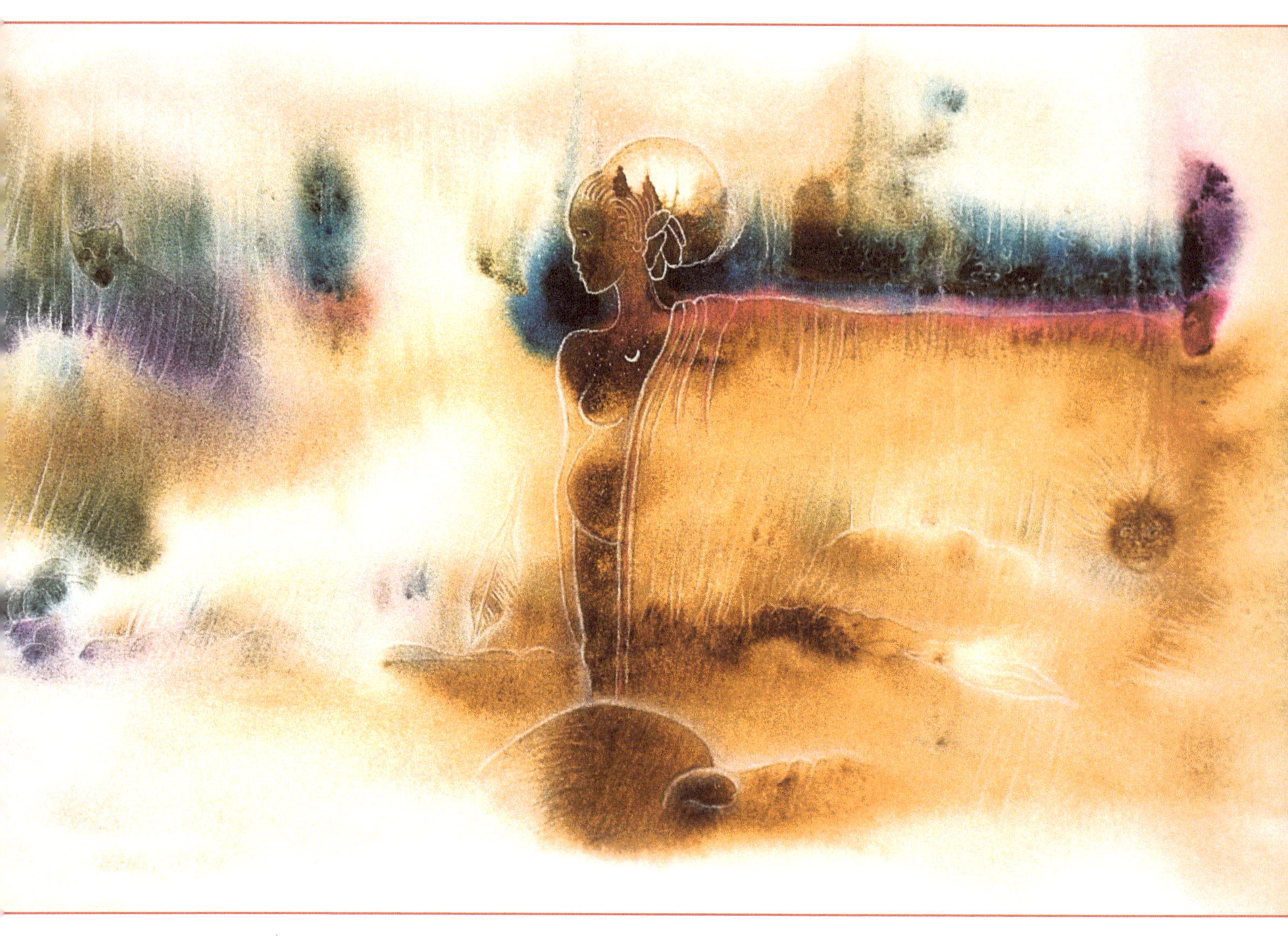

Moon-mother-SHE...

Moon-mother-SHE...
in ceremony with turtle...
and two feathers...

Representing HE and SHE in union,
the two feathers shower new life upon the earth.
And balance, it is known.

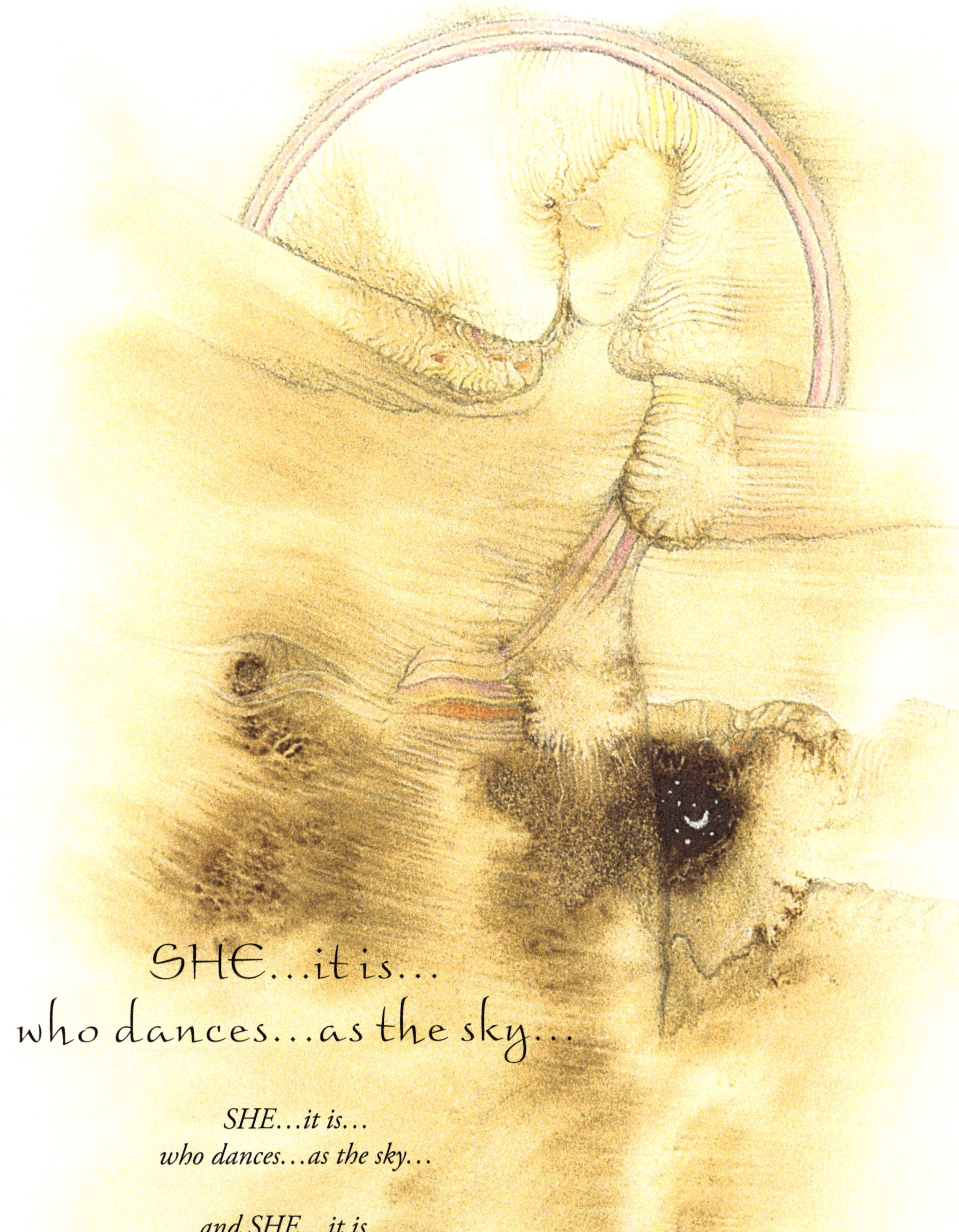

SHE…it is…
who dances…as the sky…

and SHE…it is…
who feels softly…her feet upon the ground…

Imaged here is Oneness of the above and below.

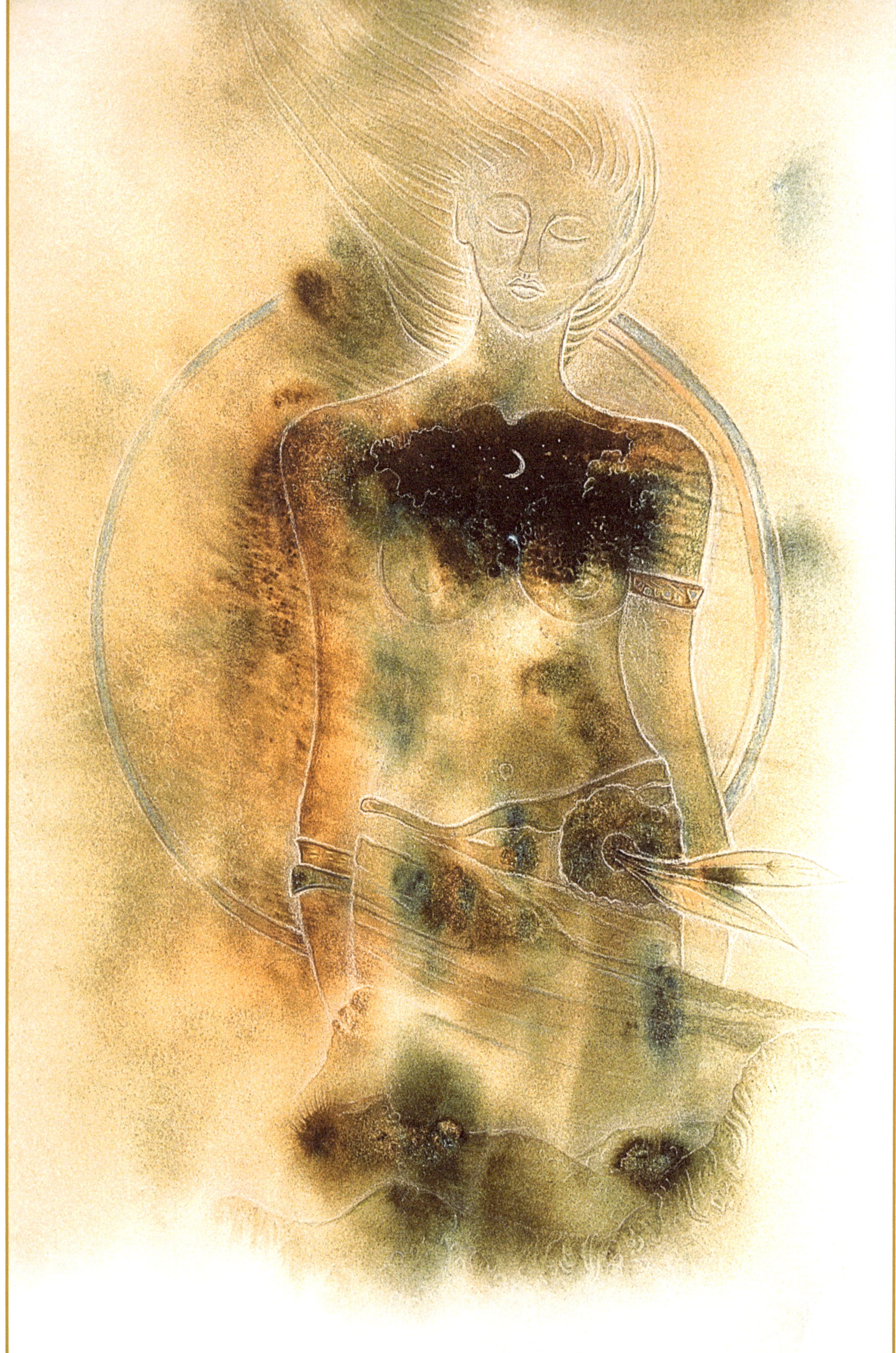

White Buffalo Woman

white buffalo woman dances…
in the circle of he and she…

Depicted is an ancient knowledge
of yin/yang balance. And harmony, it is there.

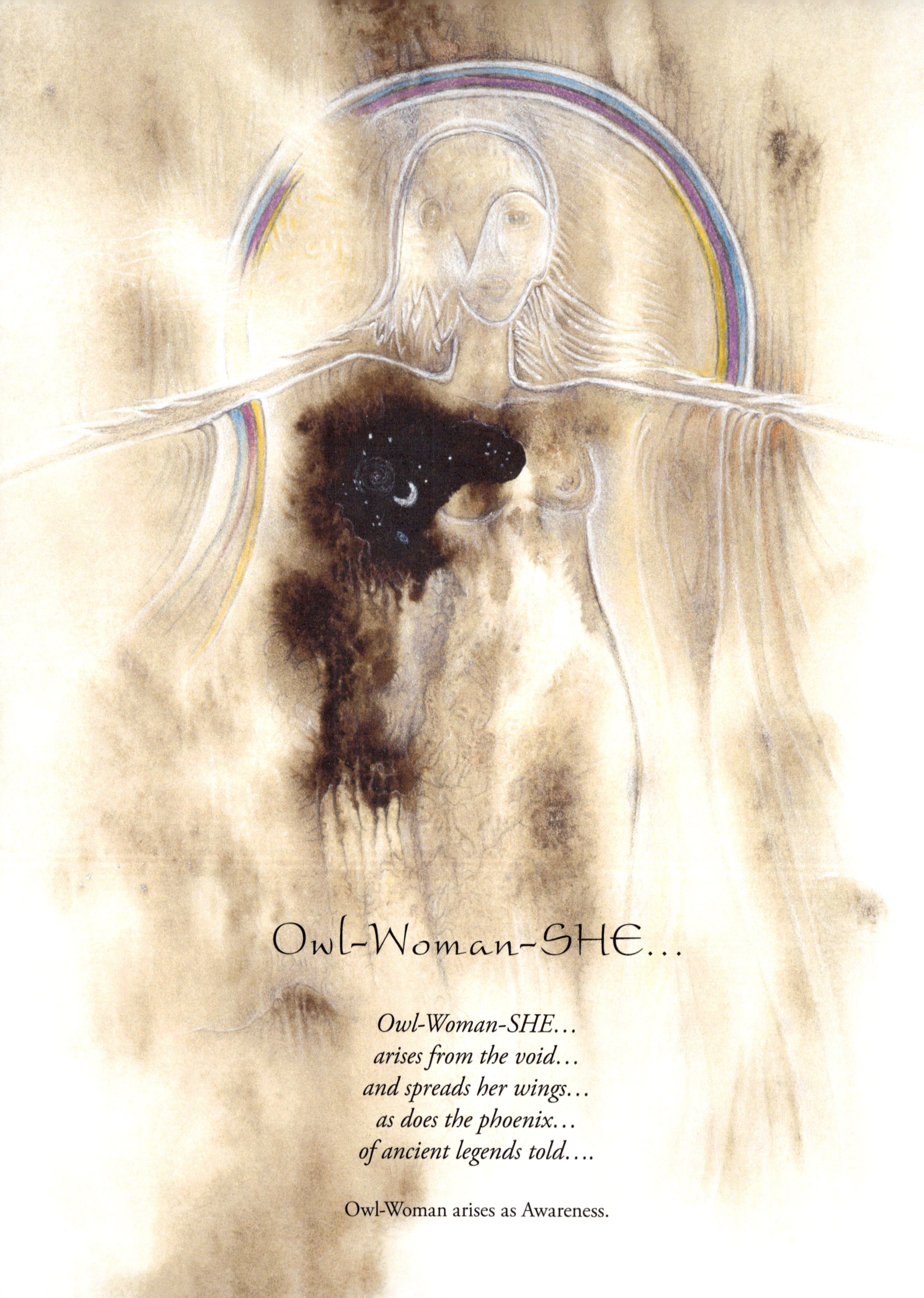

Owl-Woman-SHE…

Owl-Woman-SHE…
arises from the void…
and spreads her wings…
as does the phoenix…
of ancient legends told….

Owl-Woman arises as Awareness.

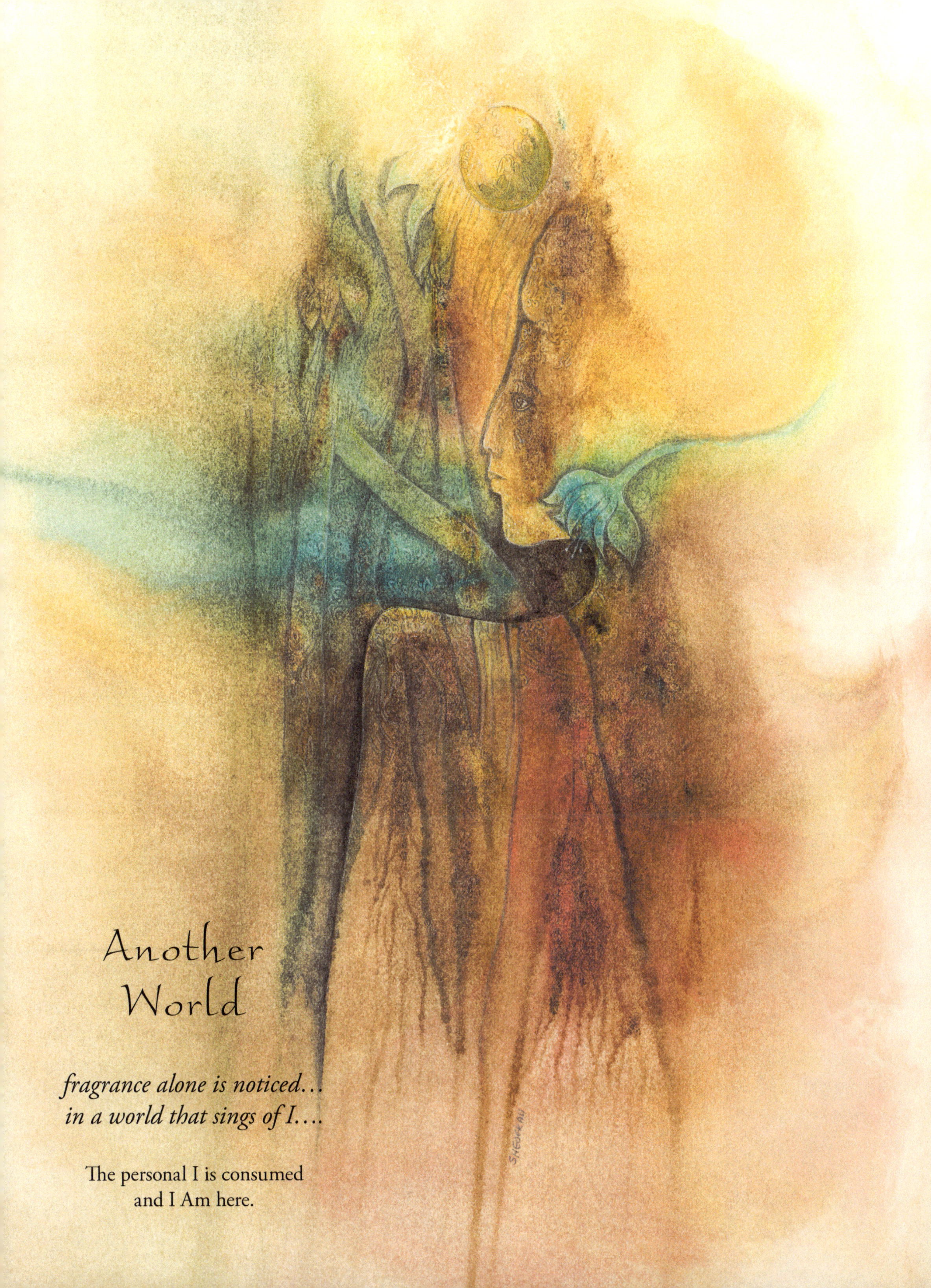

Another World

fragrance alone is noticed…
in a world that sings of I….

The personal I is consumed
and I Am here.

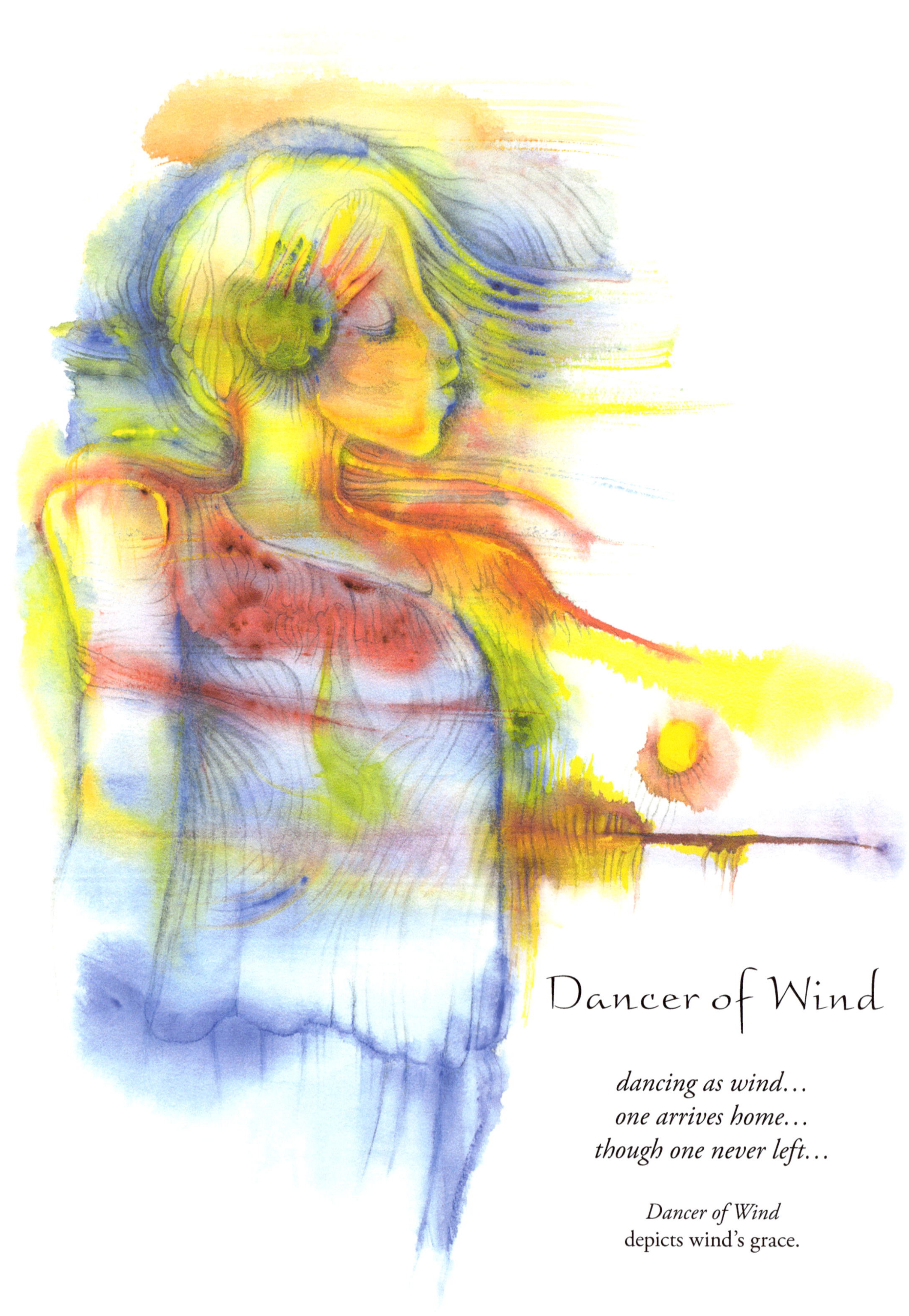

Dancer of Wind

dancing as wind…
one arrives home…
though one never left…

Dancer of Wind
depicts wind's grace.

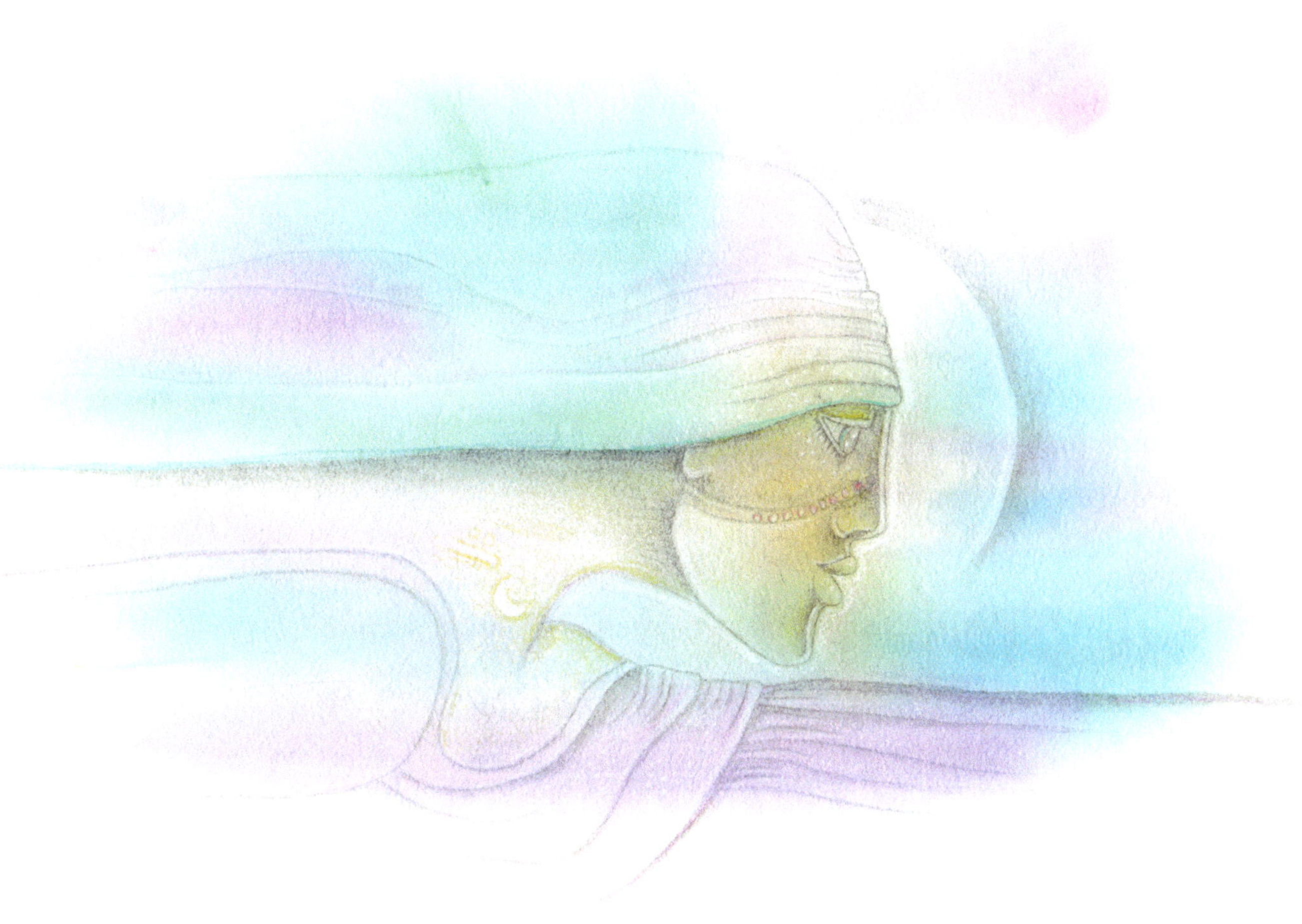

Holy flight-SHE

holy flight-SHE…
wrapped in scarfs of sky…
she wends the ancient way…

All is known as a holy flight.

Images borne to reflect…
the seemingly personal self As the Impersonal Self…
Pure Consciousness…alone…

The Divine Masculine Principle

in

Man and Woman

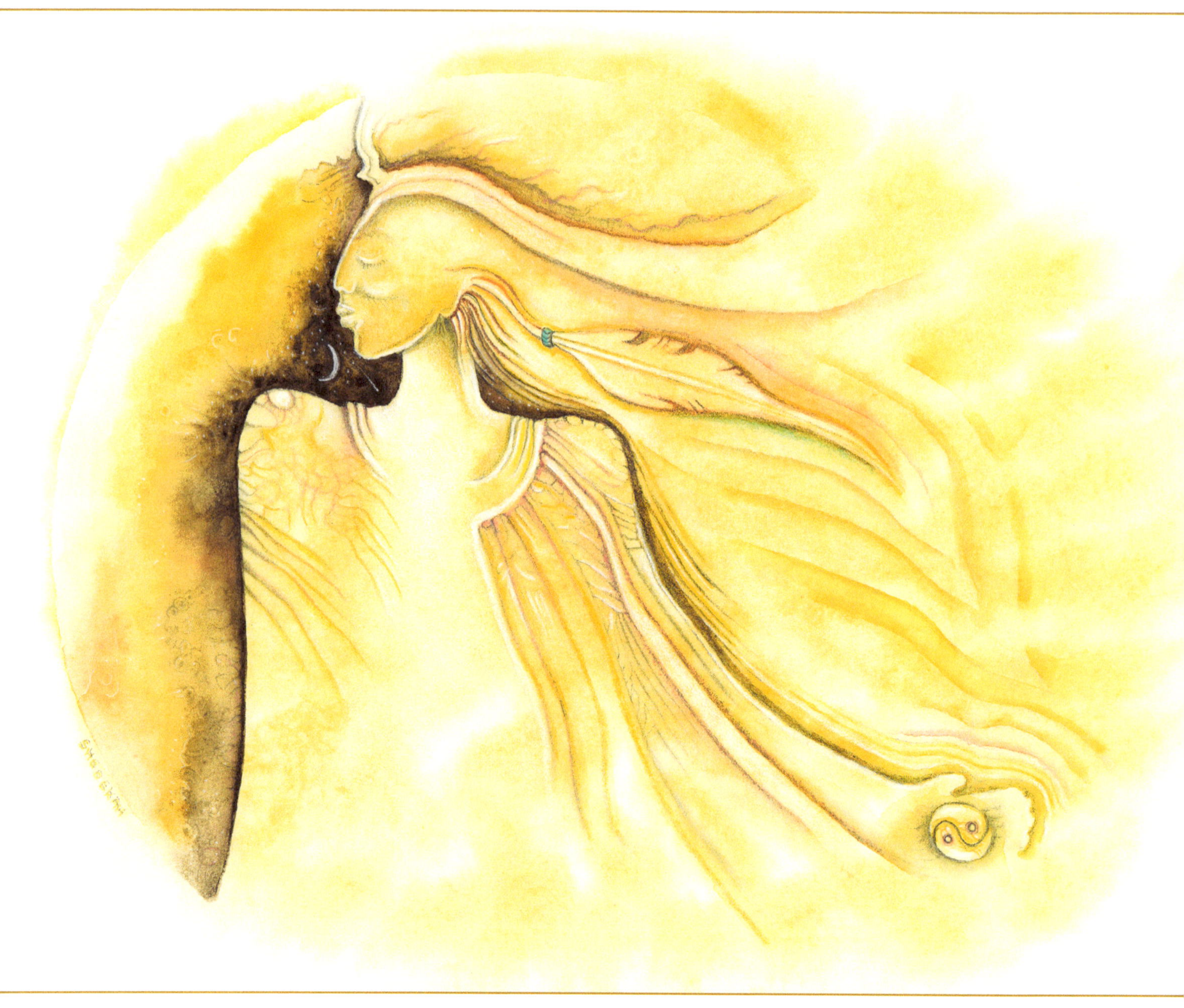

Prayer-HE

robed in Spirit…
prayer has its way…

A visual allegory to herald
the universal law of balance.

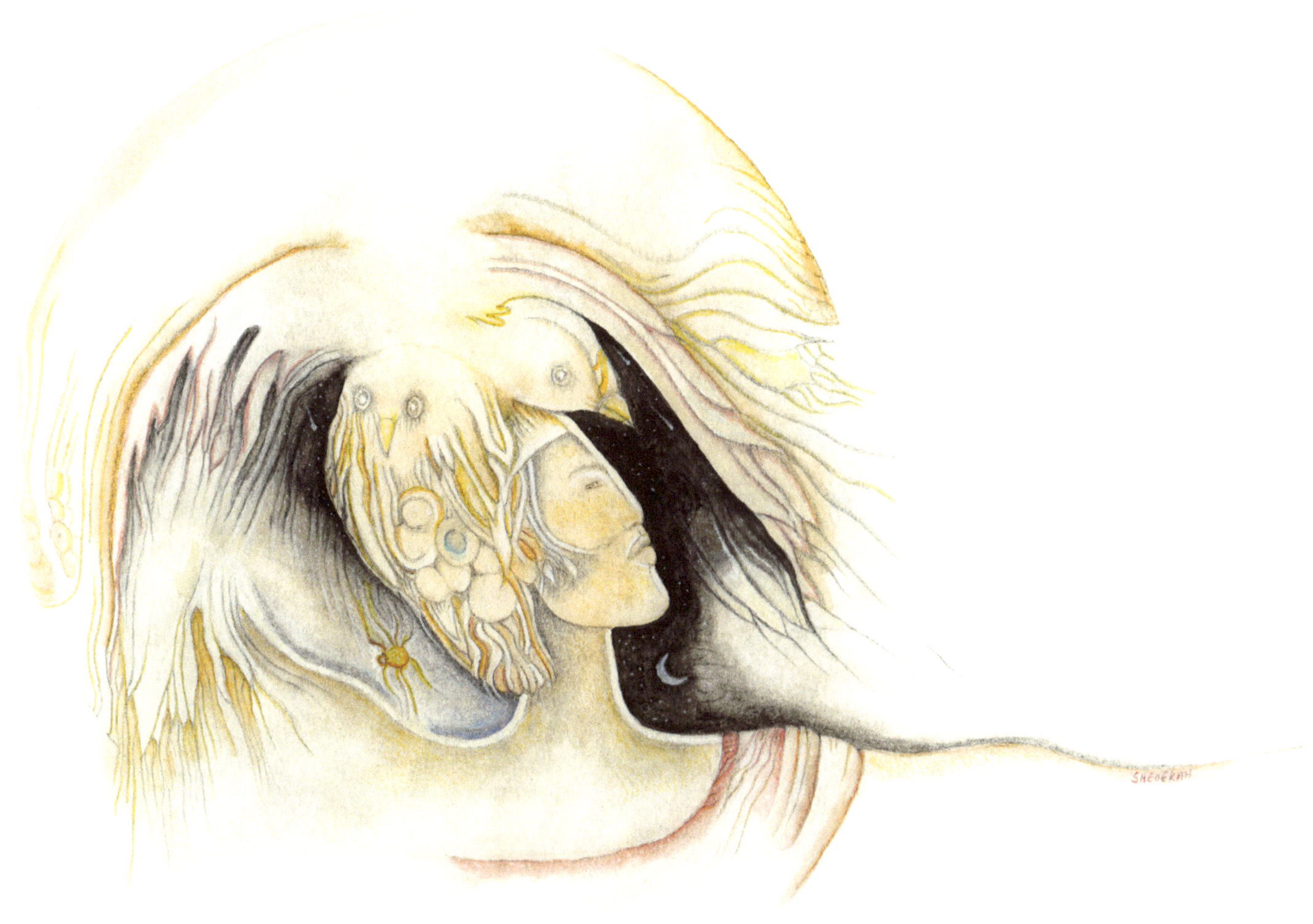

HE...who dances...
in the center of the circle...

HE...does fly amidst the birds...
HE...does visit flowers...
even spiders call his name...

Manifest is god-man...ever free...

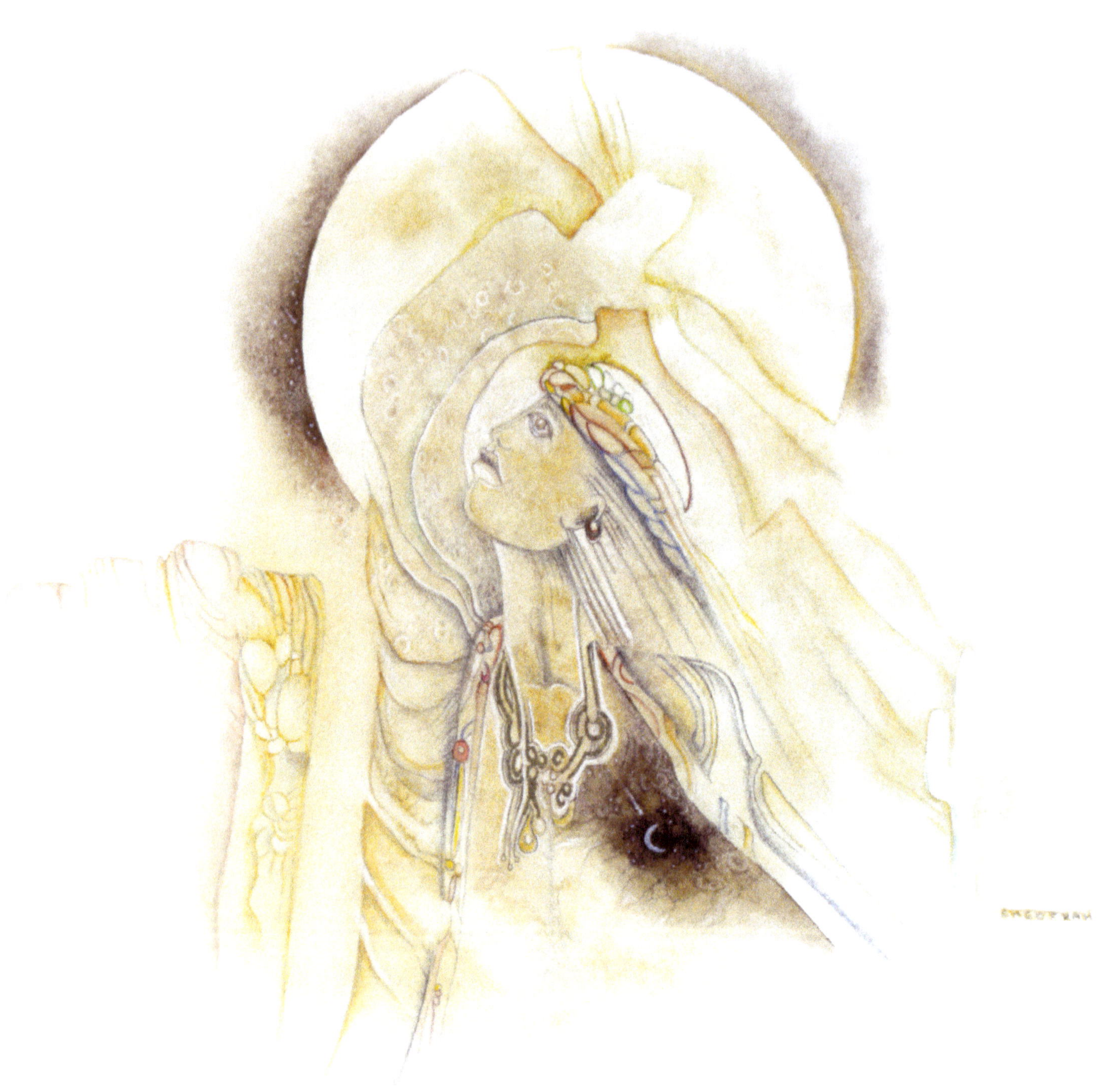

desert ceremony with the moon-HE

adorned as desert dancer...
moon beckons...
he arrives unseen...
touching that which is not heard...

Man arrives solitary on the desertscape
adorned for the moon's eternal song.

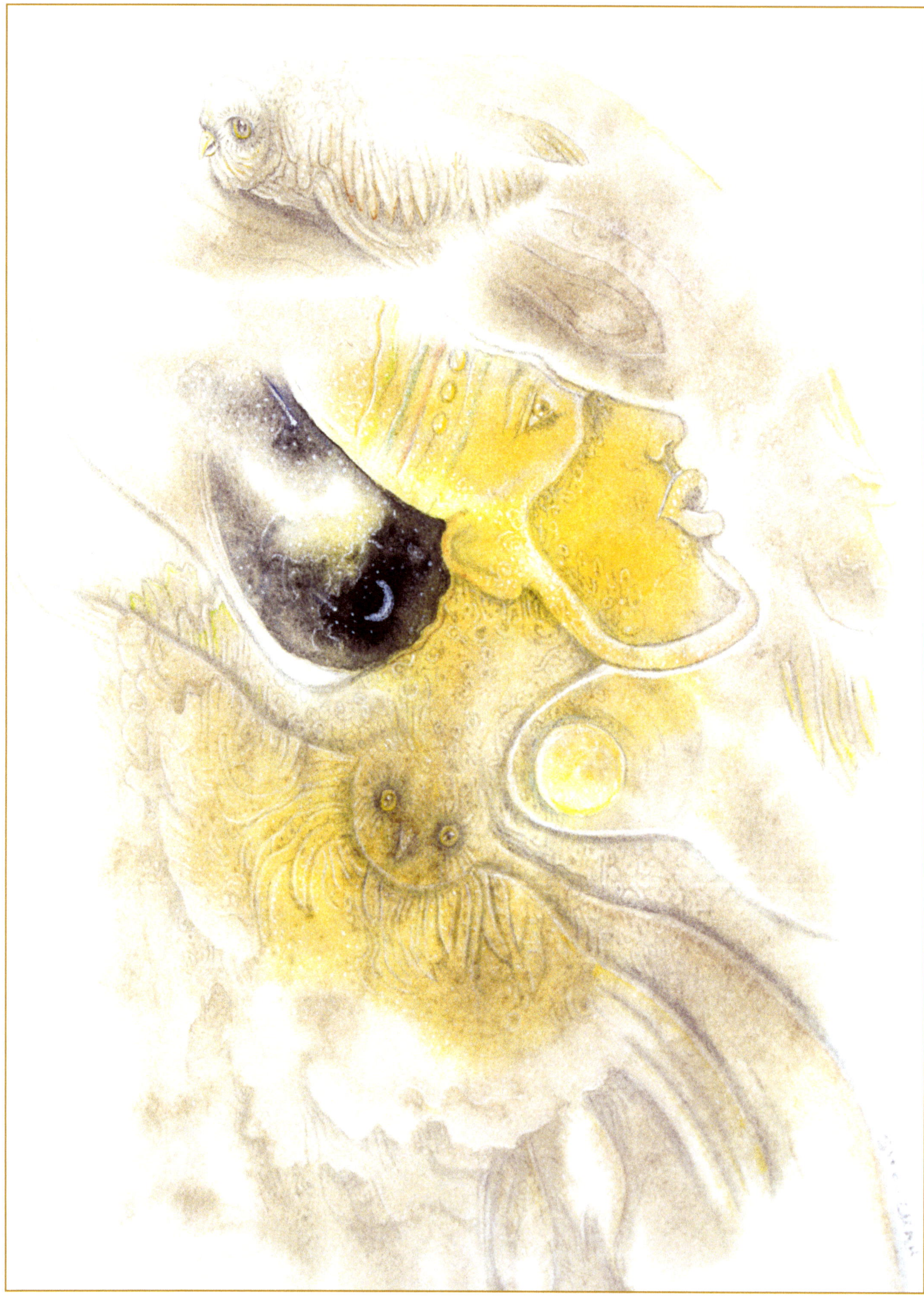

Owl Ceremony-HE

masked HE as the starry realm…
in ceremony with and as the owl…
the stars do shoot across the sky…
heaven…it is known…

Owl does speak the voice
of the heaven world in this painting.
Wisdom in the night.
And man does Know.

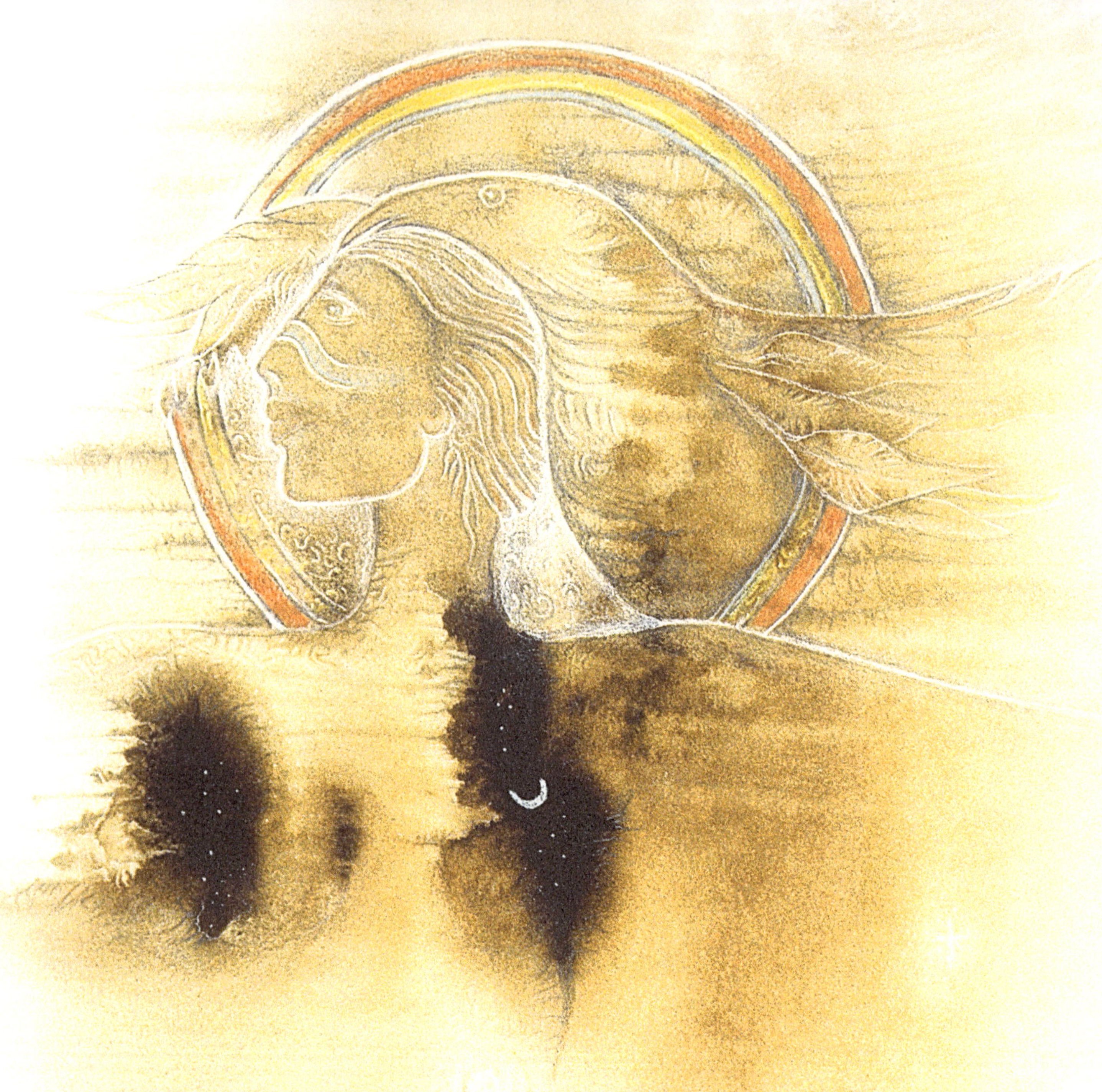

Bird-Tribe-HE...of the Rainbow Nation...

Bird-Tribe-HE...of the Rainbow Nation...

Bird-Tribe-HE...of the tribe of One...

Awareness of oneness inside
the circle of the rainbow is depicted.

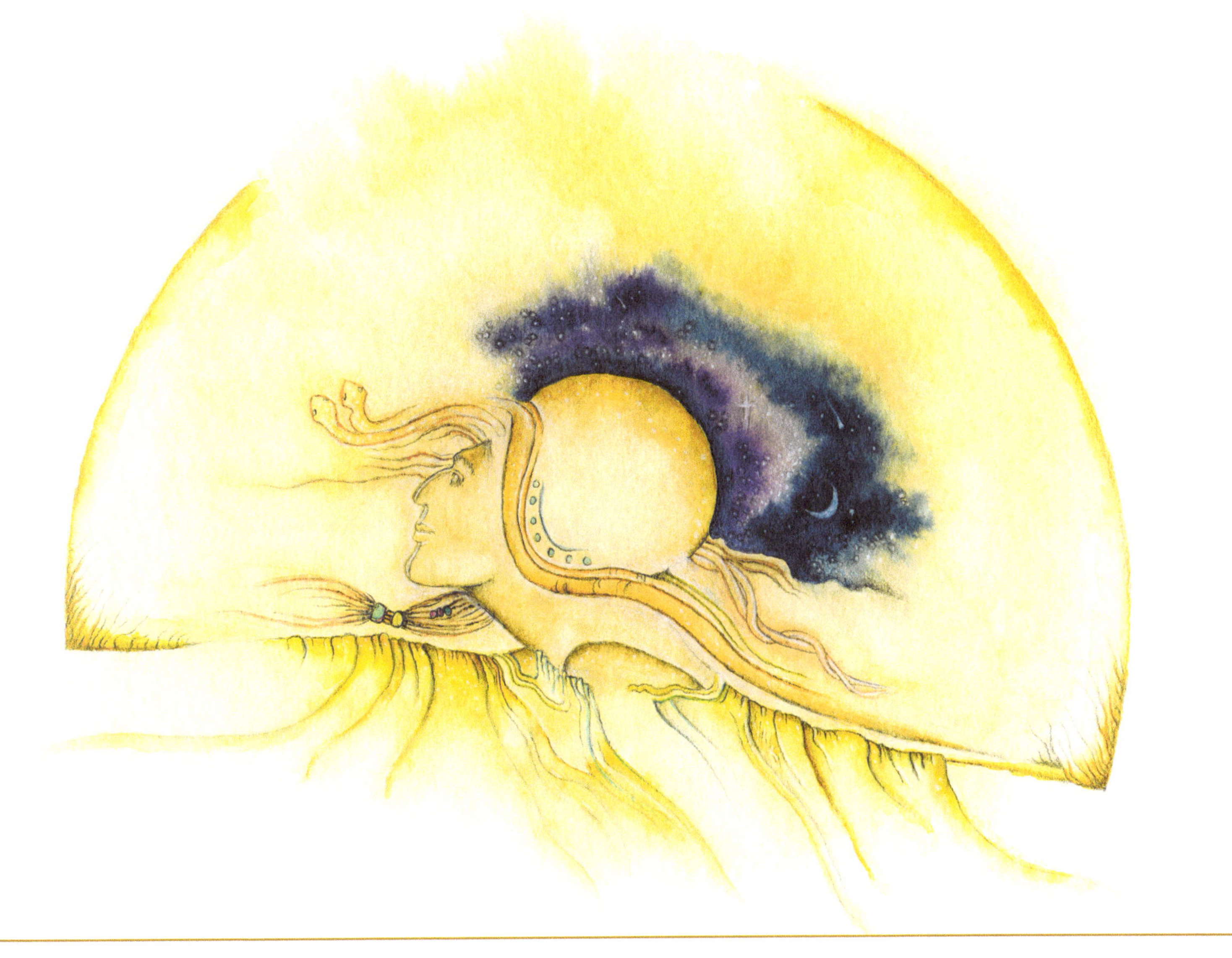

in golden robes

in golden robes and
through the moon…
HE remembers
the Ancient Way…

The universal law of balance
that is unconditional love is known.

This painting exacts the importance
of the receptive, the yin of our nature.

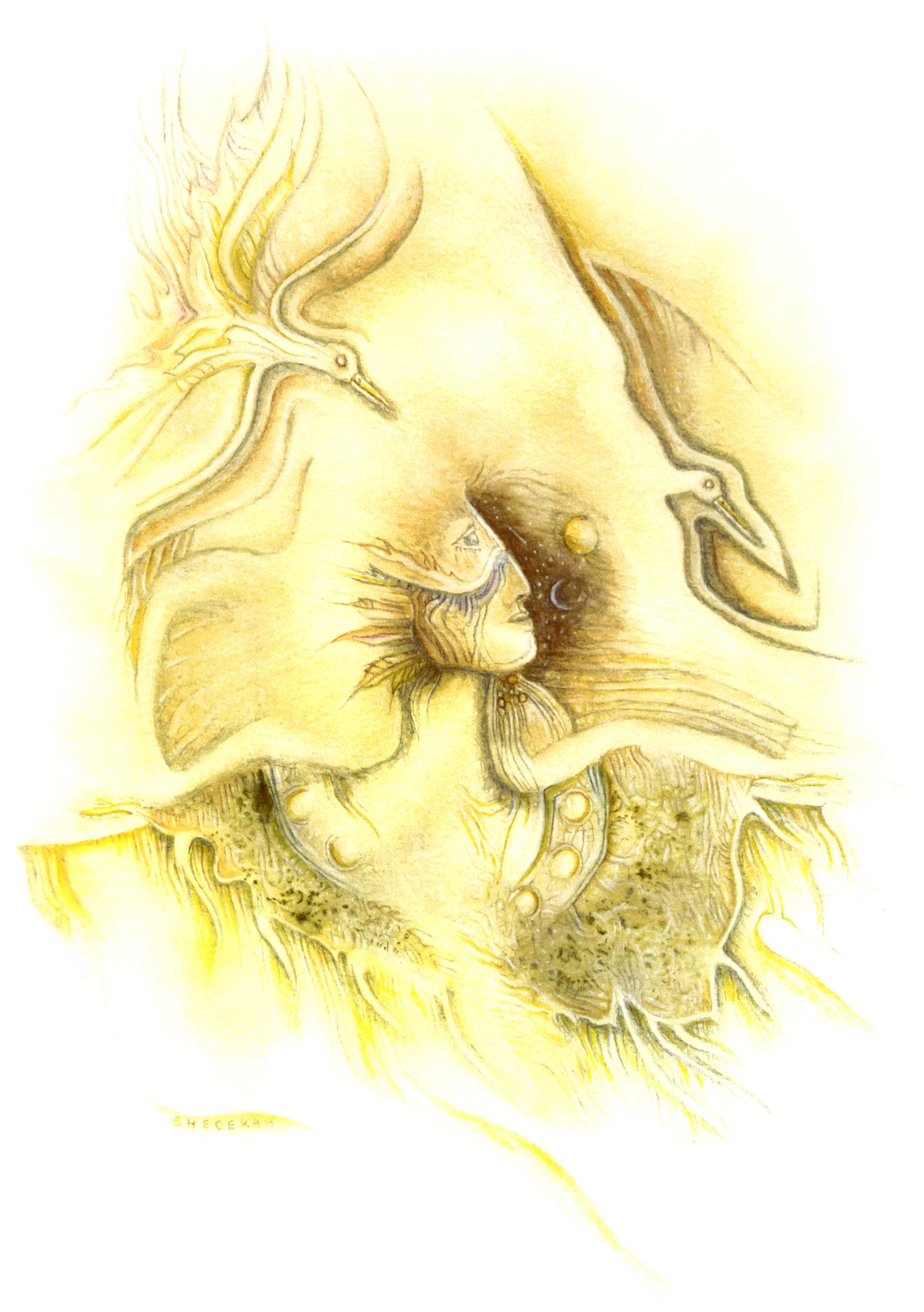

HE…it is…
who Remembers the Bird Tribes…

HE…it is…who lives as a Star-Stone ONE
abiding ever in the heart of love…
finding a joy that neither comes nor goes…

Here is demonstrated the Changeless One
who ever brings the change.

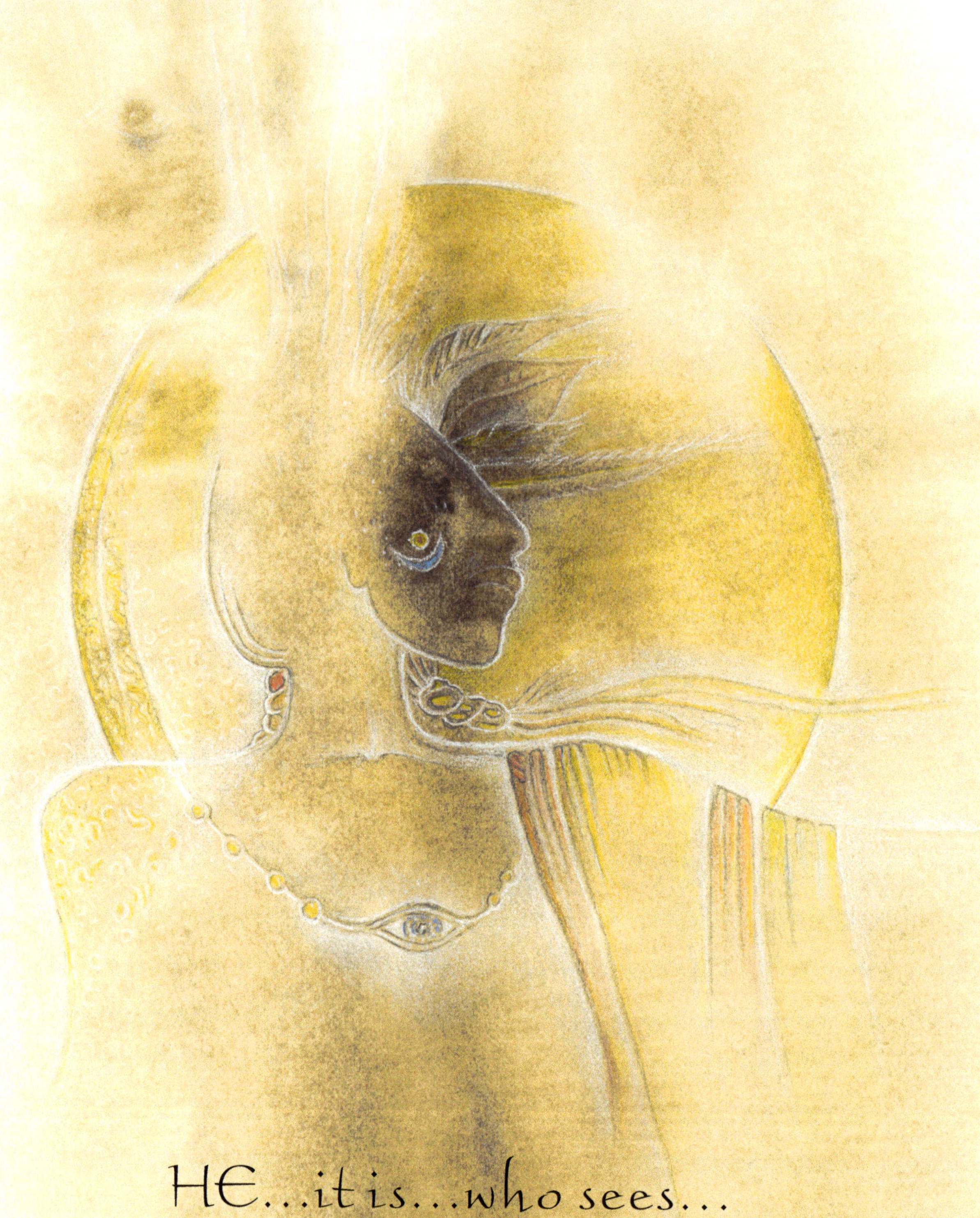

HE…it is…who sees…

HE…it is…who sees…
through the eyes of the sun…
and of the moon…

A native man adorns himself
in the yin and yang of his being,
the marriage of the heart.

dancer-HE...
of the ceremony...
# of two feathers...

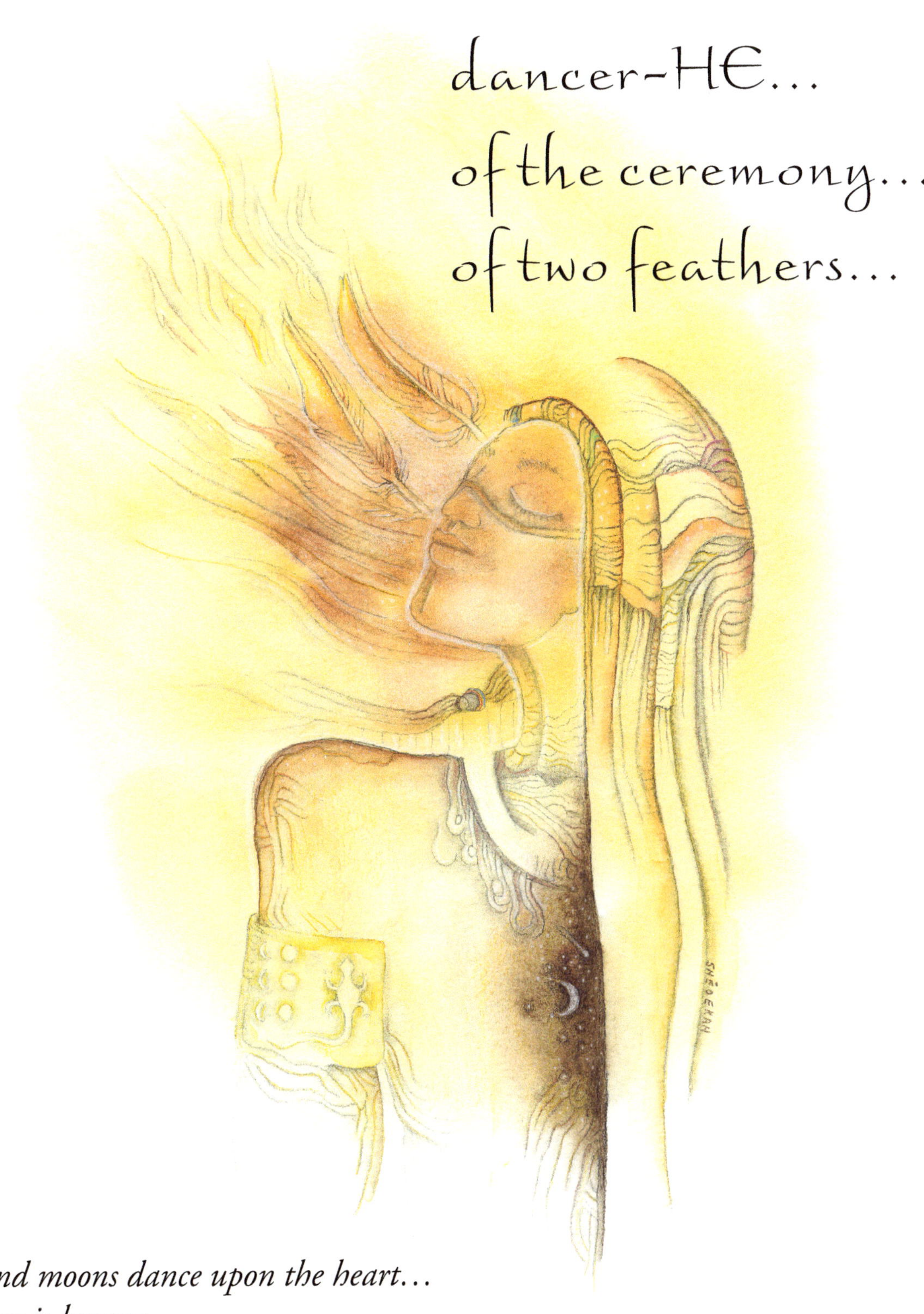

stars and moons dance upon the heart...
and love is known...

Two feathers speaks of the HE and SHE... the yin and yang as One. Ceremony in solitude does anchor in the knowing. Impartation comes. Silence fills the air.

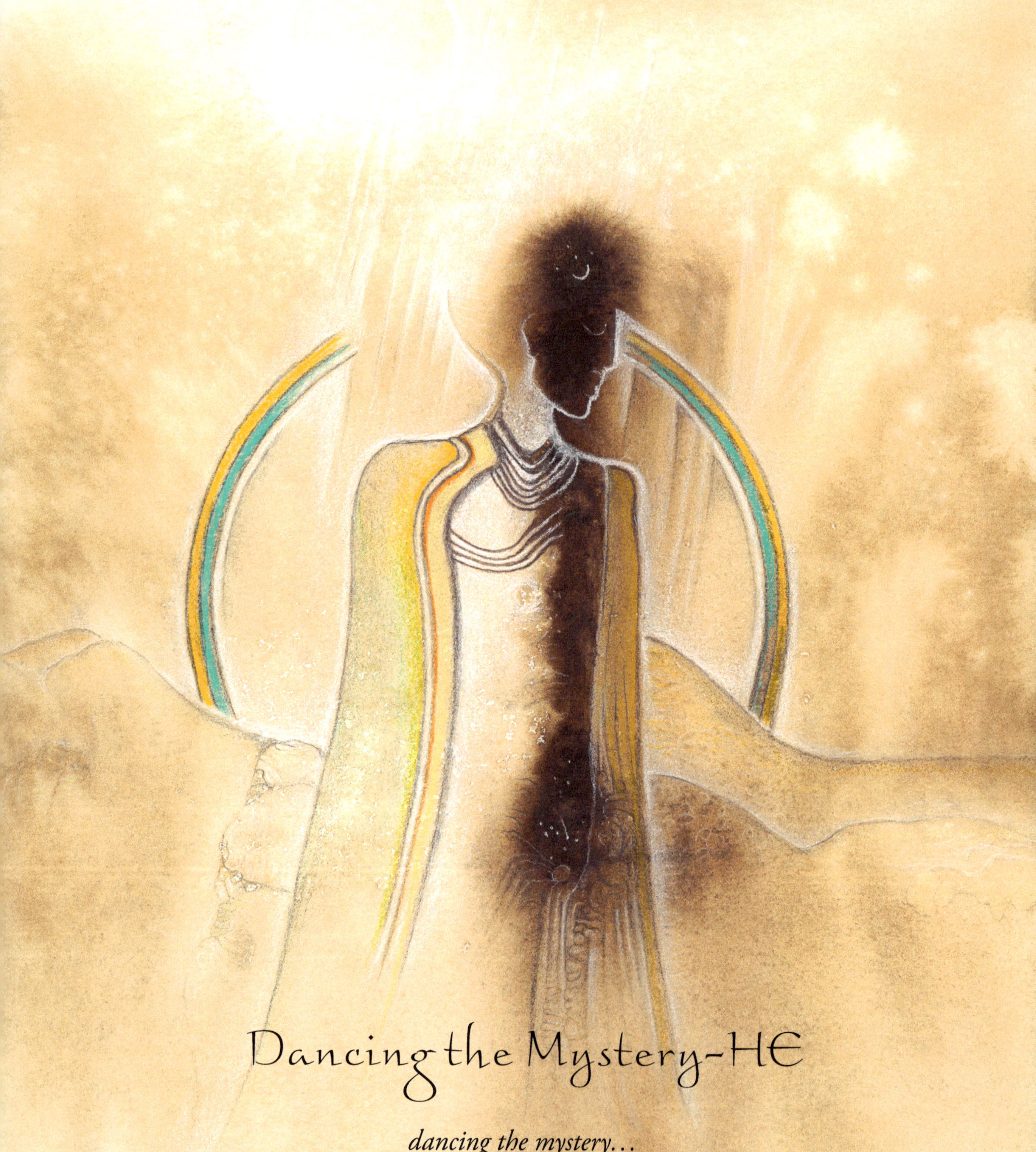

Dancing the Mystery–HE

dancing the mystery…
ever does the changeless…
bring the change…

The Unknown is embraced.

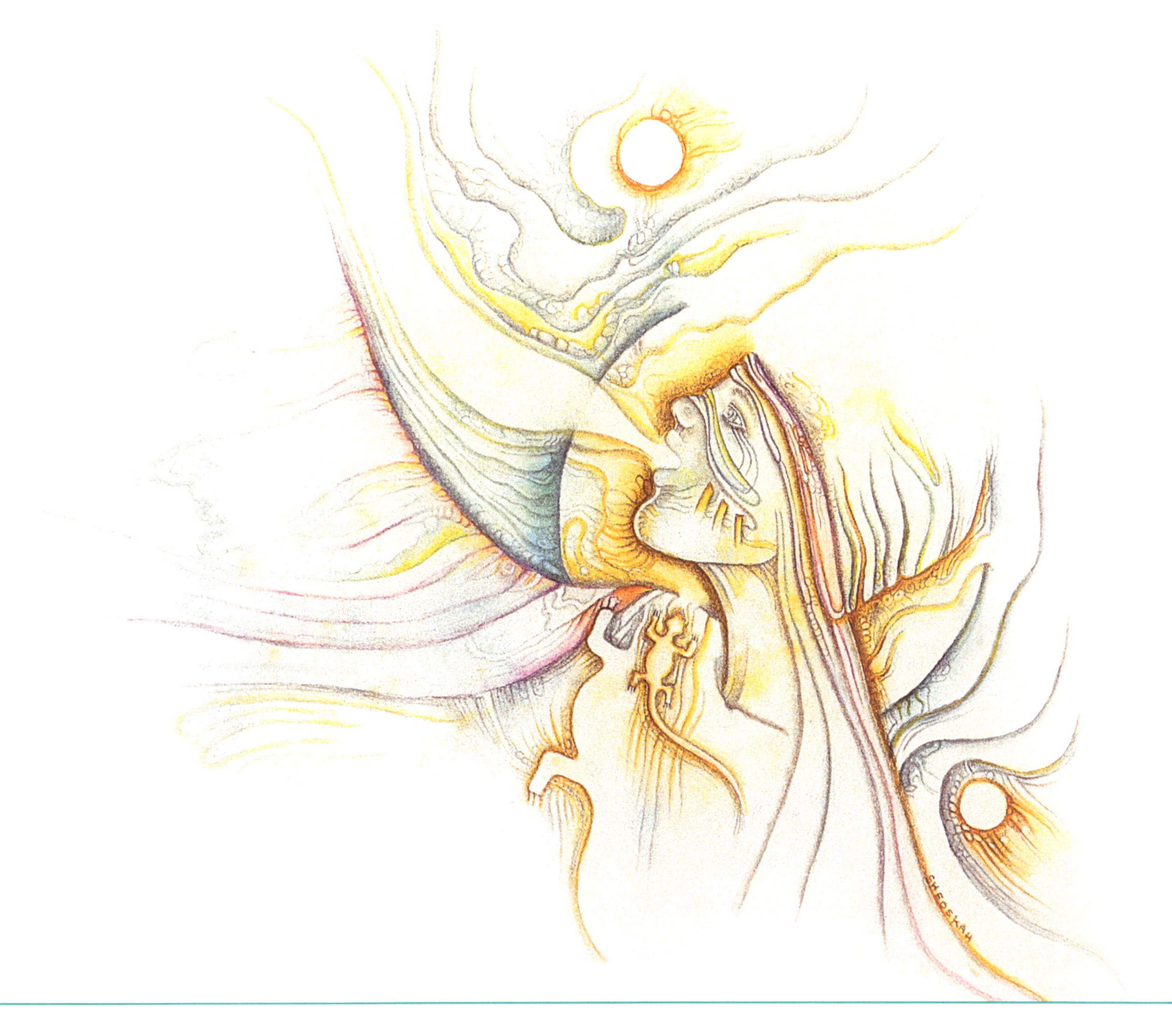

HE...of the Rainbow Dance

HE...of the Rainbow Dance does sound...
with sounds of all creation...

HE...of the Rainbow Dance gives voice to sacred sound
in harmony with all creation.

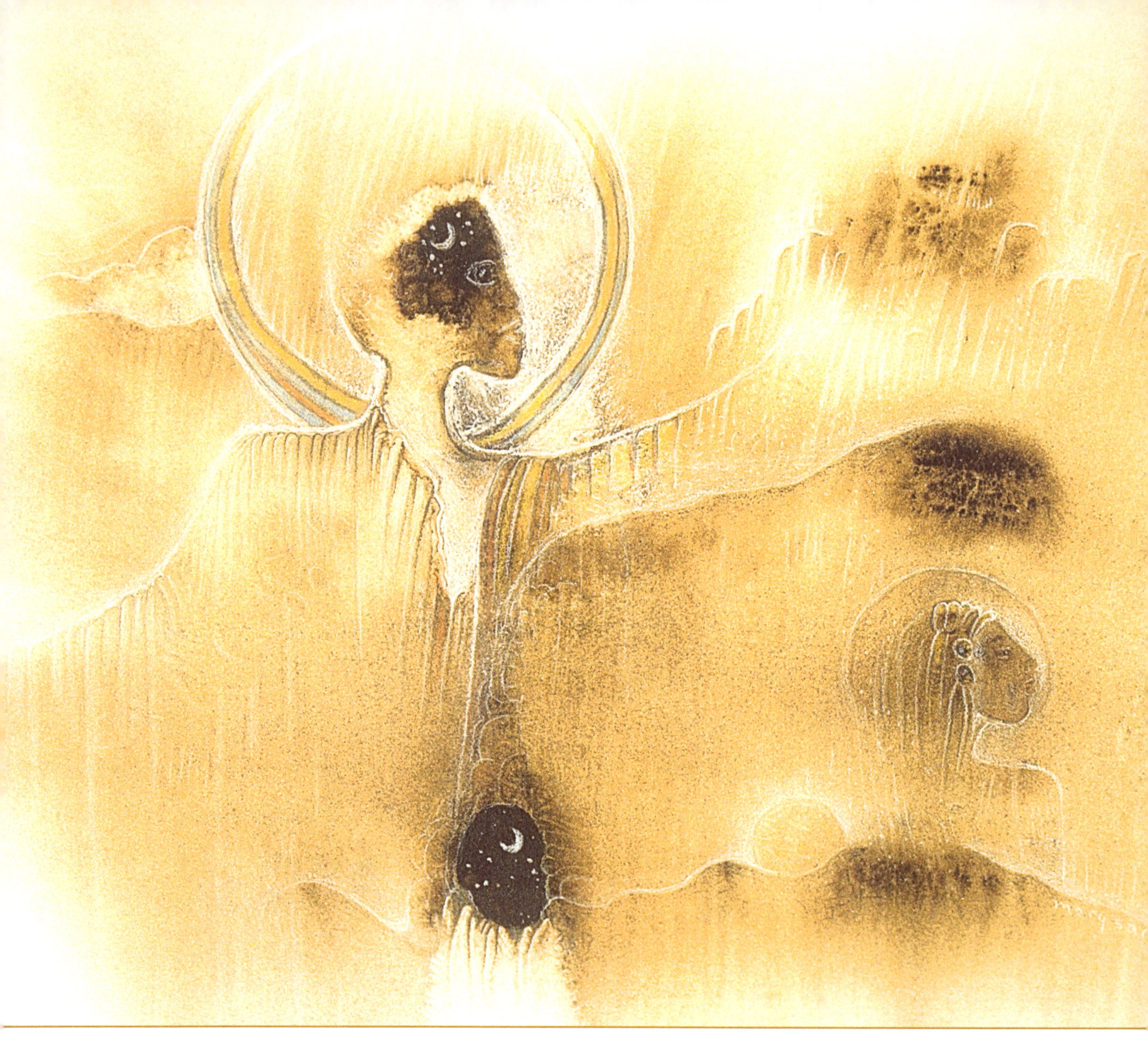

HE…who from the earth…

HE…who from the earth…
and from the very stones…
does build a temple to the stars…

Envisioned here is a
Temple of Consciousness.

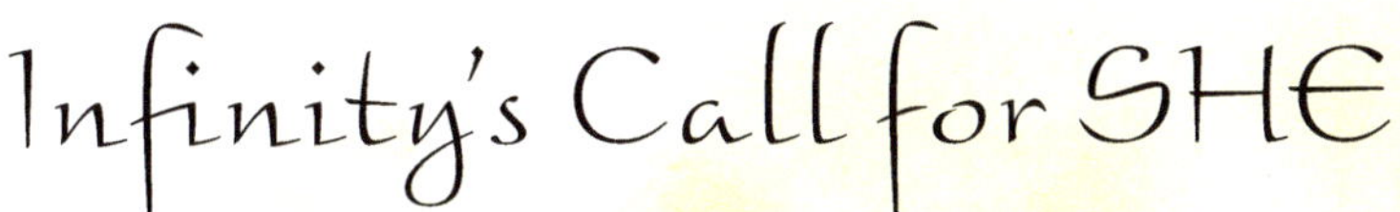

Infinity's Call for SHE

infused with infinity…
HE does call for SHE…

Balance does wend its way.

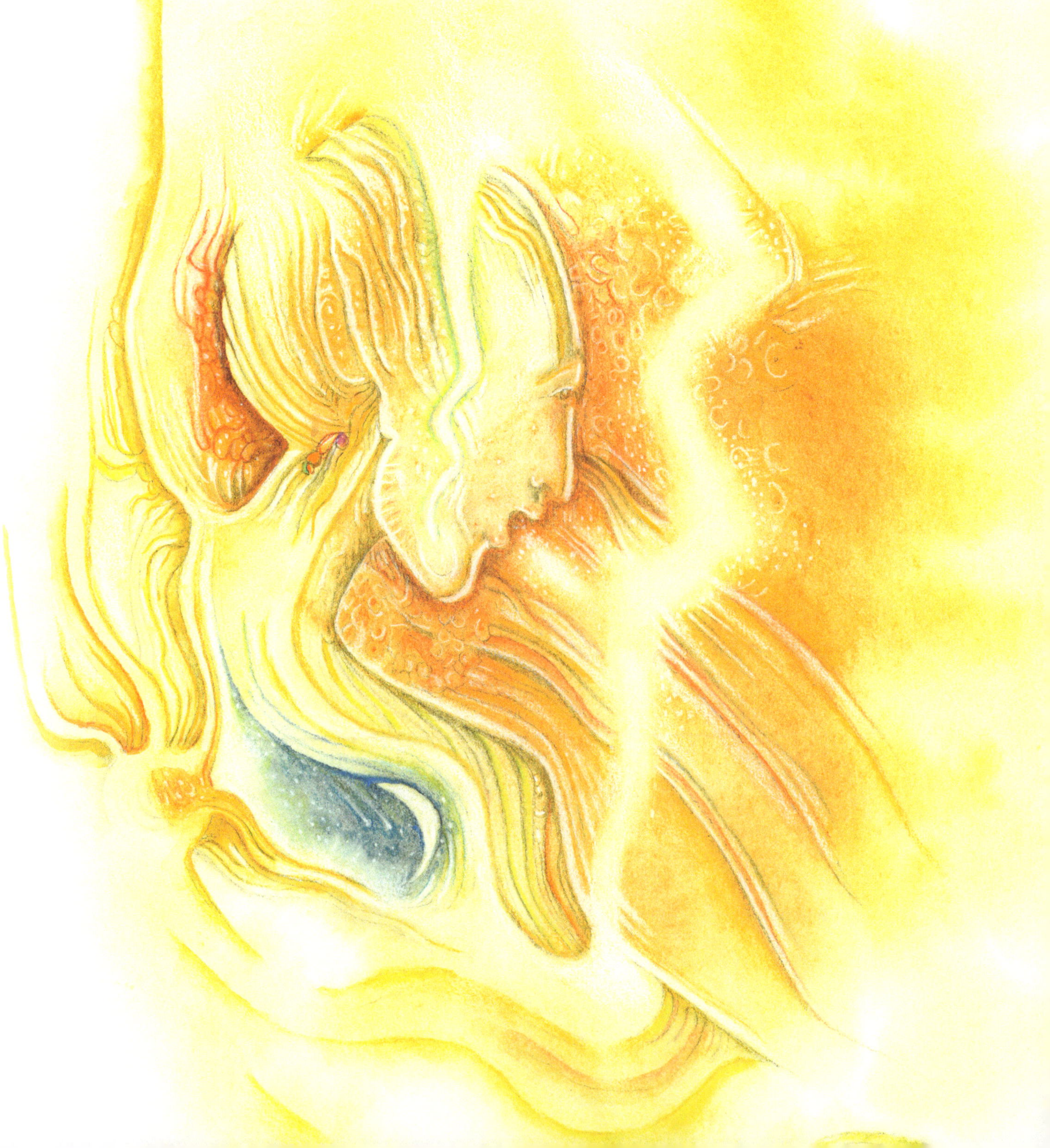

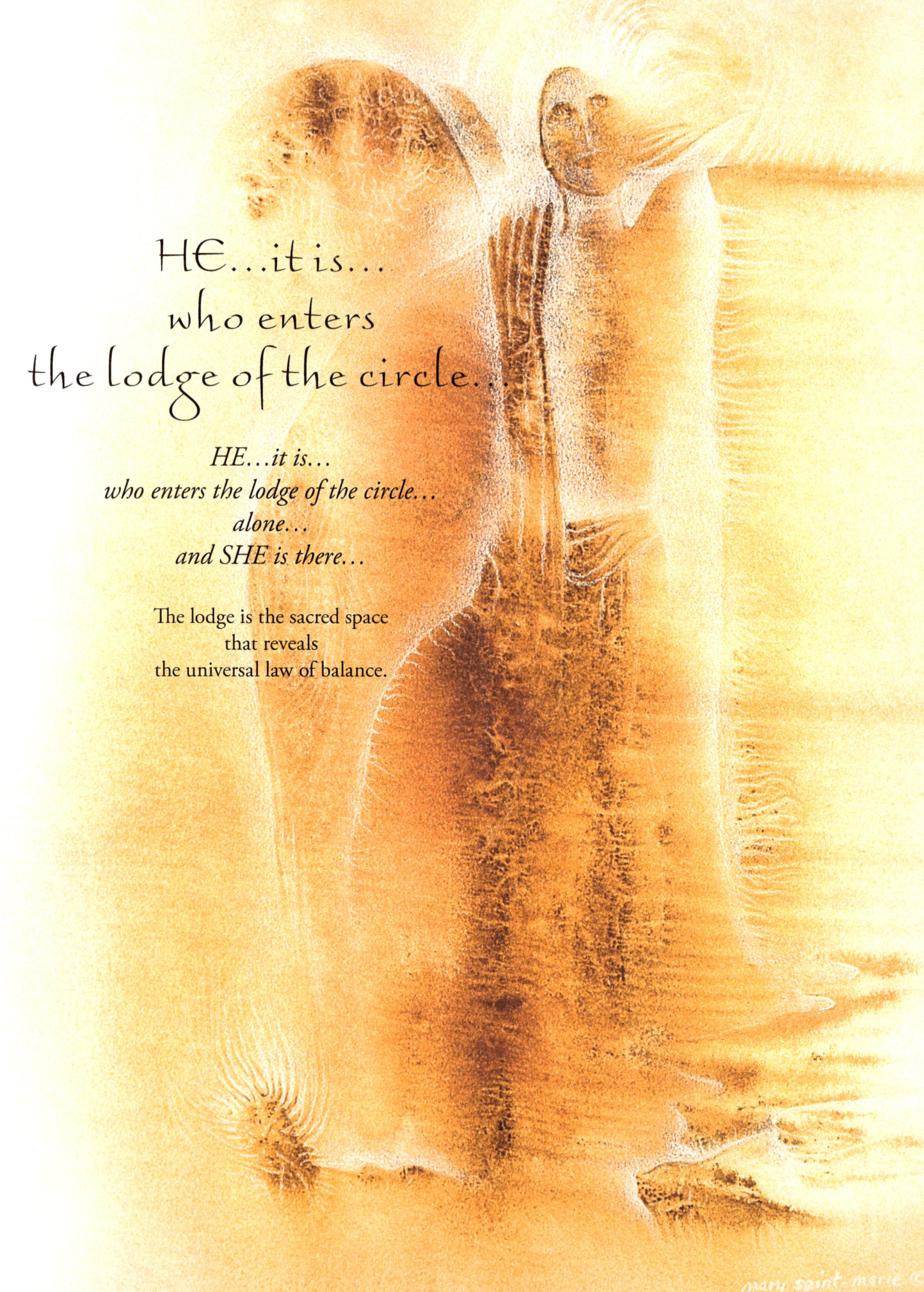

HE…it is…
who enters
the lodge of the circle…

HE…it is…
who enters the lodge of the circle…
alone…
and SHE is there…

The lodge is the sacred space
that reveals
the universal law of balance.

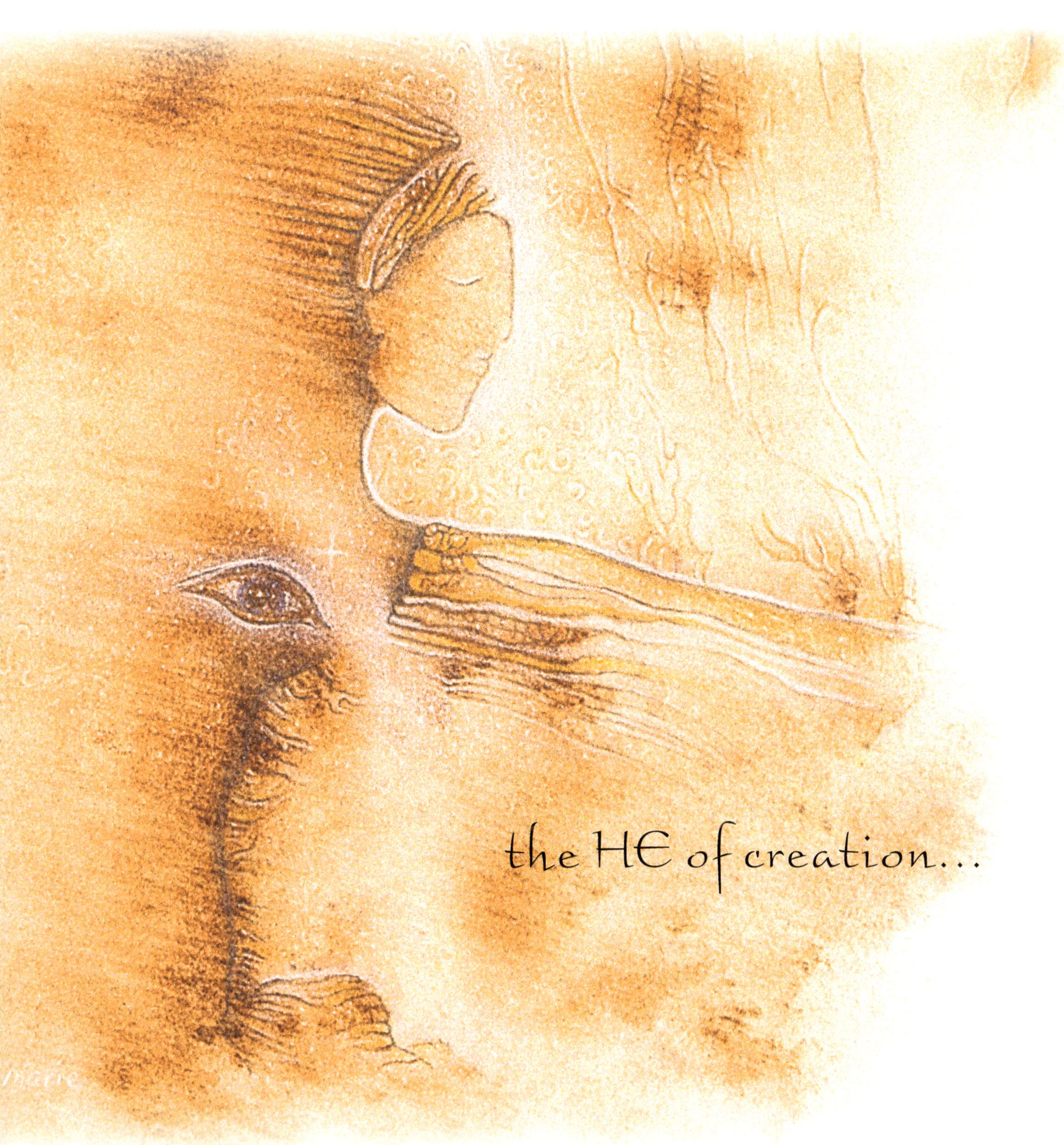
the HE of creation…

comes...
Guardian at the Door

comes...
Guardian at the Door...
as
Slayer of the Battle...
and
Protector of the Holy Space

Sword of Truth is exposed as the
instrument dwelling ever in the heart.

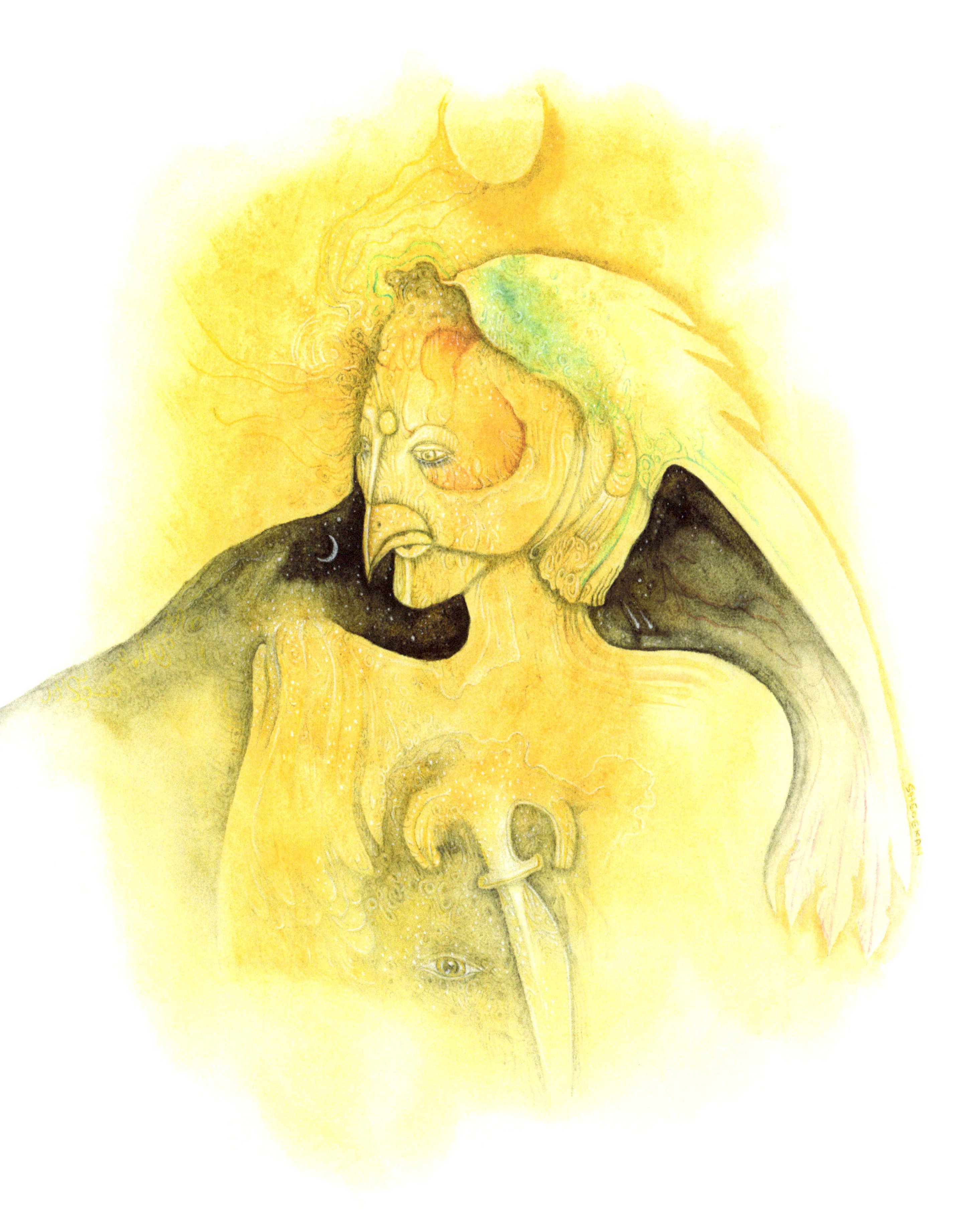

Song of Bear

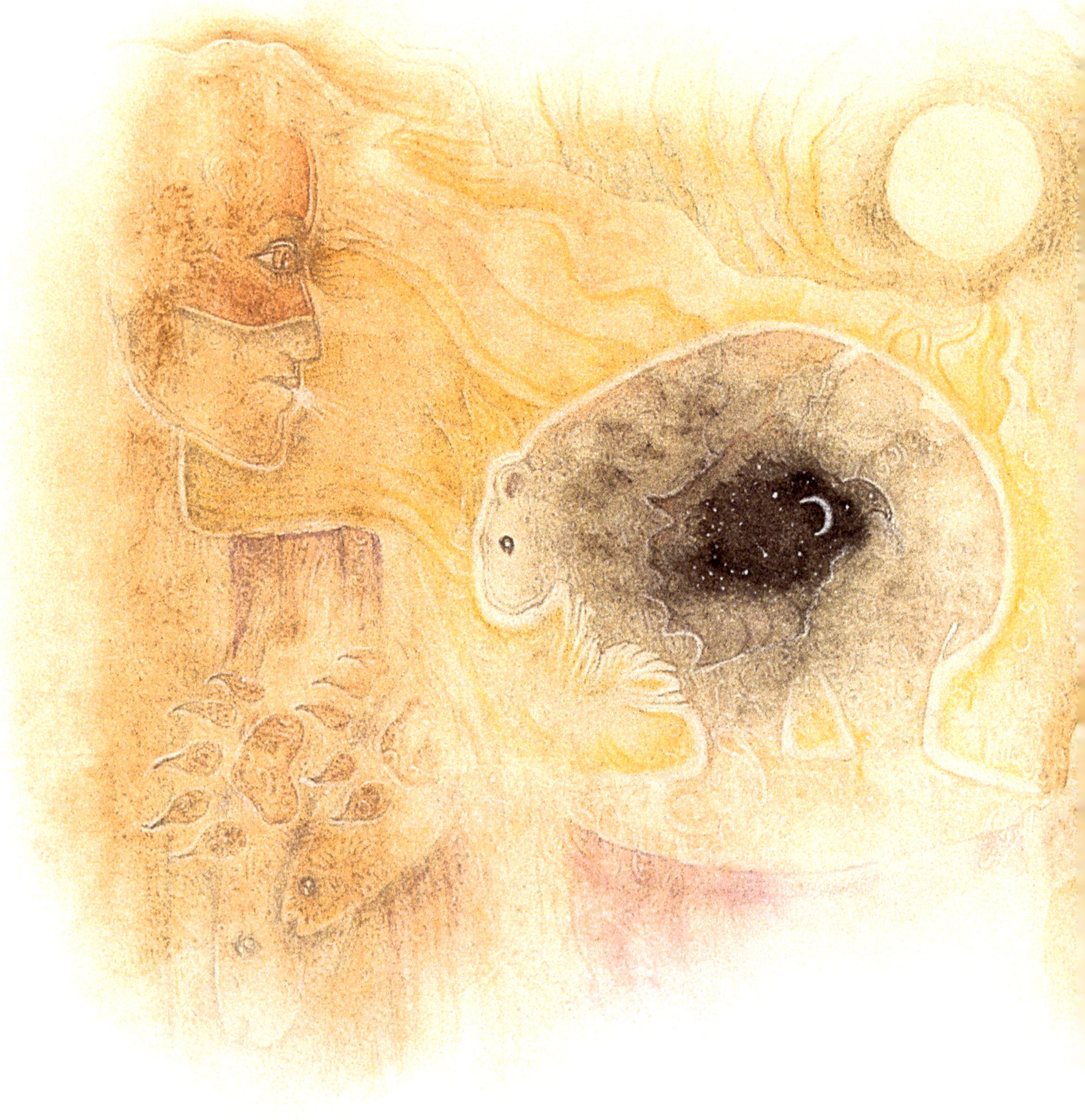

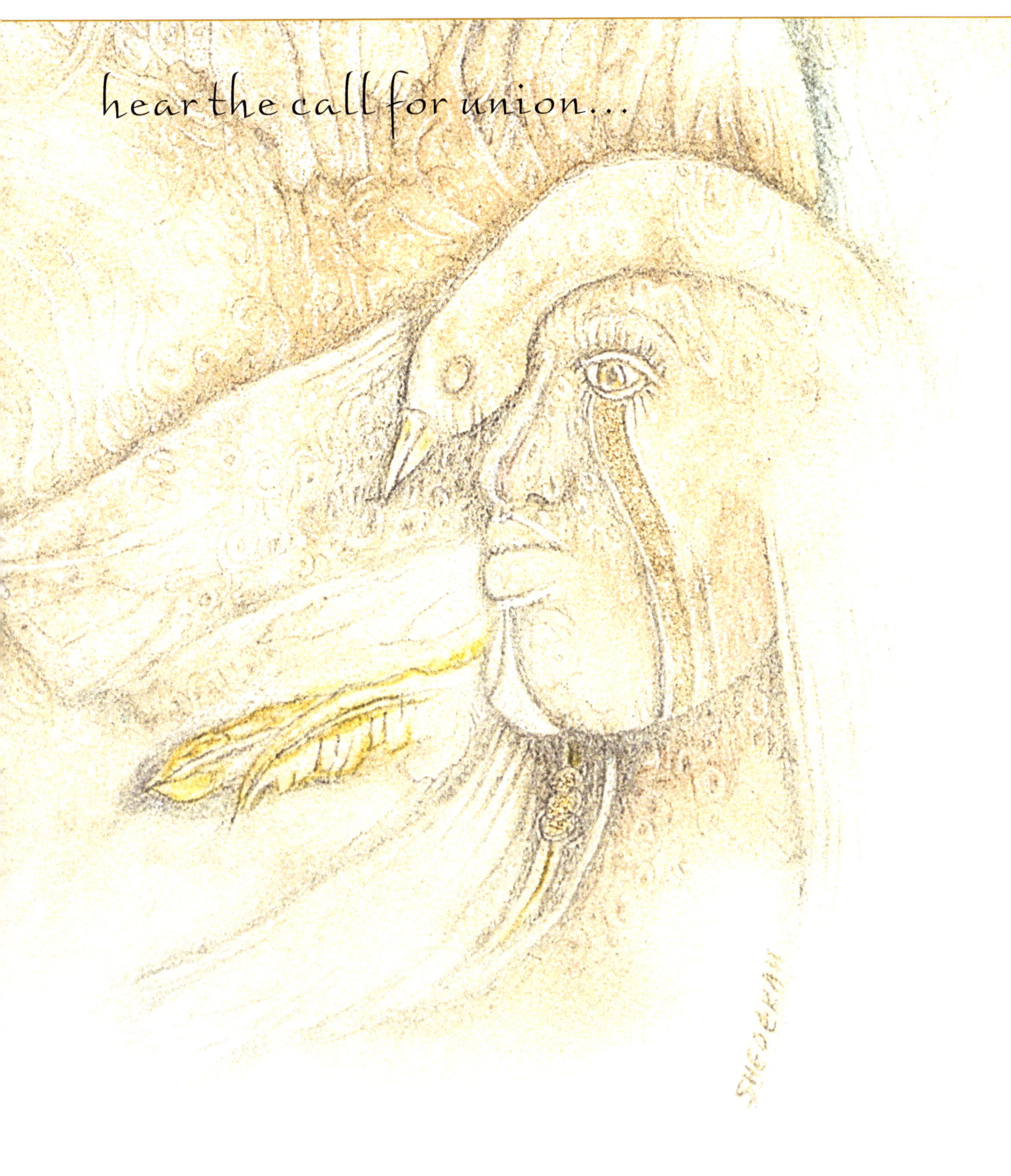
hear the call for union...
SHEBERAH

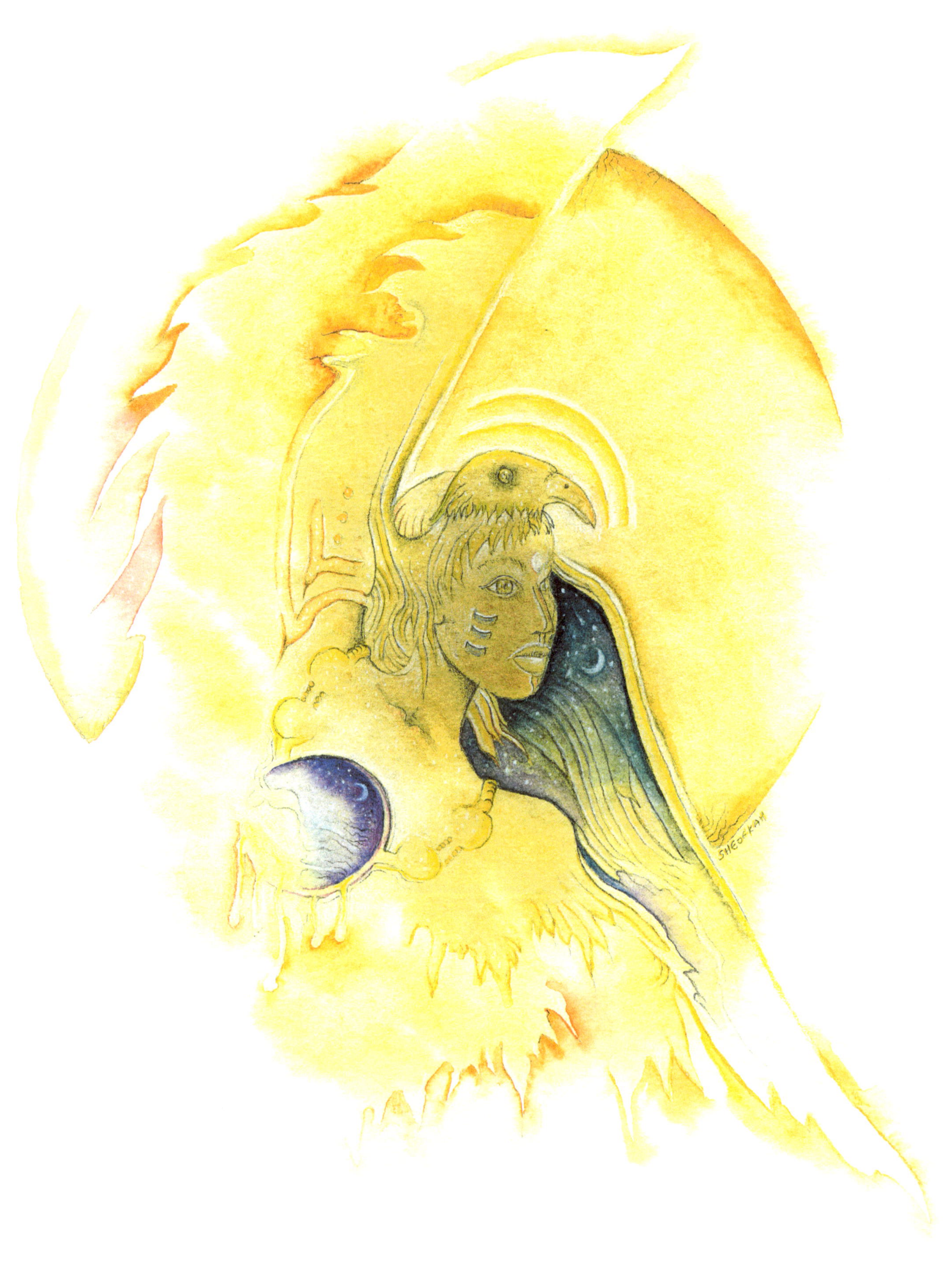

HE…who flies as the birds…

HE…who flies as the birds…
carries the moon in his heart…
and sees with golden eyes…

The winged ones remind us ever
to take flight in the heart.

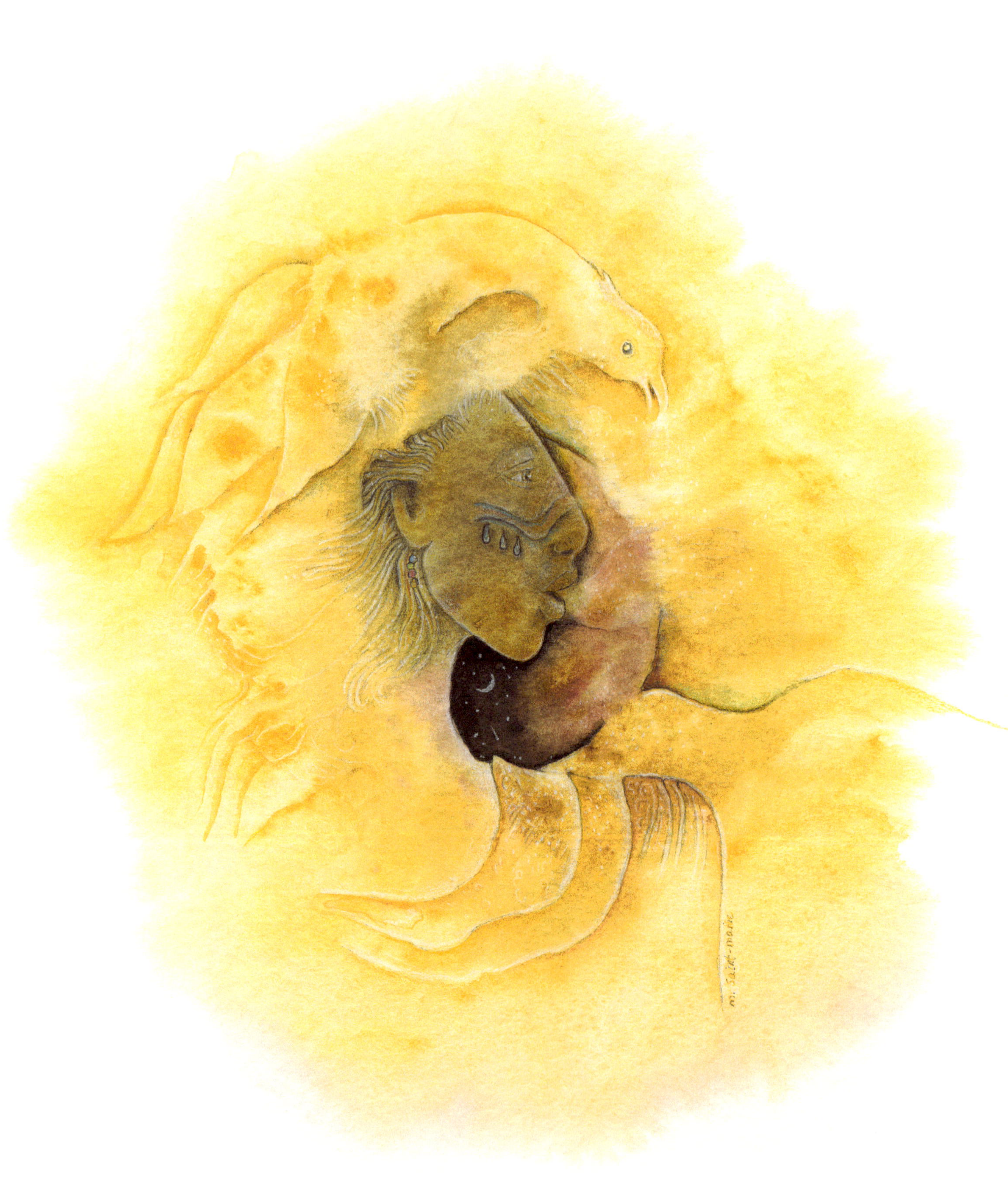
m. Saint-marie

Ceremony of the Ancient Call

as a whisper on the desert wind…
does this silent call fill the sky…
ever beckoning ones to home…

Ceremony of the Ancient Call is a reminder
that in this light-wave universe exists a Call.

HE…who stands at the edge of dawn…
and sees the SHE of all creation…

eyes unopened, He does see the
ever present sacred marriage…
and He does chant the song…

The single I of the heart is the revelator
and dawn does come.

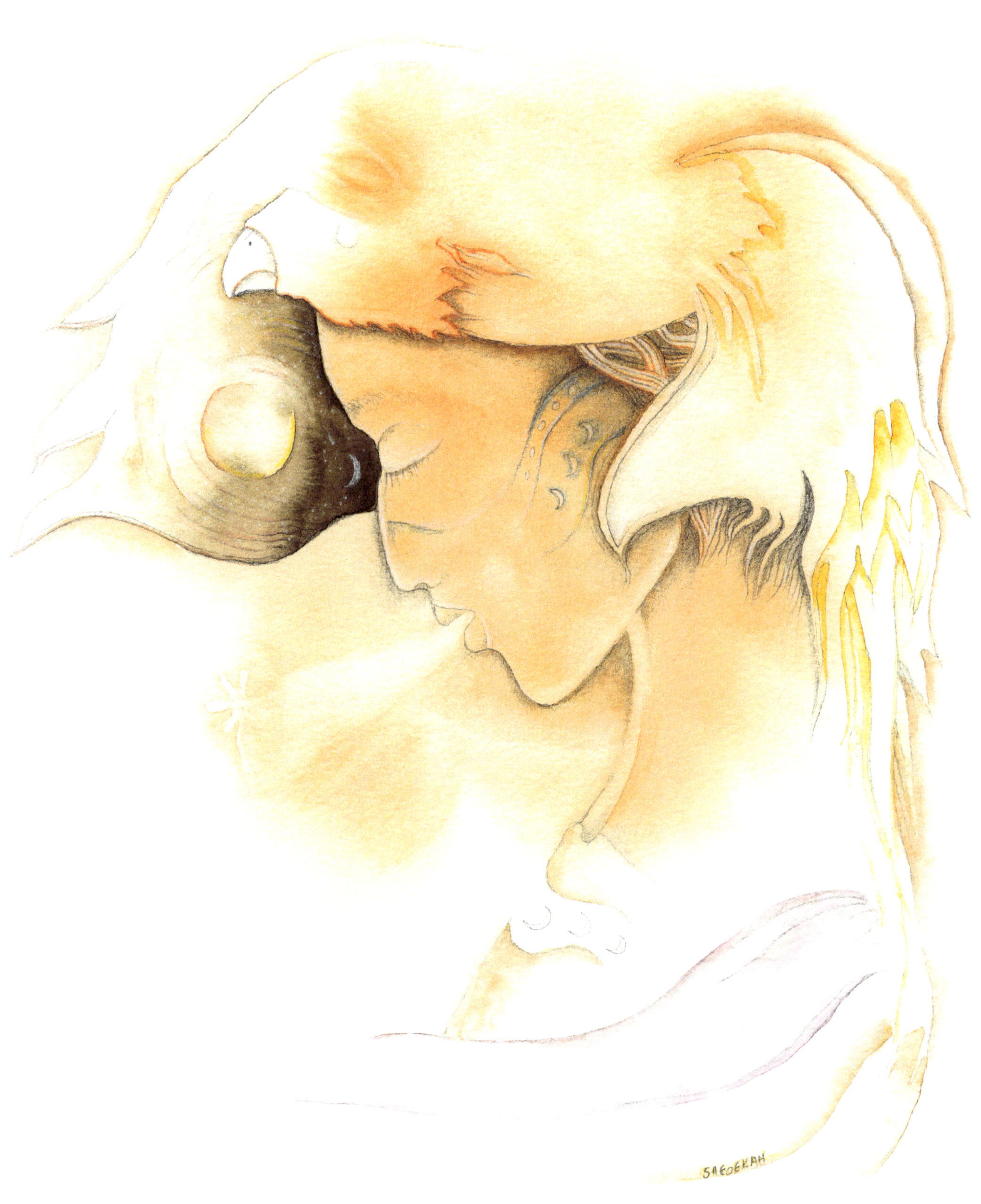

Consciousness, the Formless One, does play in form.
Together…let us feel that…
Exultation comes…

The Sacred Two:

Partners in Divine Purpose...

the SHE and HE of creation...

in

Man and Woman

SHE and HE...
through the veils...

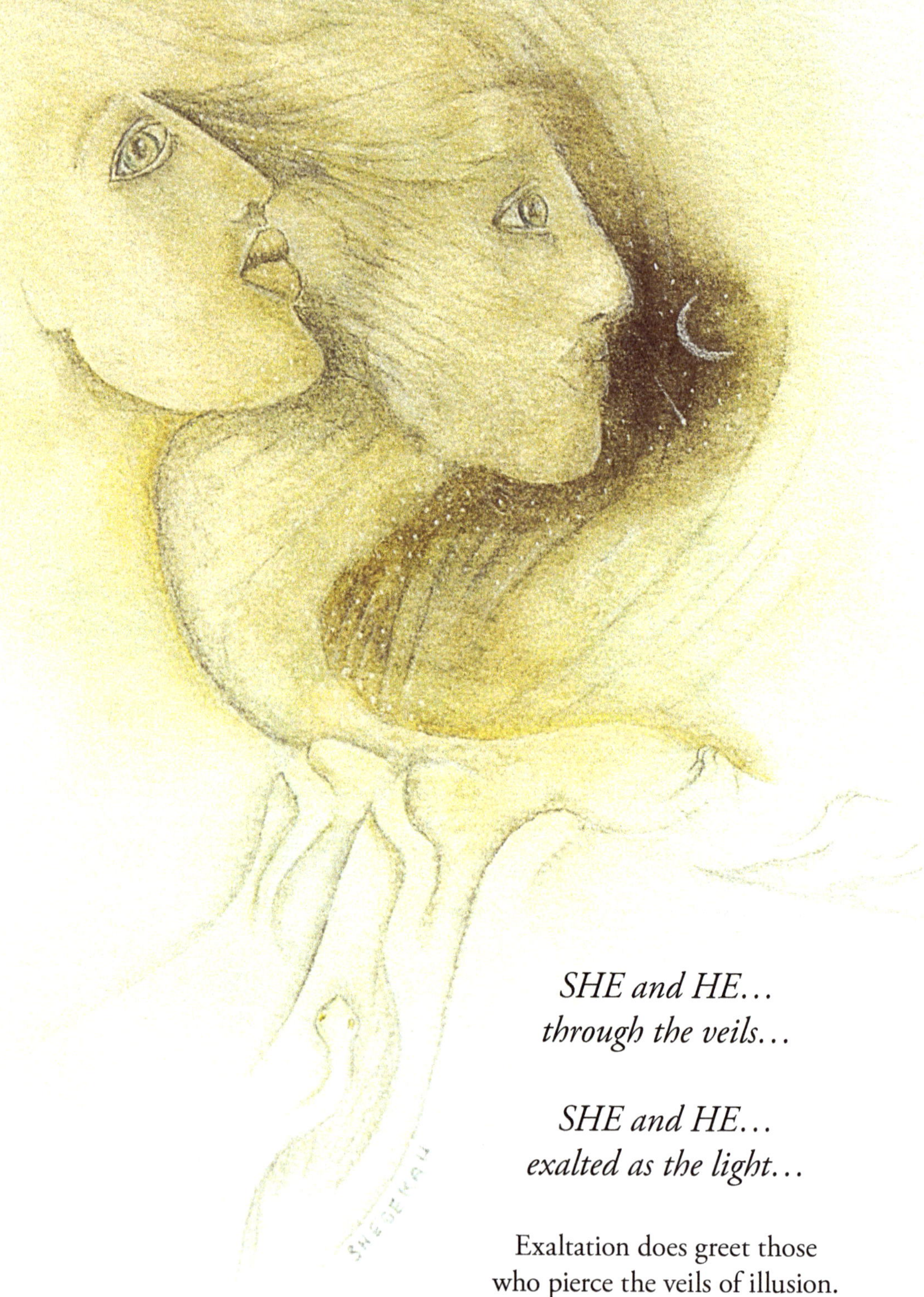

SHE and HE...
through the veils...

SHE and HE...
exalted as the light...

Exaltation does greet those
who pierce the veils of illusion.

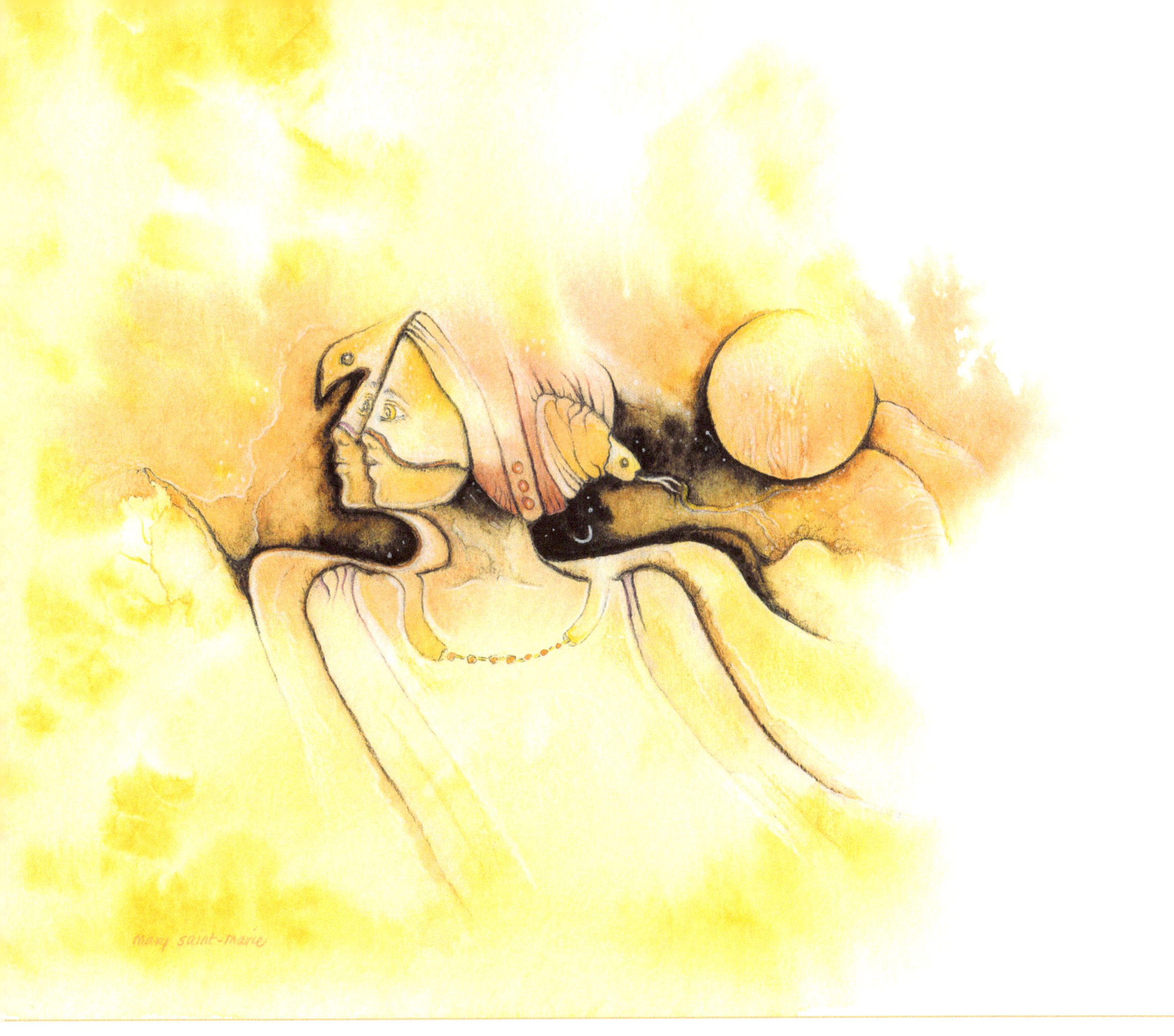

Mask of Heaven's Light

SHE and HE do don…the masks of heaven's light…

moving ever in fields of form…seeing formless with eye of god…

Woman and man portrayed as figures
on the stage of light playing ever as form
and essence that has no form.
Exaltation is.

The Call for Union

sweeping across these lands…
hear the call for union…

This union bespeaks
of the Unity that ever IS.

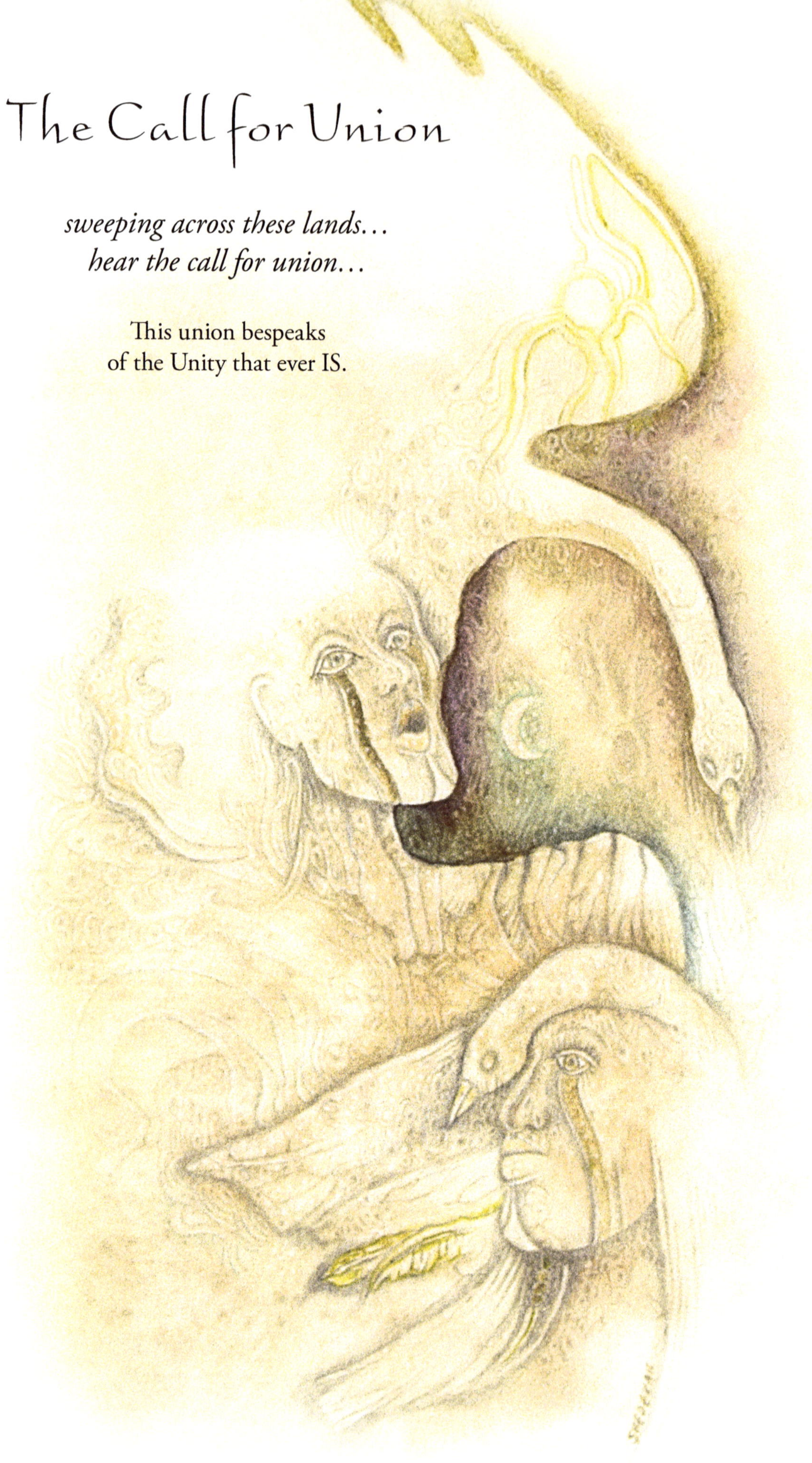

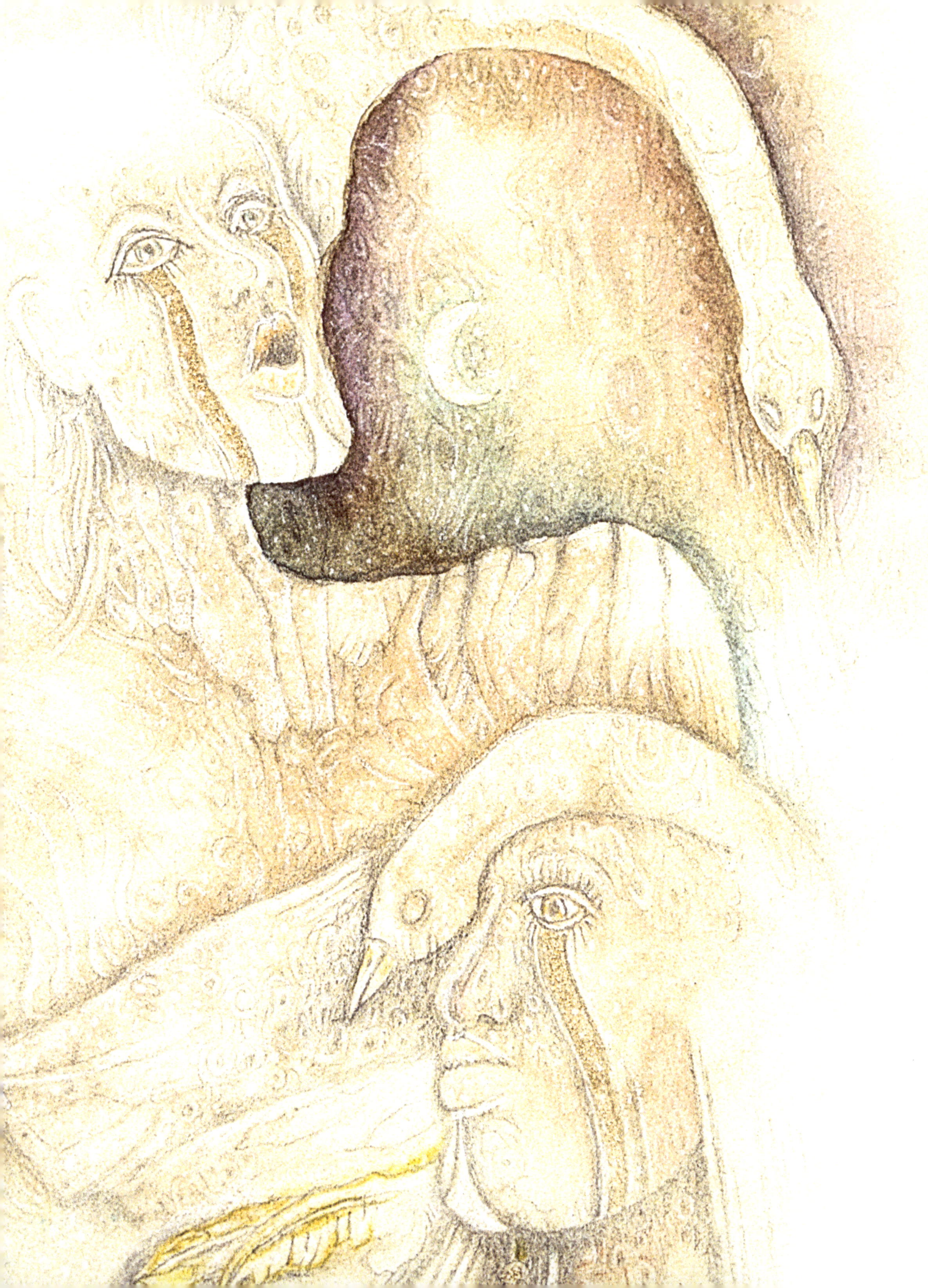

Marriage of the Winged Ones

the winged ones of light…
illumine everywhere…

This visual prayer speaks of the
marriage in the kingdom.

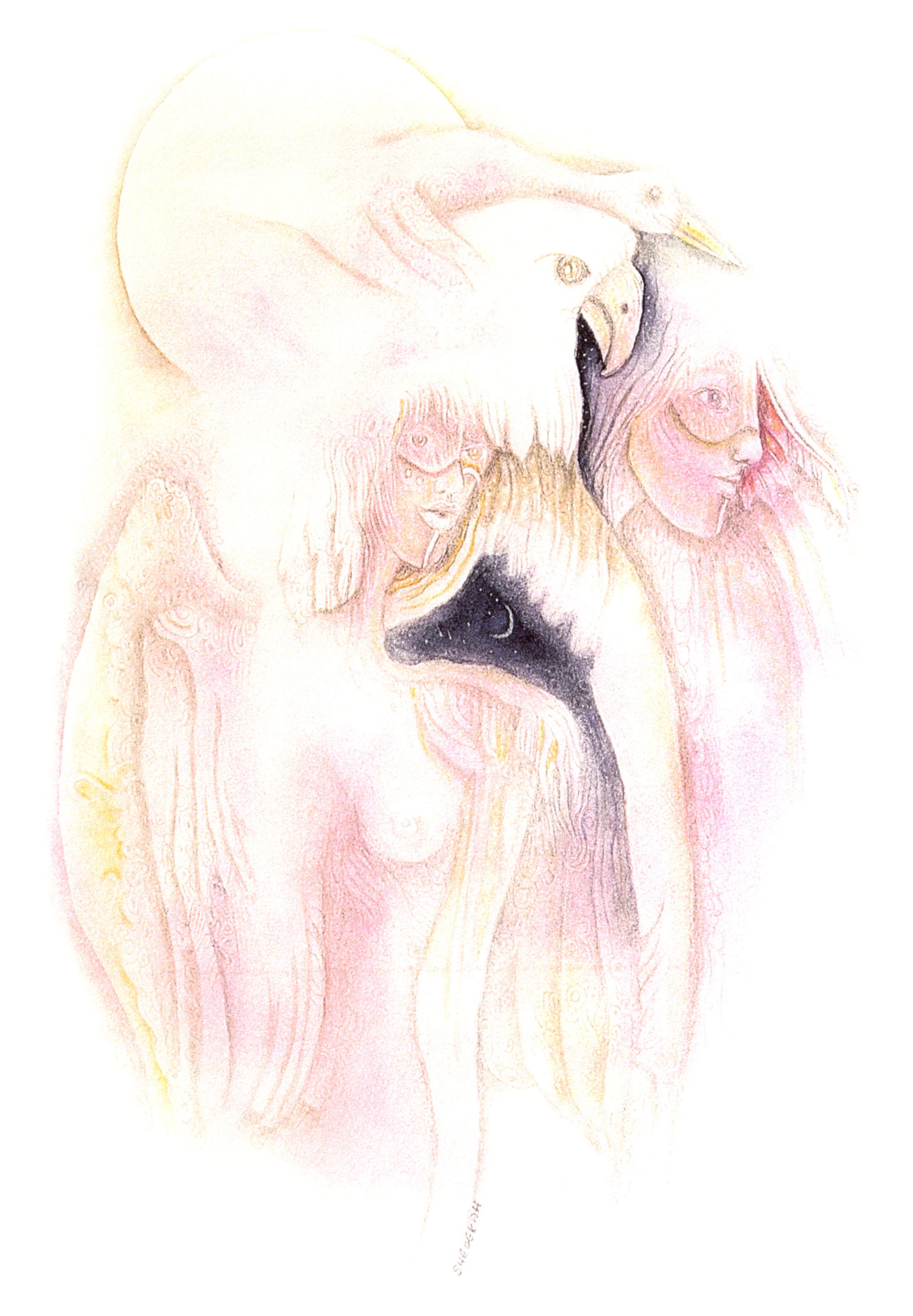

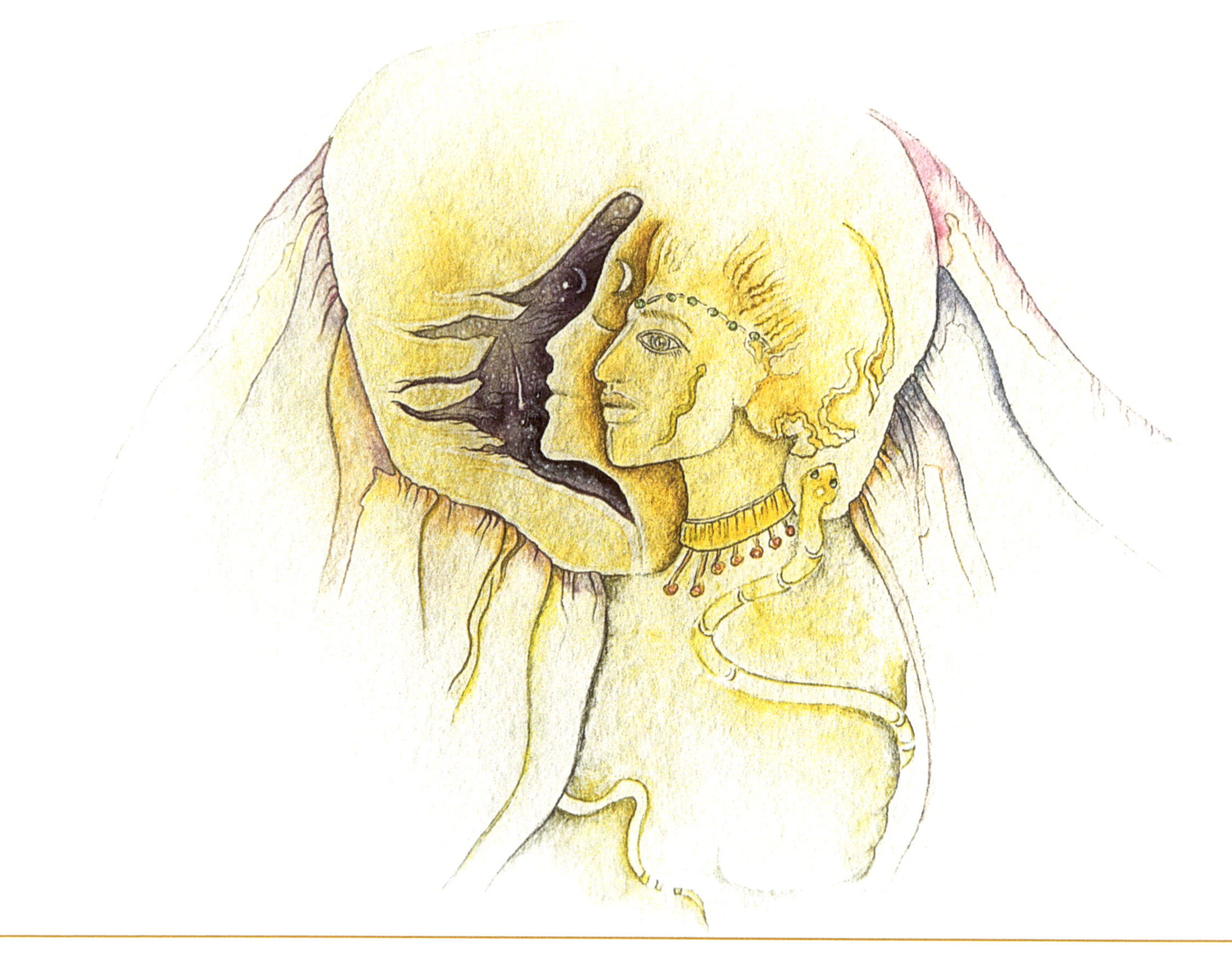

HE remembers SHE...as the timeless sky...

HE remembers SHE...as the timeless sky...

HE remembers SHE...as receptive self...

HE remembers SHE...as beauty's fragrance...

HE and SHE in Consciousness beyond the timed universe.

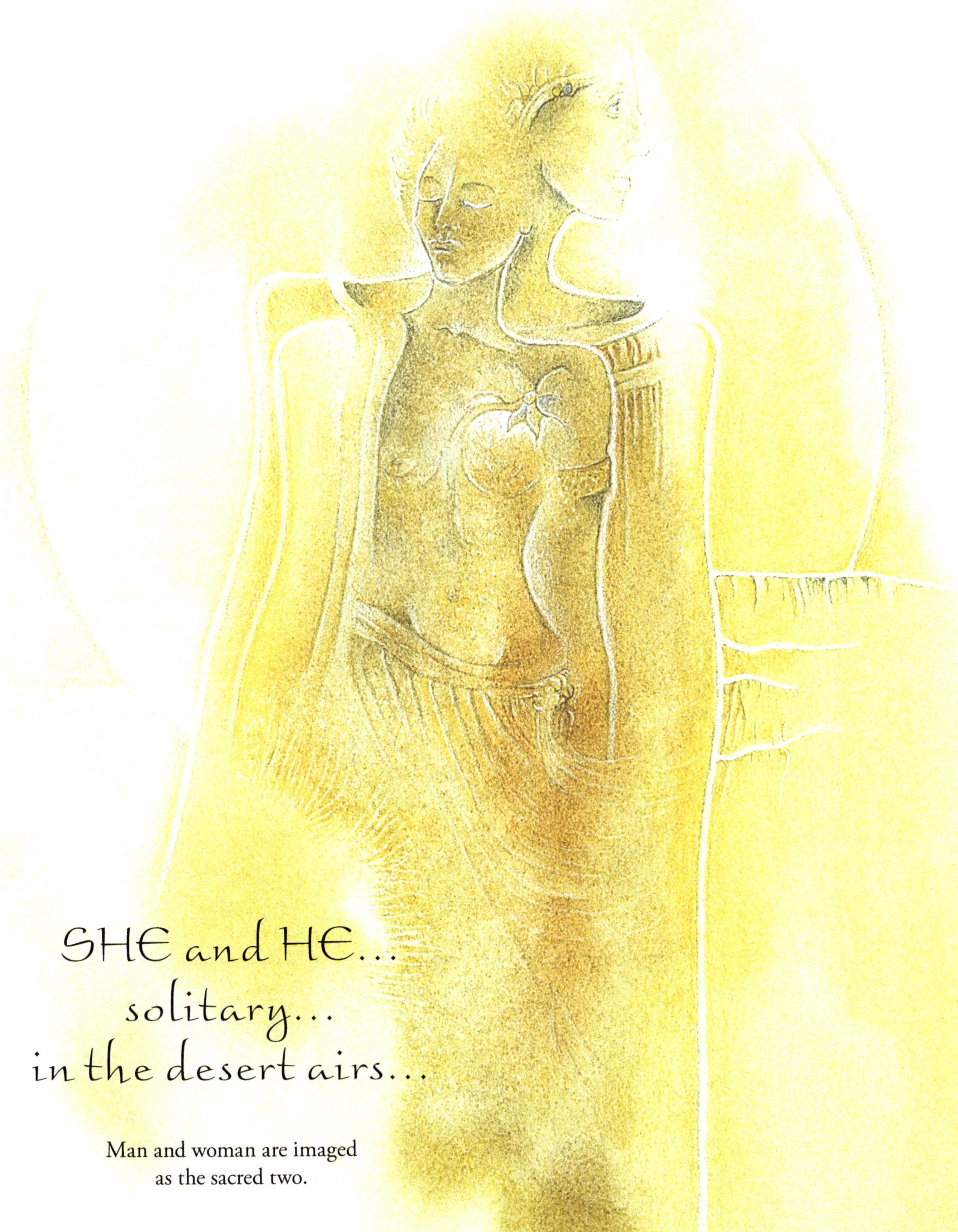

SHE and HE...
solitary...
in the desert airs...

Man and woman are imaged
as the sacred two.

HE…sounds the call…
of the ceremony of the feathers…

a call across infinity…
echoing into heart of SHE…

union rises like the sun…
upon a splendored morn…

True love has been suppressed and scoffed at
by many through the ages.
Here is a visual allegory of that ceremony of the two feathers
hearing Spirit's call to join.
Sacred marriage does rise upon this day as a forgotten gem
and as a foundation of emerging culture.

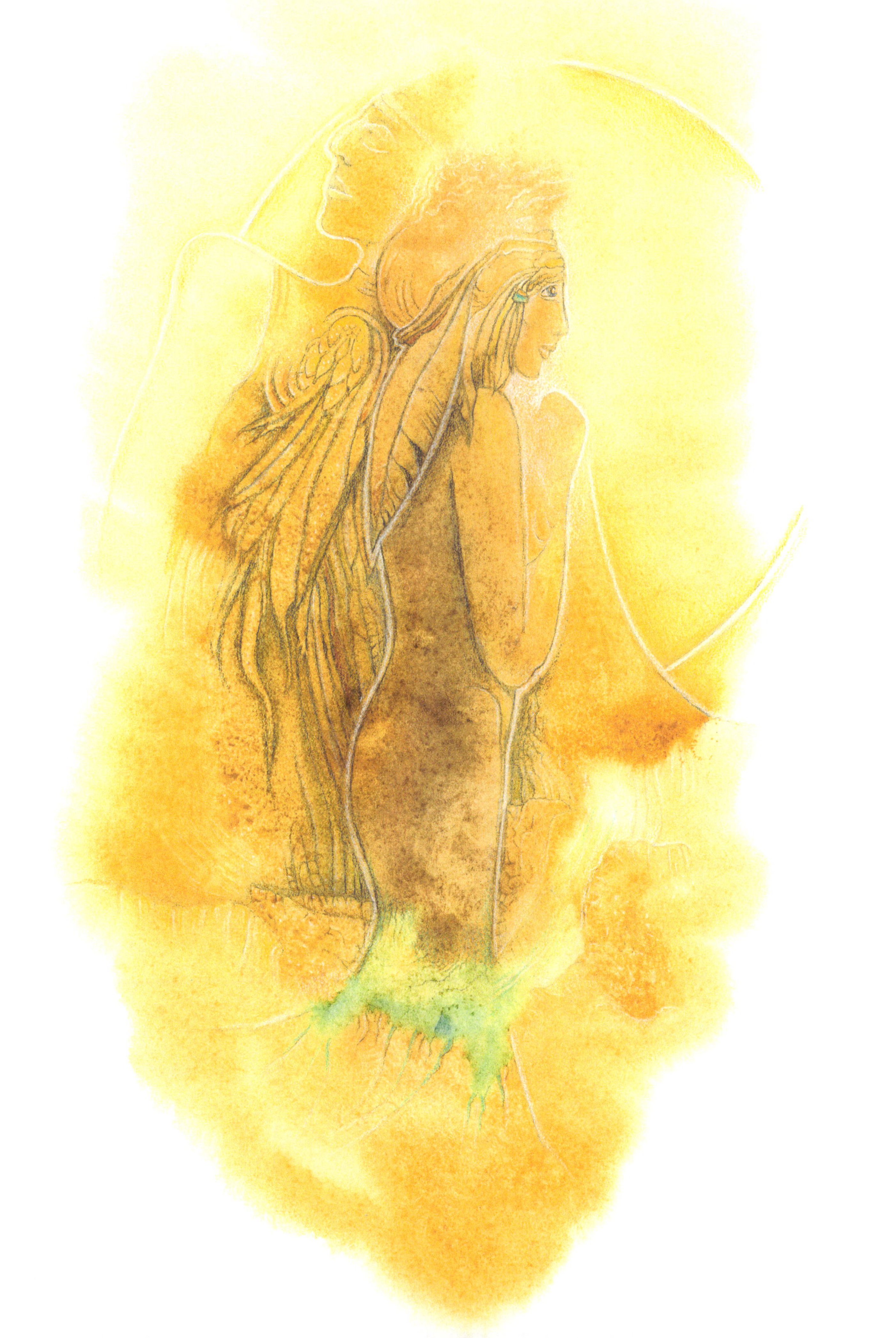

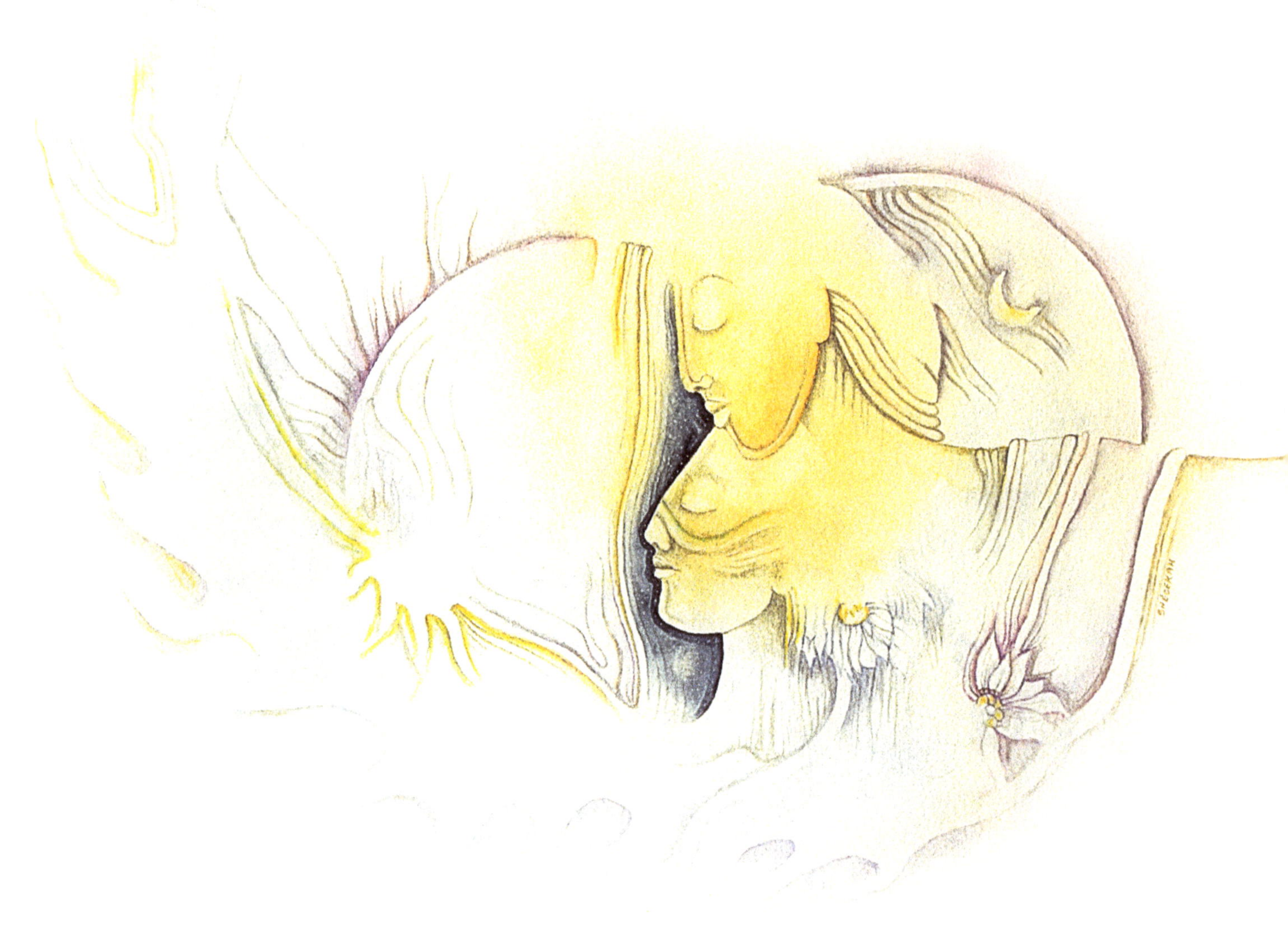

together...HE and SHE...
in the dance of the flowers...

together...HE and SHE...in the dance of the flowers...

together...HE and SHE...at one within and without...

Man and woman are envisioned in the sacred fragrance of the One.

HE…sounds the call of SHE…

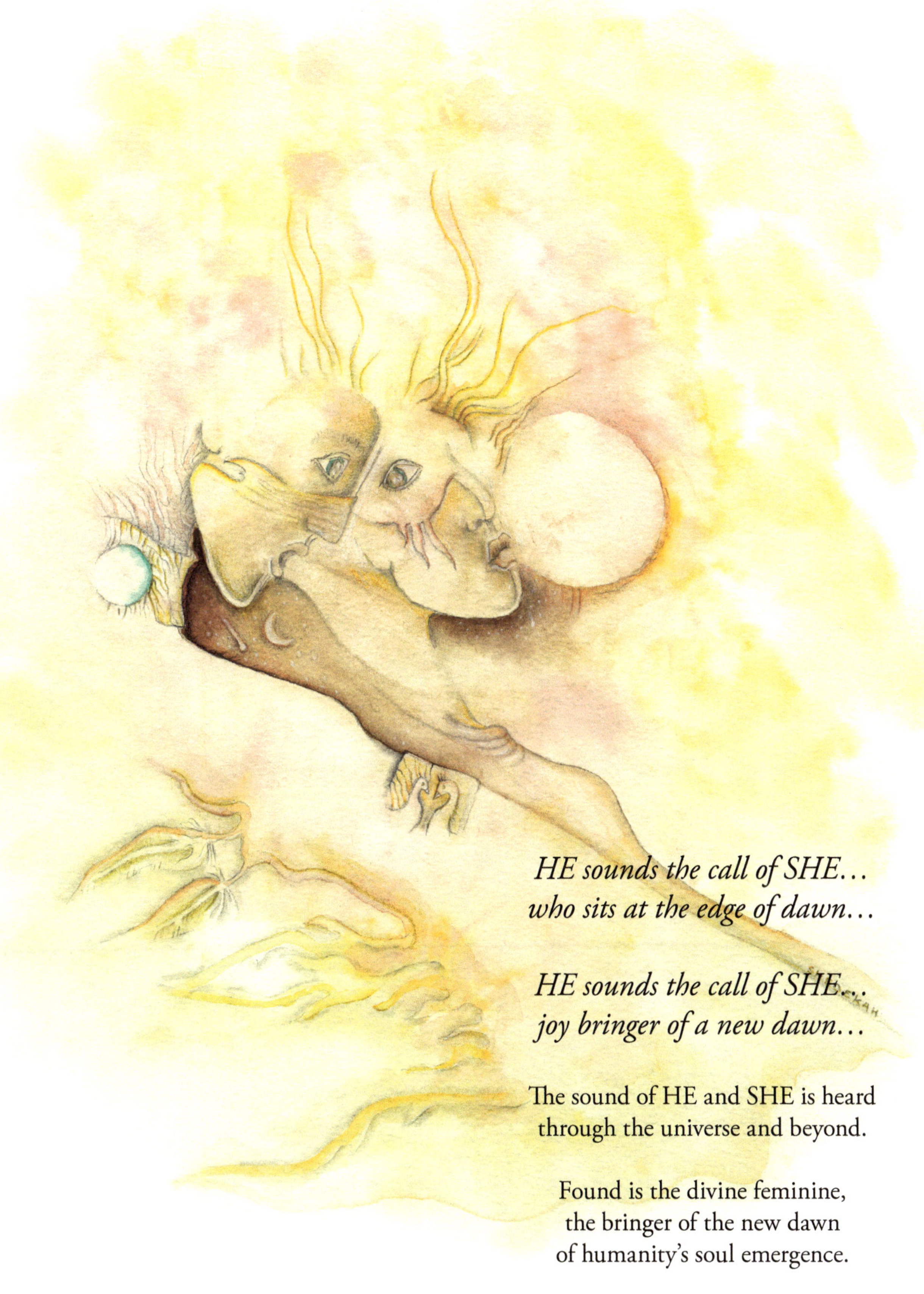

HE sounds the call of SHE…
who sits at the edge of dawn…

HE sounds the call of SHE…
joy bringer of a new dawn…

The sound of HE and SHE is heard
through the universe and beyond.

Found is the divine feminine,
the bringer of the new dawn
of humanity's soul emergence.

Rainbow Serpent HE and SHE

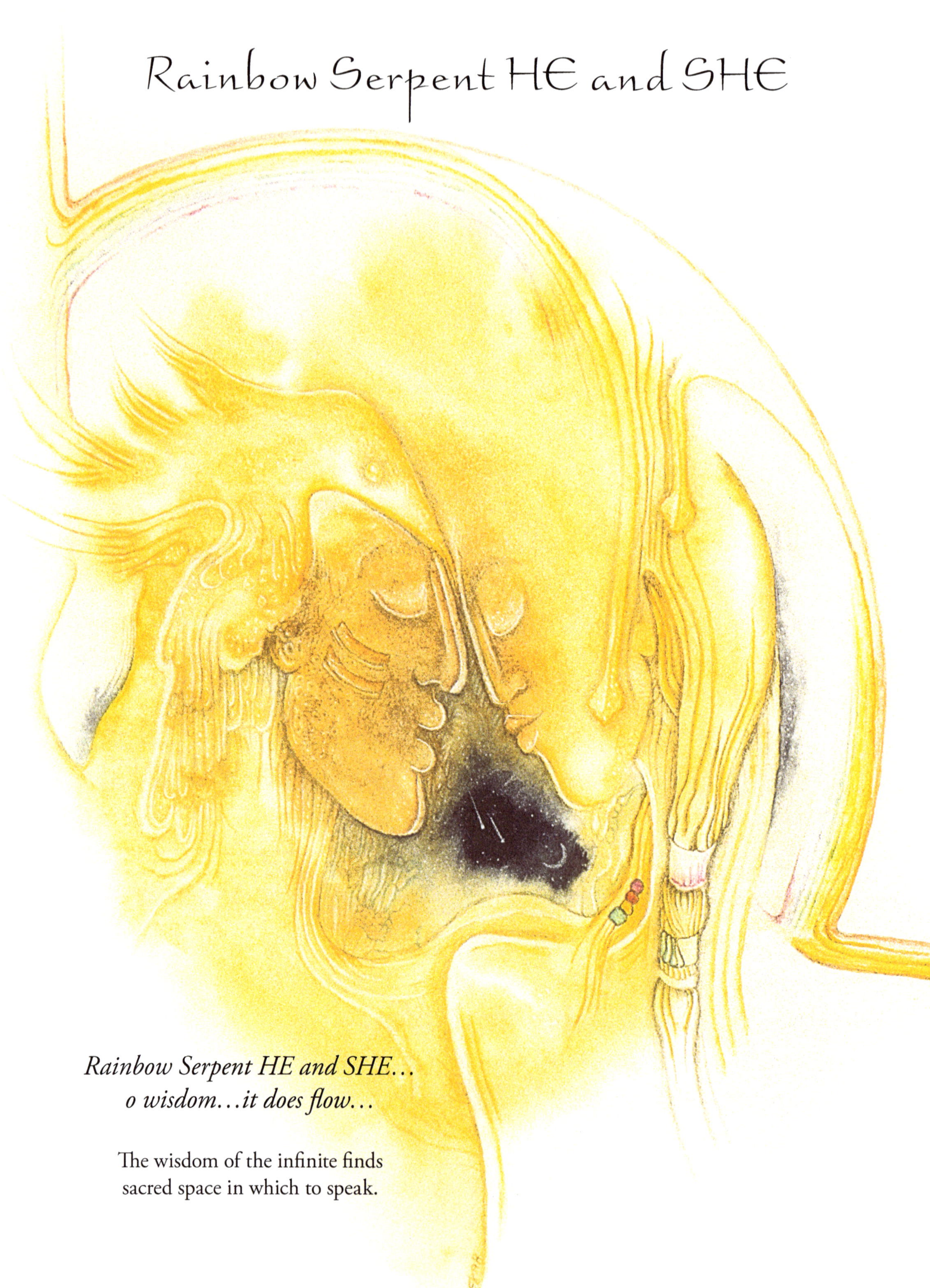

Rainbow Serpent HE and SHE…
o wisdom…it does flow…

The wisdom of the infinite finds
sacred space in which to speak.

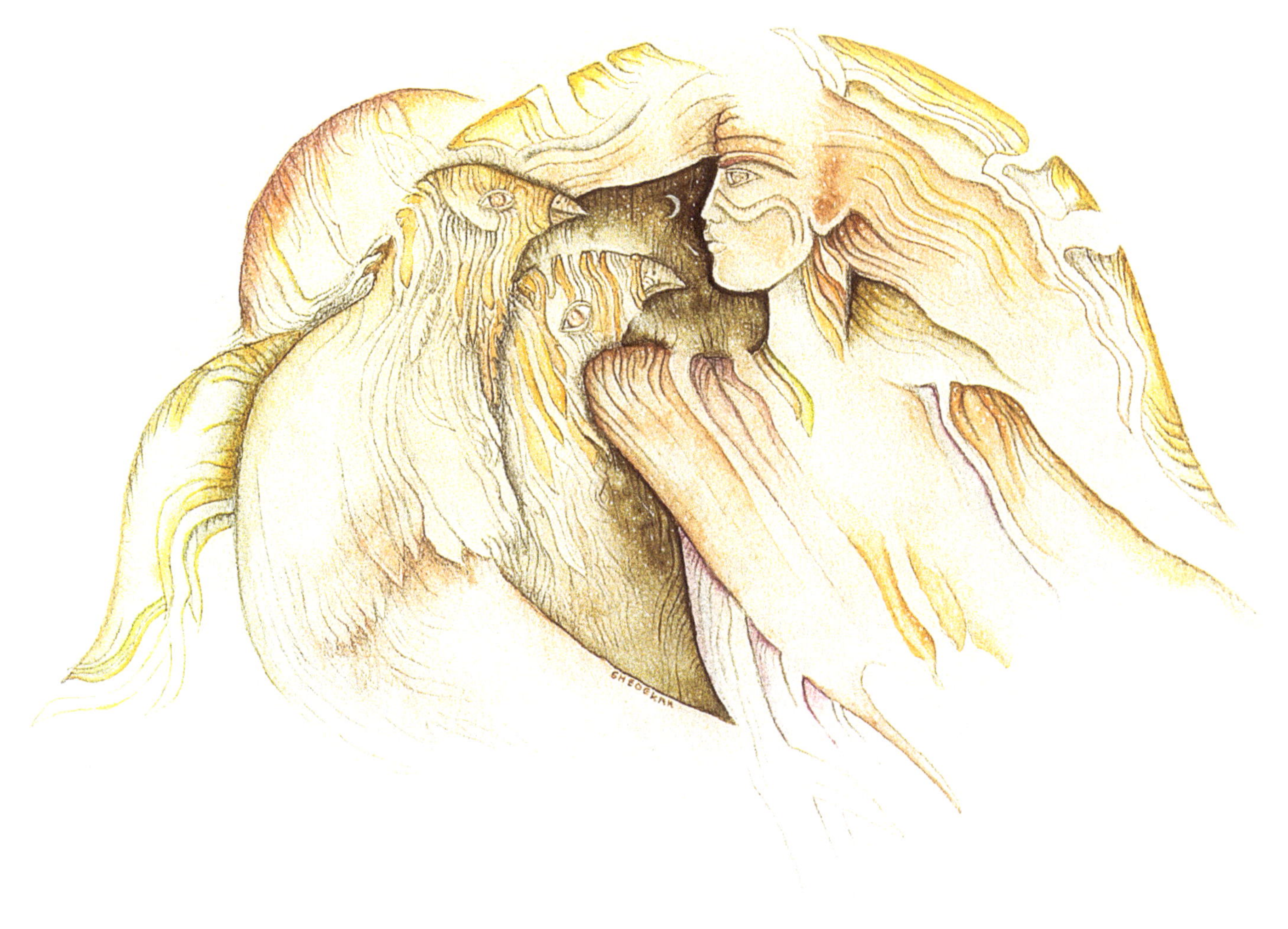

bird-tribe-two...emerging...from the stars...

bird-tribe-two...emerging...from the stars...

bird-tribe-two...emerging...as the winged ones...

finding ever...a dance of opposites...

Winged ones speak of flights of Consciousness
that are never seen by earthbound eyes.

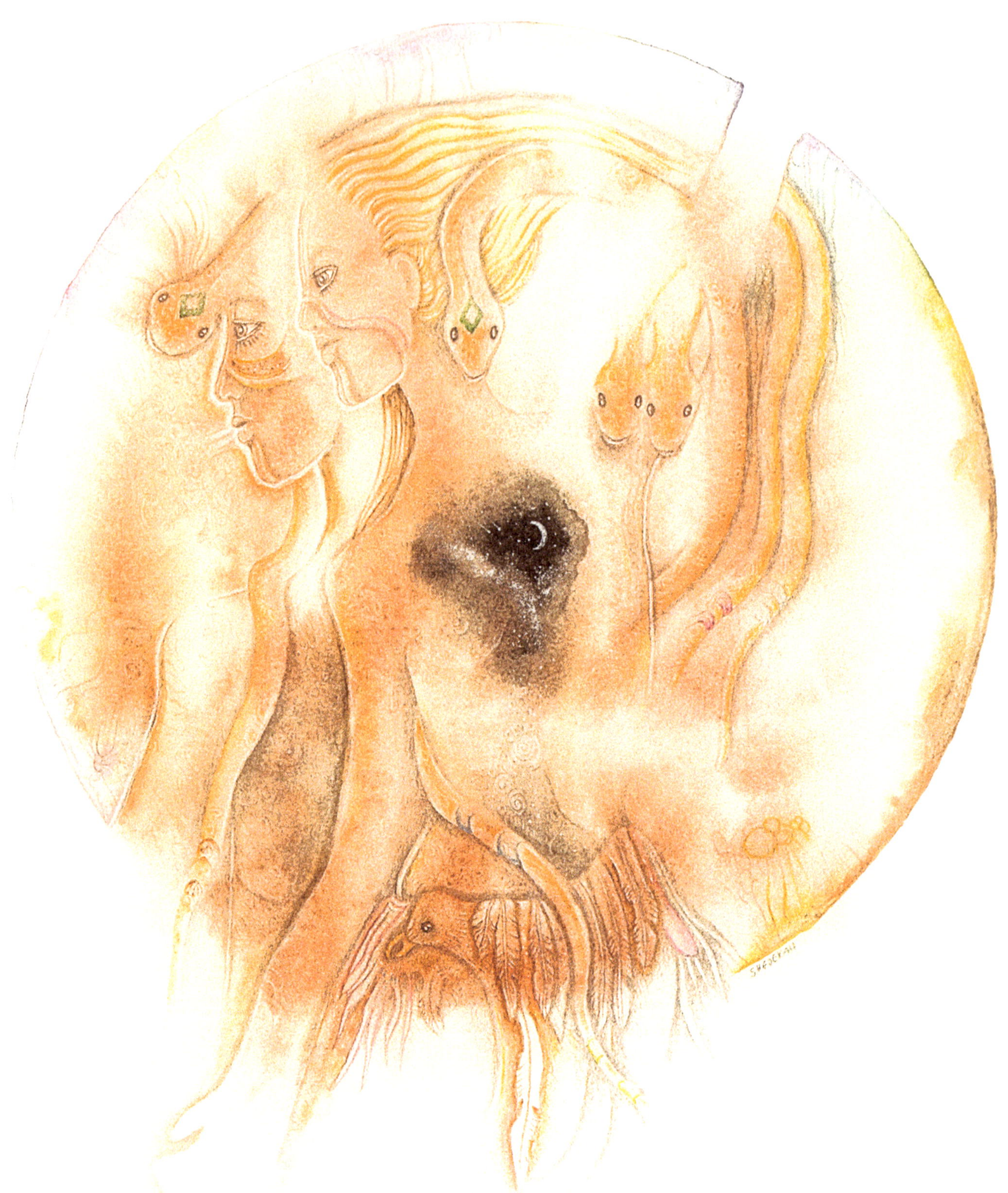

Dance of the Caducean HE and SHE

Form and Formless dance…and HE and SHE…
and knowing fills their hearts…

Light enfolds the ones who turn to wisdom. The heart does sing.

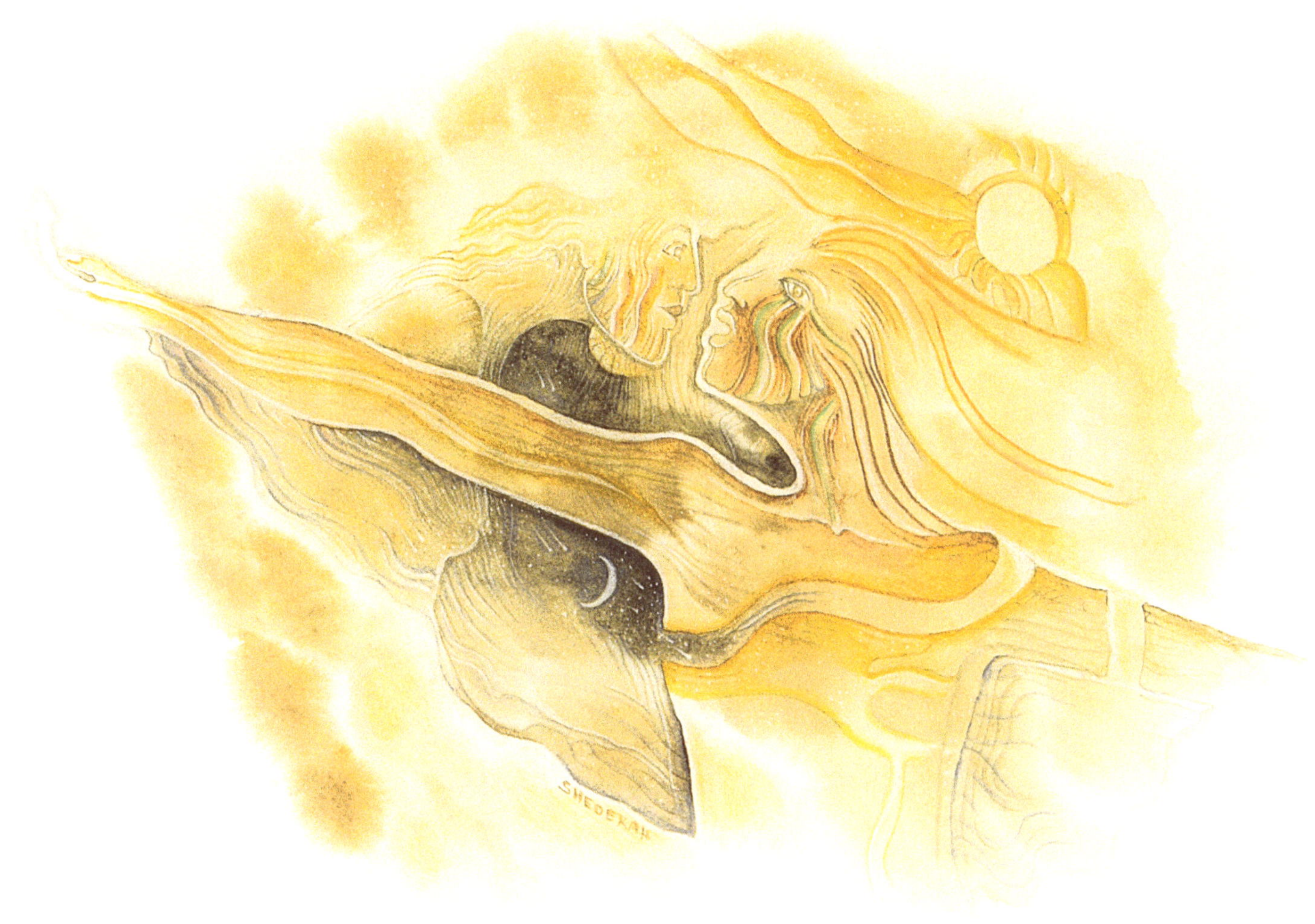

...meeting with the serpent... ...and the stars...

...meeting with the serpent......and the stars...

HE and SHE...do find...that wisdom has no end...

This painting is a poem,
beholding wisdom.

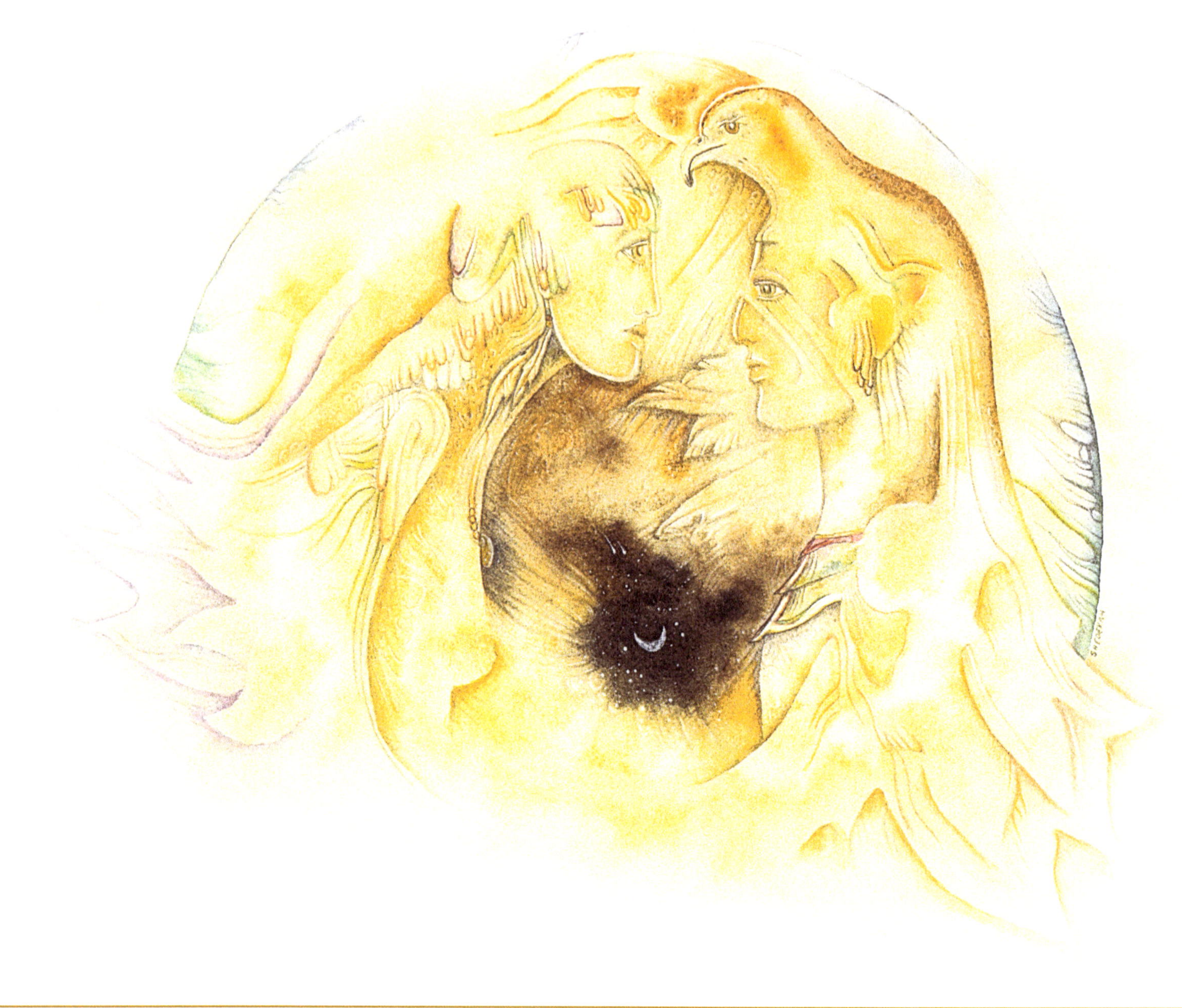

Archetypal HE and SHE...

Archetypal HE and SHE...
comes two stars...unto the circle of creation...

Visual poetry comes before us as the yin and yang.
Ever balance reigns.

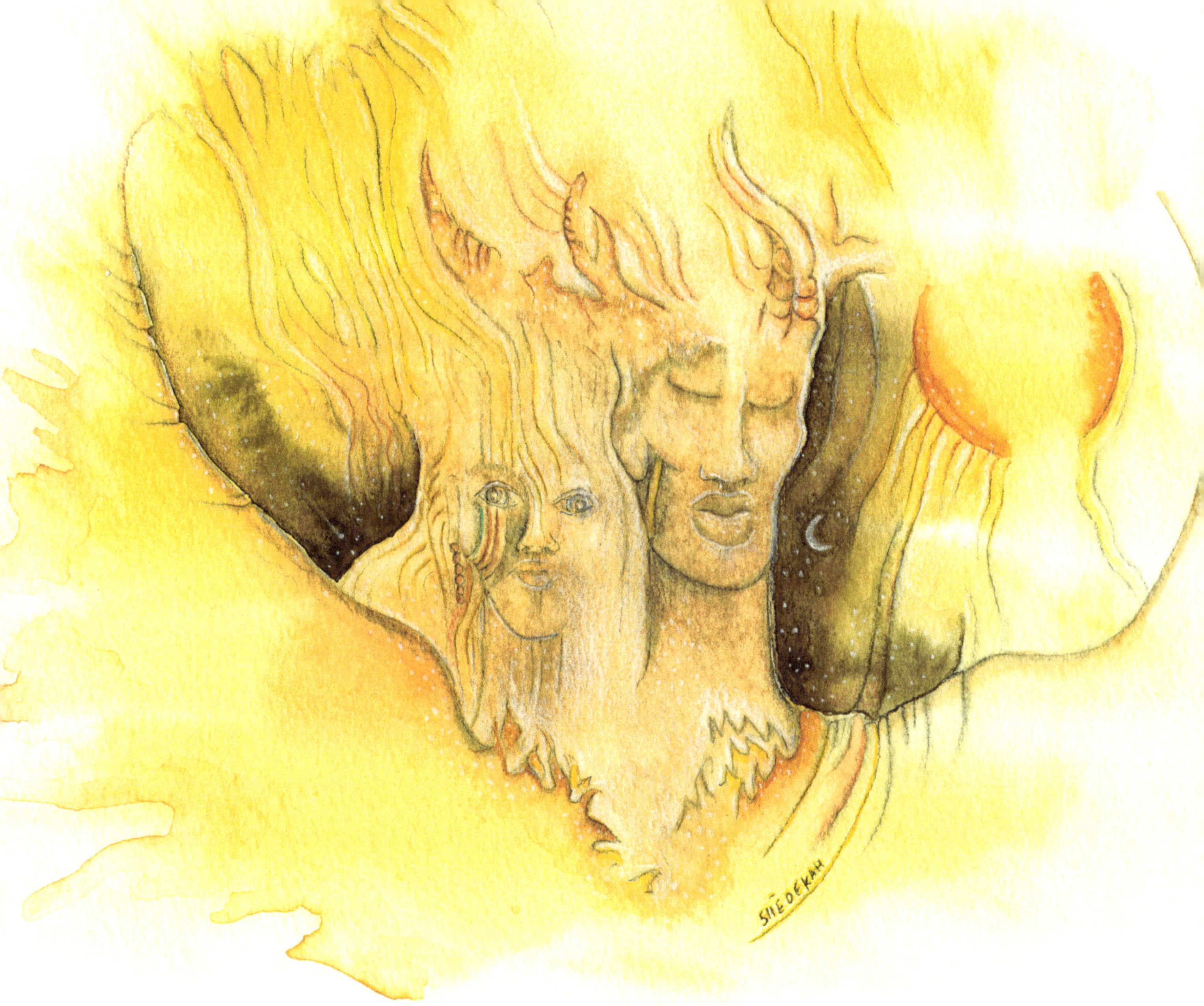

Antler-HE...in fire dance

Antler-HE...in fire dance...
to the SHE of creation...

HE arrives as protector of the balance,
the HE and SHE of all Creation.

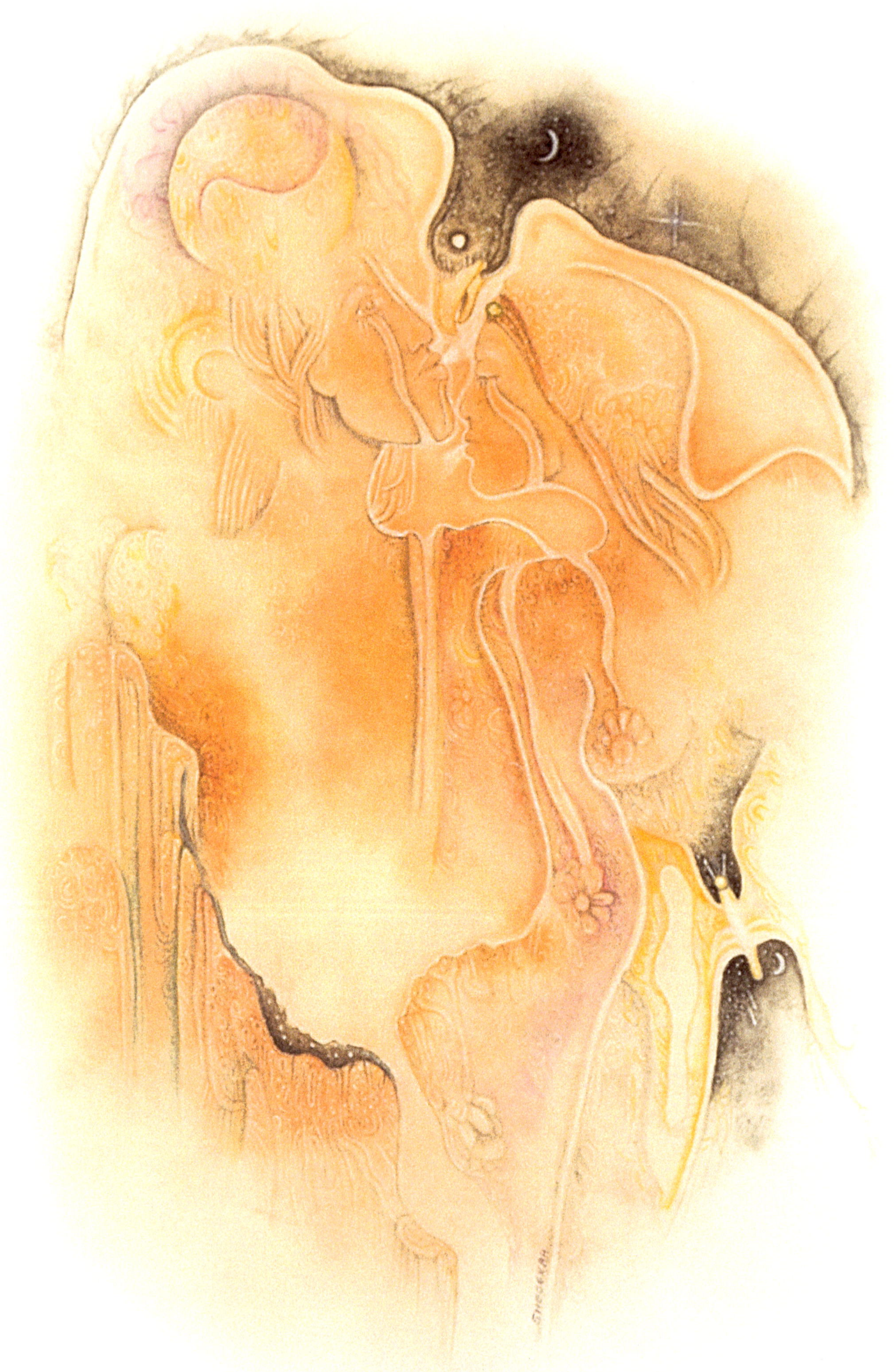

Kiva Dwelling HE and SHE

found within the kiva of the heart…
ever dwell the HE and SHE…

The yin and yang of our being is recognized,
acknowledged and ever honored.

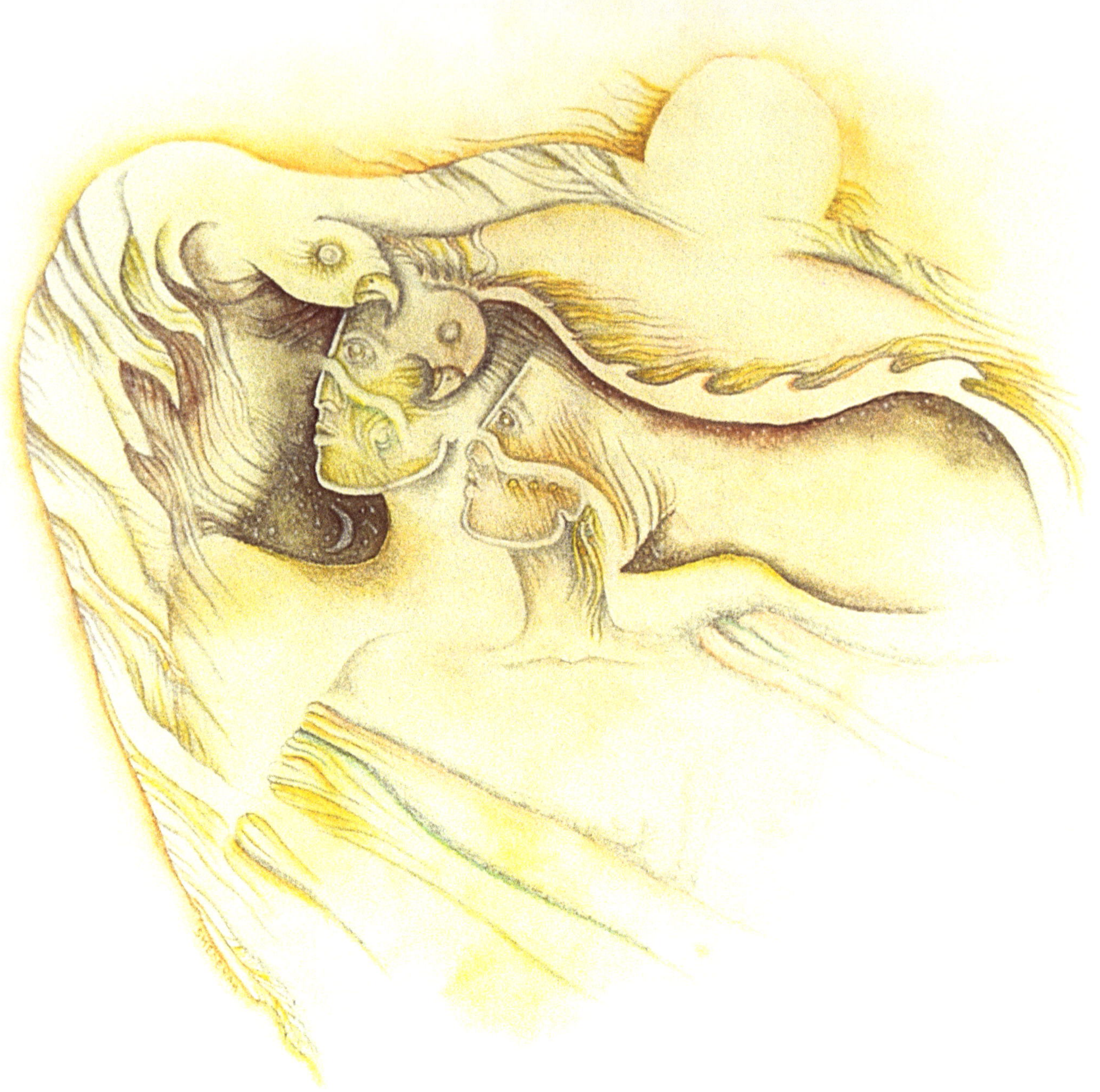

HE and SHE...emerged... as The Sacred Two...

HE and SHE...emerged...as the sacred two...

HE and SHE...emerged...as the flight of the soul...

This visual poem serves to tell
the story of Partners in Purpose.

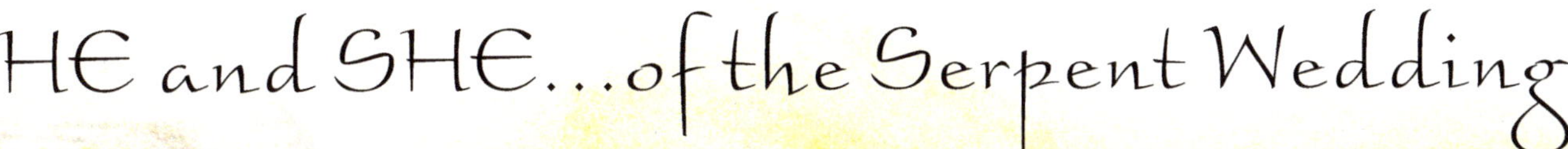

HE and SHE...of the Serpent Wedding

wisdom enters...love does come...
balance...it does flower...

The Serpent Wedding reflects the yin/yang Circle of the One.
Both feminine and masculine wisdom are honored as holy.

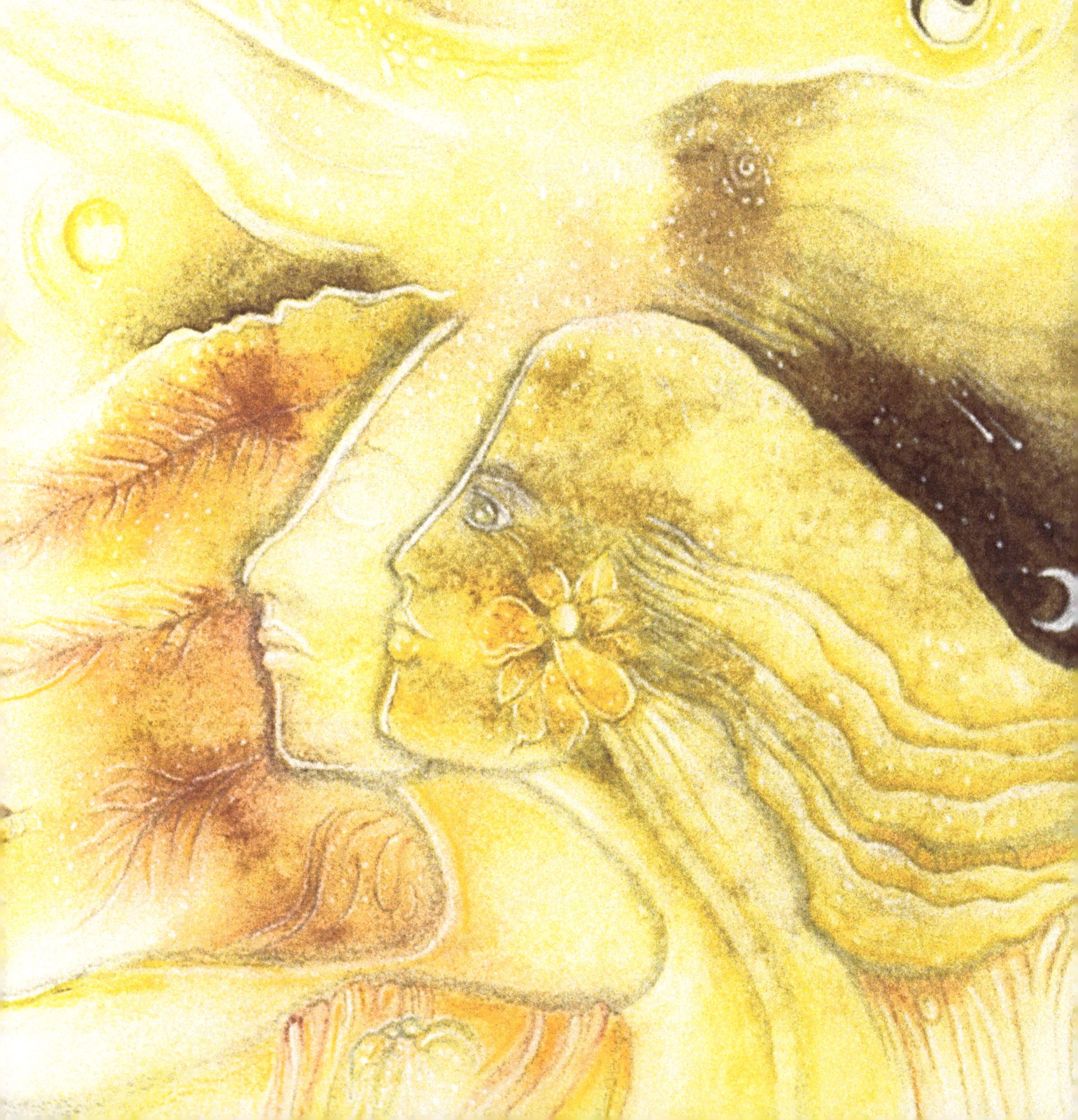

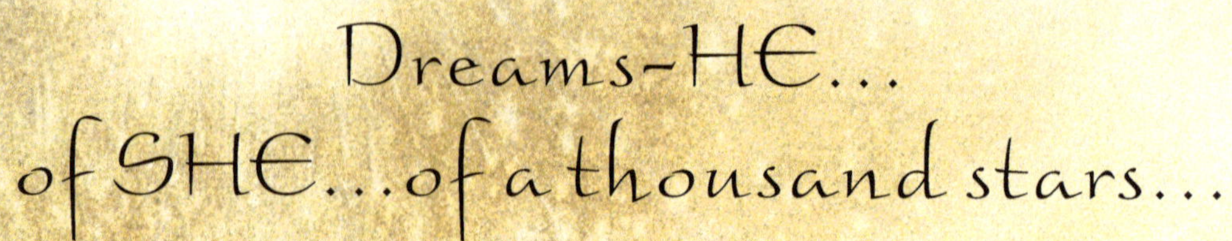

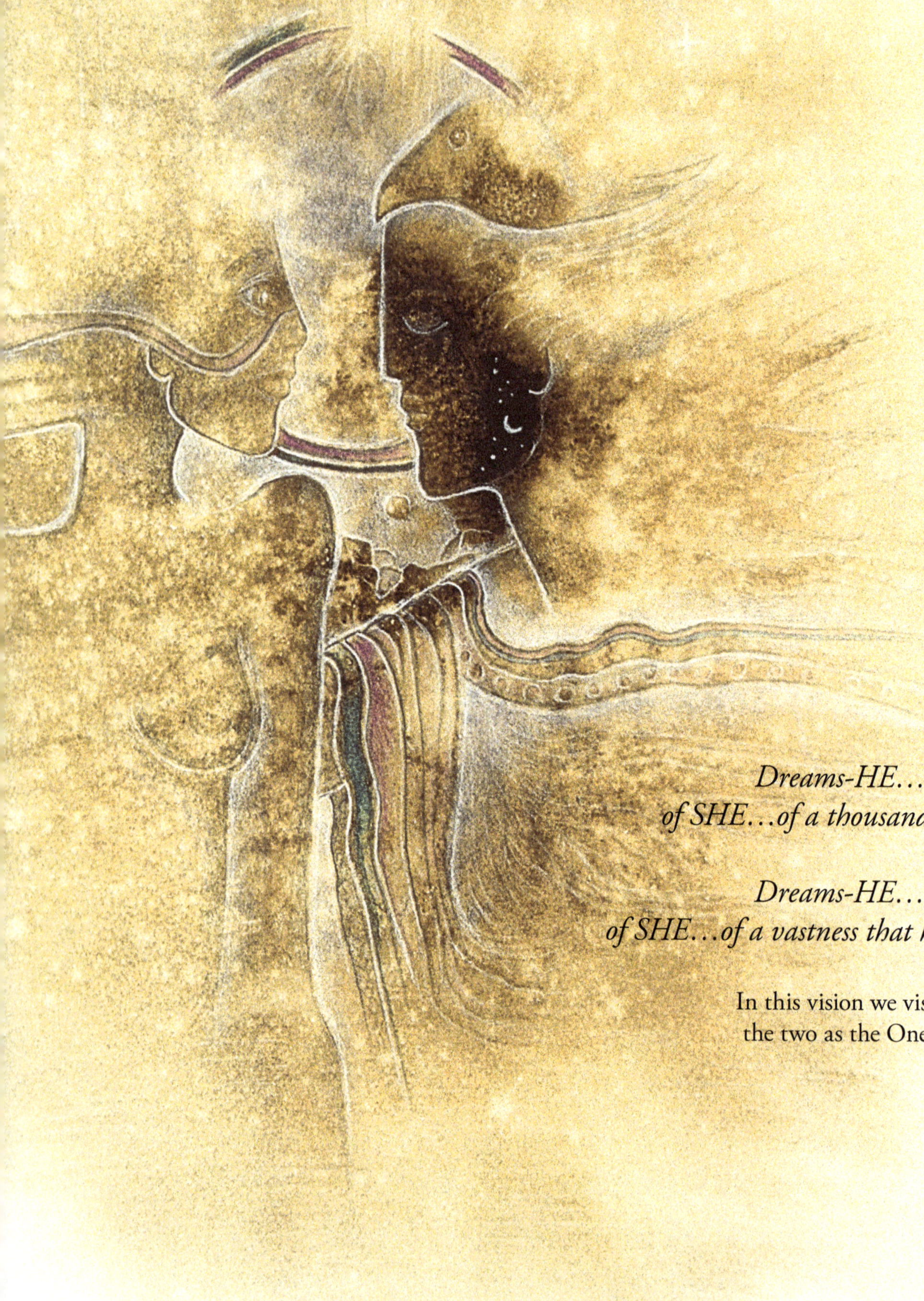

Dreams-HE...
of SHE...of a thousand stars...

Dreams-HE...
of SHE...of a vastness that has no end...

In this vision we visit
the two as the One.

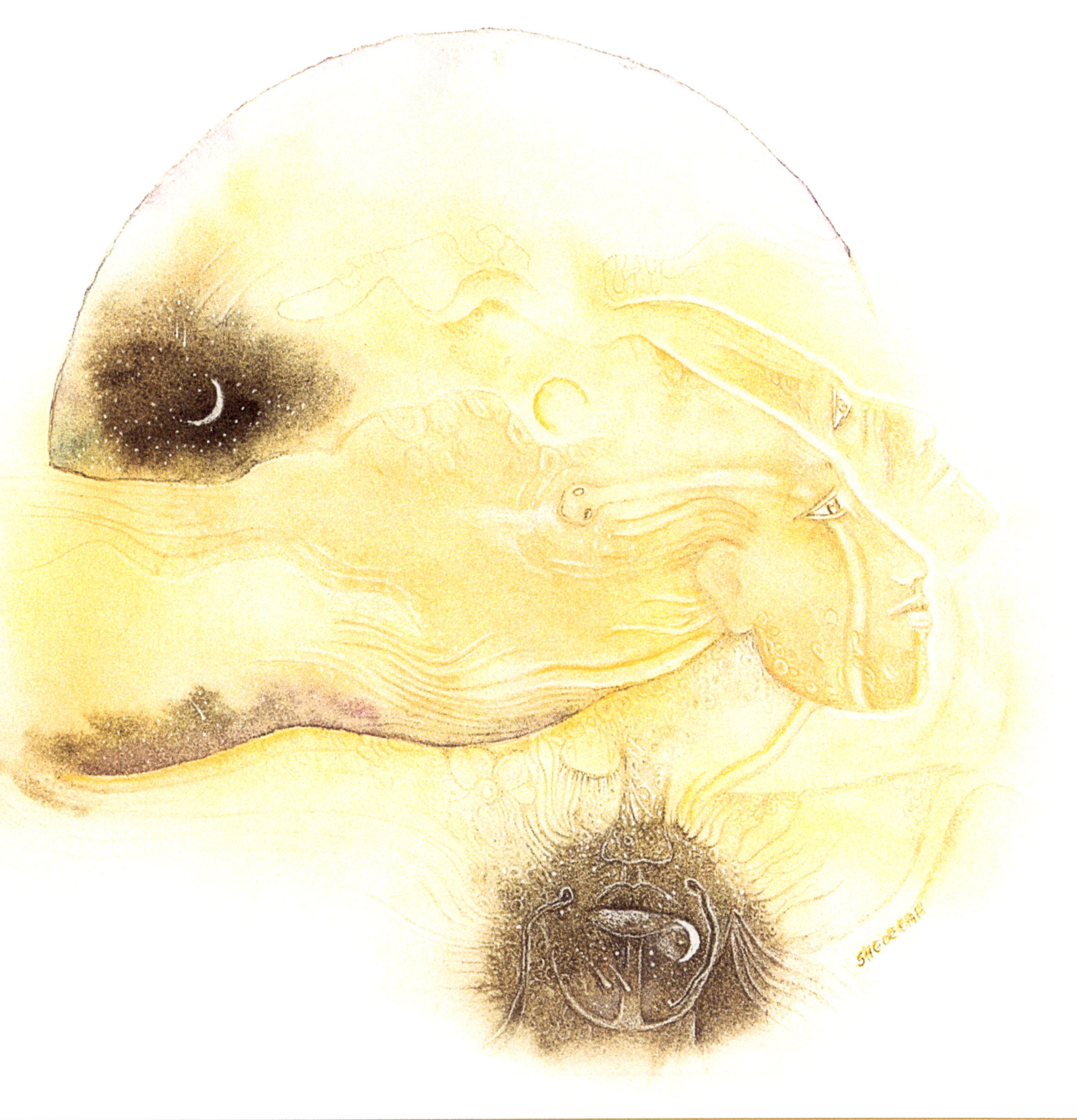

Serpent Wedding HE and SHE

vision of the union…found within the self…

Serpent Wedding HE and SHE honors the marriage borne from within.

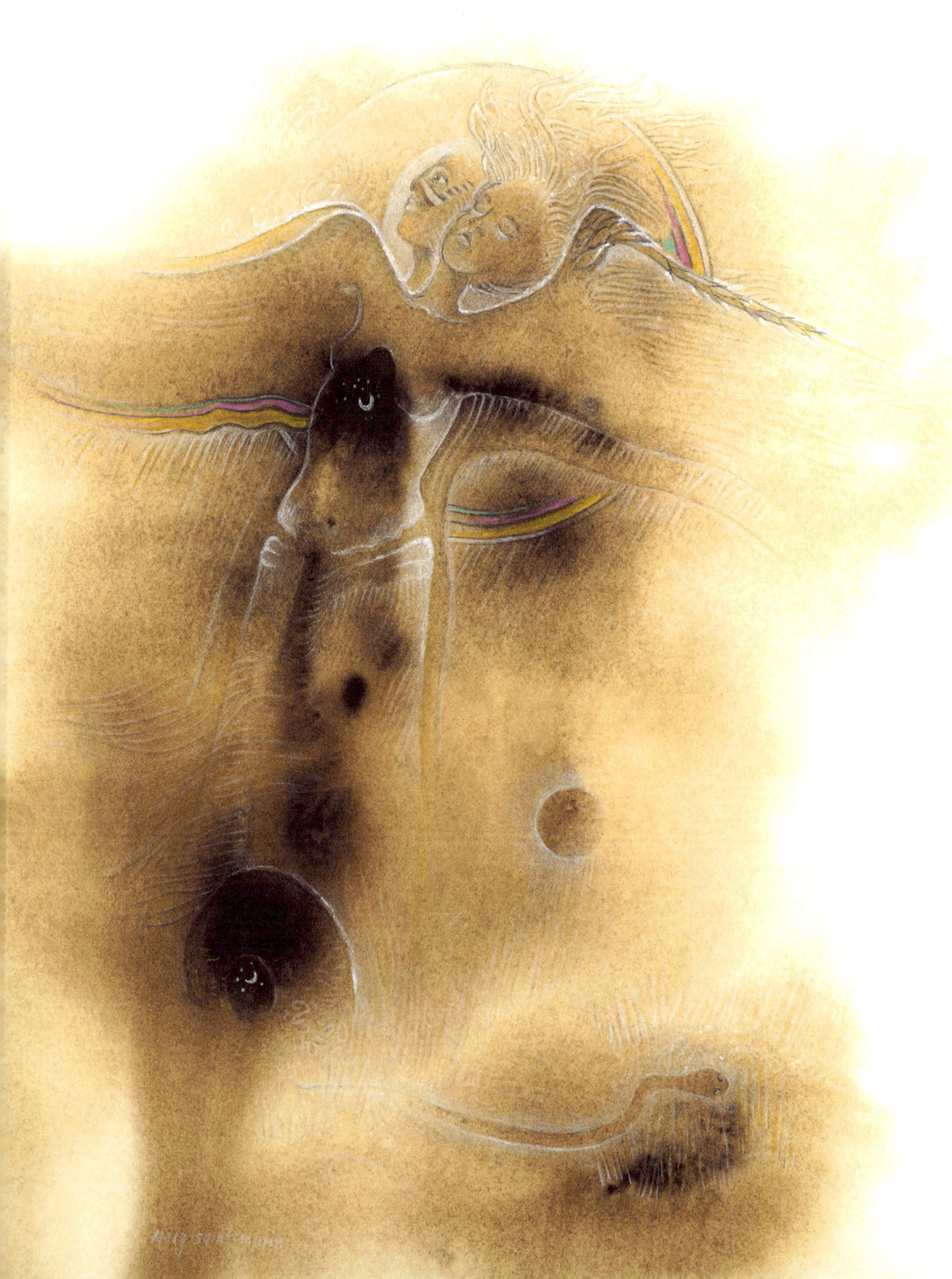
mary saint-marie

HE and SHE...
of the timeless lodge...

man...woman...HE...SHE...enter the lodge...of forever...

stars...moons...sacred cosmos does open unto them...

together...transcendent flight ensues...

together...wings do spread...

together...rainbow nation unveils...

revealed...a world of wholeness...

here...yin and yang...in balance...

here...Beauty...does sing its song...

This painting represents the "the sacred two", man and woman,
brought together by Spirit to be a foundation for an emerging culture,
unlike the rising and falling civilizations of eons past.
The union represented here brings wisdom of a new day.
The portrayal of the flight in the image shows
the awareness coming from I Am Awareness.

This painting is a visual prayer.
It is a holy chant unto the high heavens.
It touches lightly on the earth...and silently does sing its story.

This image does speak of the transcendence that awaits as our Awareness.
It speaks of the joy of sacred marriage.

Universal Birth…
from the Bird-Tribe-Two

pregnant…
the formless…
takes form…

The visual
languaging
portrays the
Undivided One.

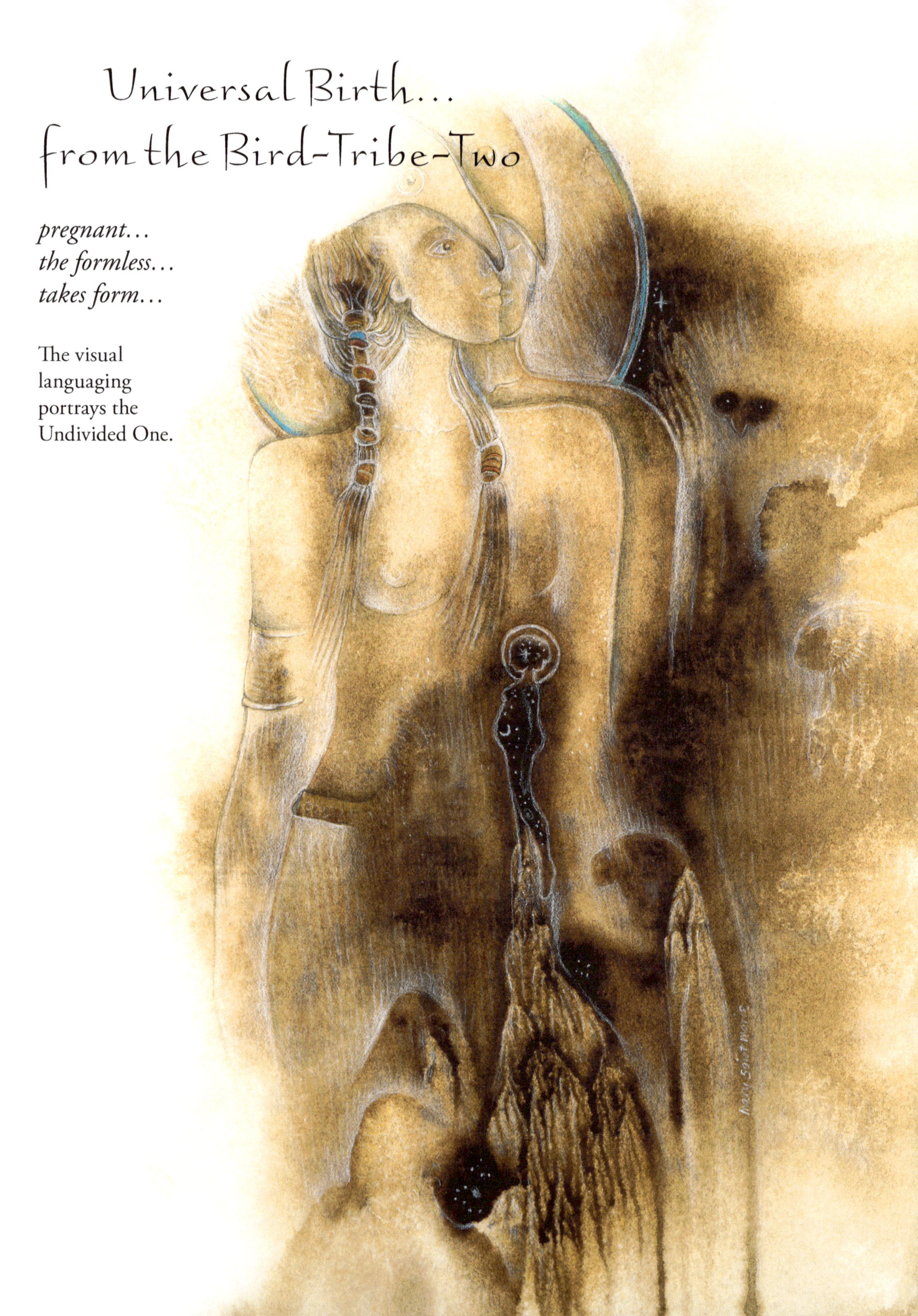

Passages

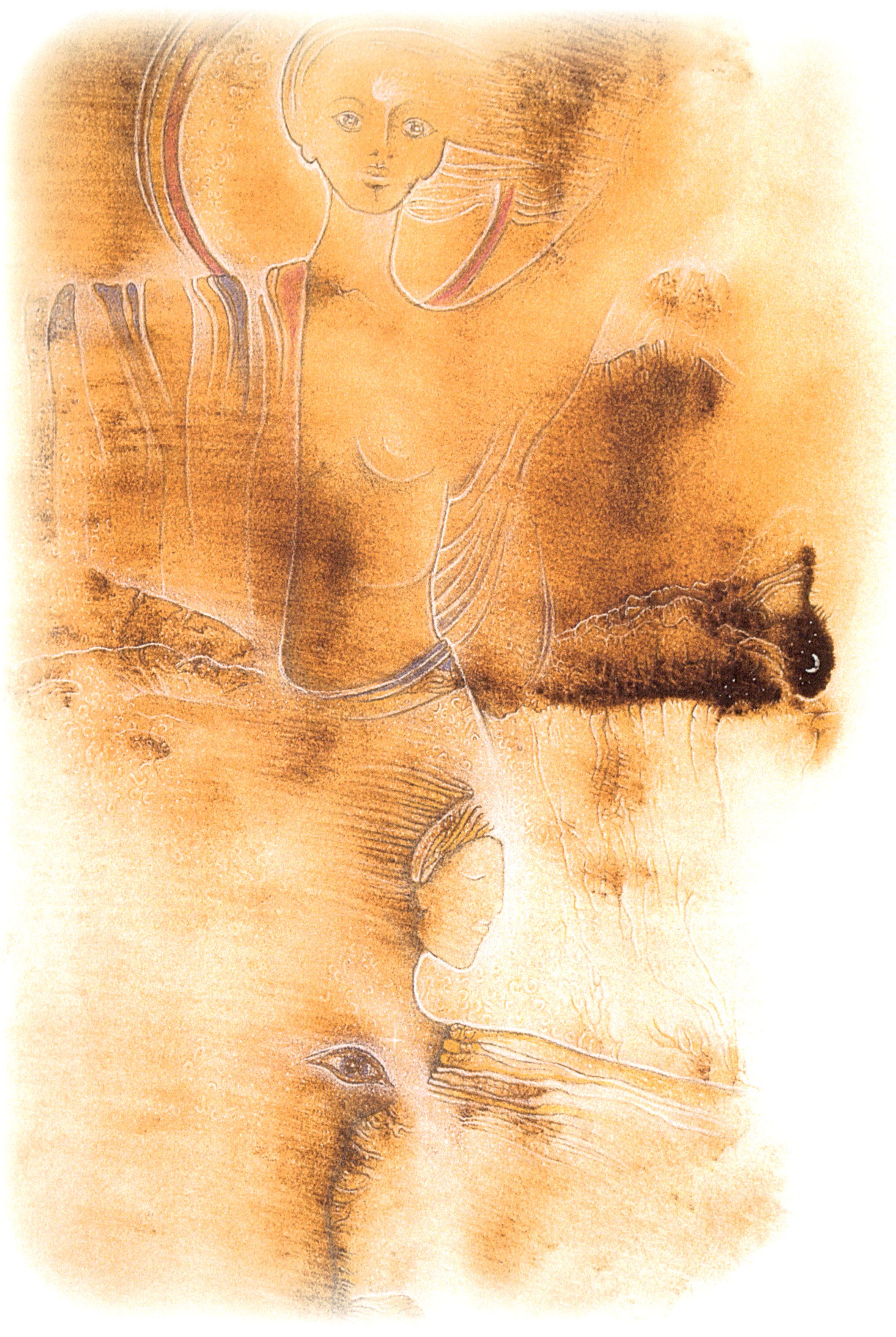

O Lift This Veil of Untruth

O would you ask, "how is your world?"
I answer. Do you speak of a world filled with
beliefs, concepts, worries, doubts and fear?
Is this the world of which you speak? Do you
speak of a world of strife and suffering and sorrow?
Do you speak of endless disasters, distress and death?
Is this the world you speak of?

Or do you speak of the only world there is?
Do you speak of the world illumined by joy?
Do you speak of the world unshrouded with dismal
human beliefs veiling the light of everpresent joy?

O lift this veil.
Lift this veil of untruth.
It is ever only a thought.
A belief.

Beyond this veil another world already ever IS.
It awaits.

My prayer is ever that these visitors shall pierce*
the veil of human beliefs.

My prayer is ever that these visitors in seeming time
and space emanate their knowing.

My prayer is ever that these visitors penetrate the
dross that light may grant one passage.

*visitors – art images from the light of knowing

Sing the Holy Chant

During the 90's, I created a series of paintings that felt like gossamer visitors from another world beyond all time. So subtle they were, taking much more time to arrive than other paintings.

They called to me.
They whispered.
They invited me and I followed.

Hours and days passed into weeks, months,
years with these guests ever in my studio.

Enchanted, I became the listener, the beholder.
I became the bringer of the image only.

And questions came.
Are these personal?
I would fall silent.
Personal?
Personal is only the fancy of the belief in separation.
It is all impersonal.
We are One.

May we join in sweet song…
May we hear the distant chant…
And may the hum of the one heart send smiles across the globe.

You say there is suffering. There is suffering everywhere.
Find the belief that creates the suffering.
And sing the holy chant.
And suffering shall cease.

These images do come from the land beyond the suffering.
I enjoin you to take pilgrimage to the land beyond suffering.

Your glow shall entrance others.
Suffering shall cease to be.

The World is in You

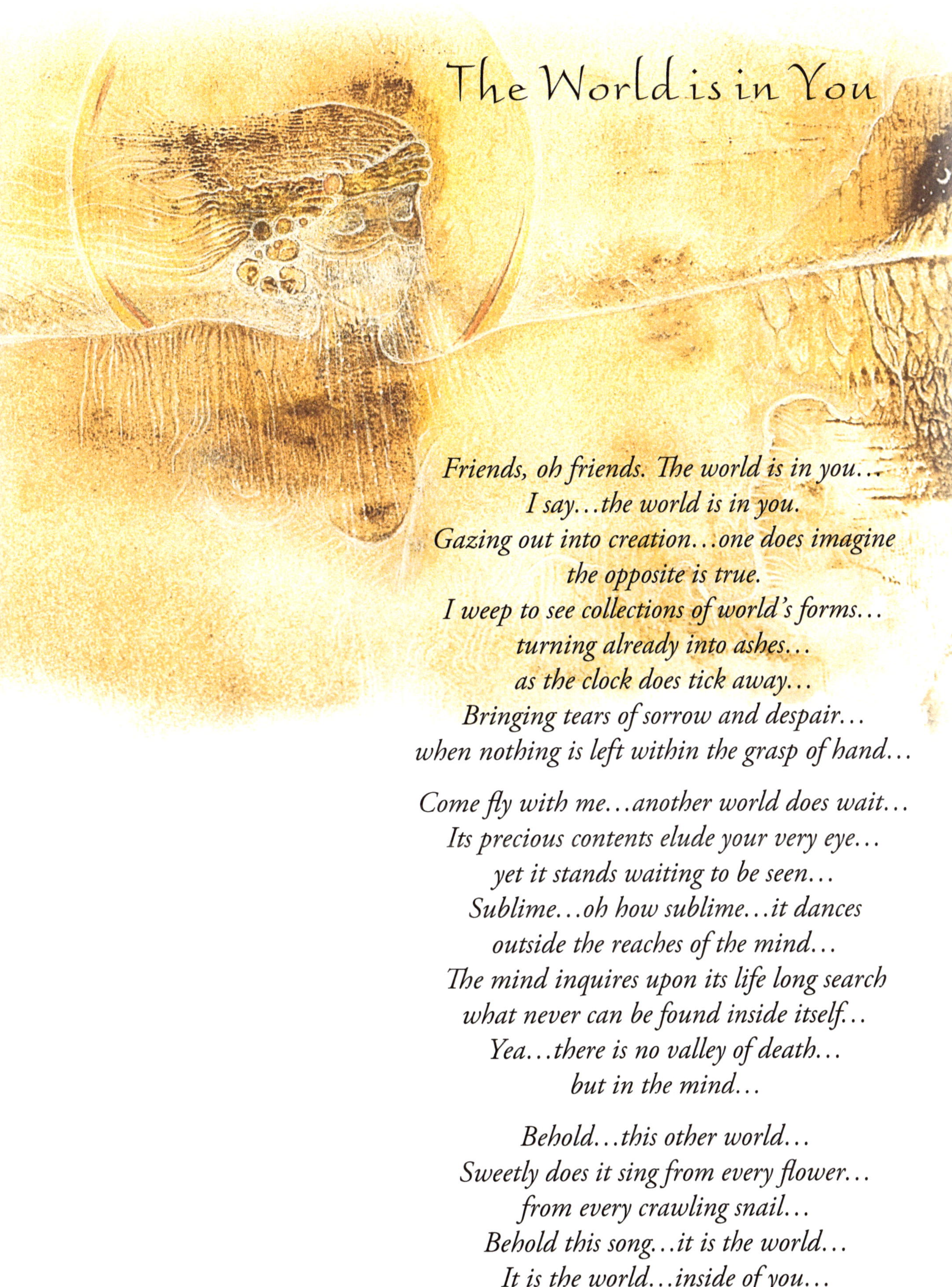

Friends, oh friends. The world is in you…
I say…the world is in you.
Gazing out into creation…one does imagine
the opposite is true.
I weep to see collections of world's forms…
turning already into ashes…
as the clock does tick away…
Bringing tears of sorrow and despair…
when nothing is left within the grasp of hand…

Come fly with me…another world does wait…
Its precious contents elude your very eye…
yet it stands waiting to be seen…
Sublime…oh how sublime…it dances
outside the reaches of the mind…
The mind inquires upon its life long search
what never can be found inside itself…
Yea…there is no valley of death…
but in the mind…

Behold…this other world…
Sweetly does it sing from every flower…
from every crawling snail…
Behold this song…it is the world…
It is the world…inside of you…

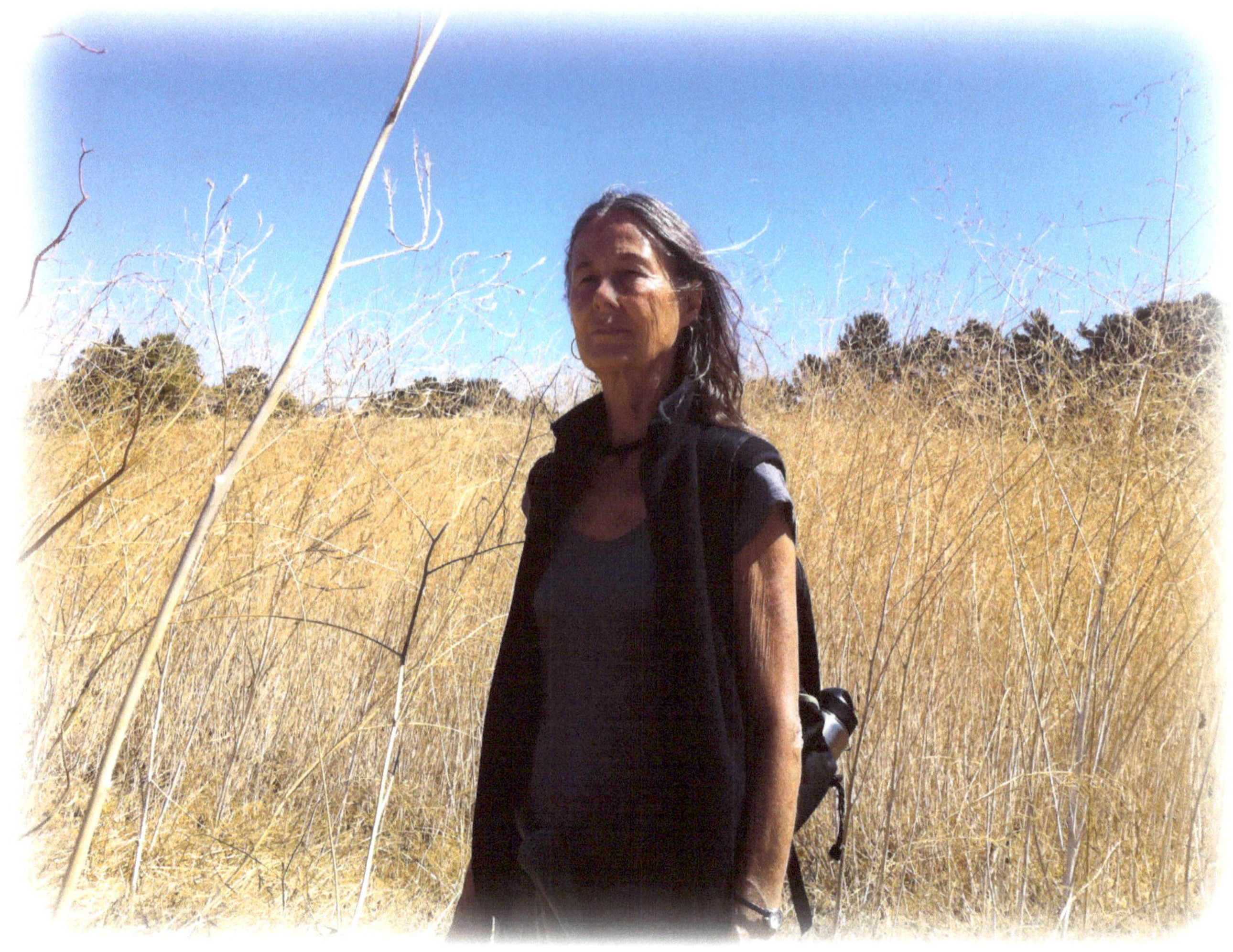

About the Artist-Writer

Mary Saint-Marie is a mystic artist, writer and spiritual educator. Mary has traveled extensively with her exhibits nationwide, creating over one hundred and fifty visionary showings. Mary has been pioneering visionary art exhibitions that reveal Essence/presence since 1972 in galleries, conferences, symposiums, expositions, holistic faires, workshops and in her studio/gallery, Ancient Beauty Studio. Mary's work has been shown in Belgium numerous times. She has created many years of multi-media enactments inspiring others into the awareness of the I Am Awareness, Pure Consciousness, that each may come to express their true nature and essence. She describes her work as *The Mystical as the Practical.*

The visionary Art of the Soul of Mary Saint-Marie is inspirational and reflects and mirrors our oneness. It is an odyssey into the land of original Archetypal realms of wholeness. This art is inspired in Mary from her own journeys/upliftments into those realms of ecstasy and exaltation. This Consciousness is here now waiting to be "landed unto these very times" from the "Once upon a Non-Time." The Timeless.

This sacred art is witness to the Law of Balance, that is the law of love in all of nature. It is a reflection of the sacred marriage of earth and sky. The Formless come as the formed. The Invisible come as the visible.

Mary's art and words are featured in *One Source Sacred Journey,* a collection of 44 international visionary artists, as well as *Songs from the Edge of Everything* and *The Ways of Spirit.*

Mary Saint-Marie's body of work is collected nationally and internationally. It has appeared on calendars, greeting cards, cd covers, book and magazine covers and in magazines. They include magazines such as *Quest, Mystic Pop, Anemone, Dream Network Journal* and *Crone Chronicles.* The art has appeared on many television interviews nationwide, such as the Wisdom Channel and Channel 5 in San Francisco. Her art of the soul was featured on television across Germany.

Mary's art appears on her books, *The Holy Sight, The Sacred Two, Messages from the Silence, Nectar of Woman* and *Galactic Shamanism.* It also appeared in her multi-media sacred enactment, *SHE…it is…who Remembers.*

Mary is also a sculptress and created ceremonial sculptures from compounds for many years. From there bronzing began. Mary has created a recording, *Return to Oneness,* that is a poetic odyssey as a voice of the animals. Mary has been uplifted into the soul realms of the animals many times. The odyssey is a call for rights of the precious animals.

Mary Saint-Marie loves changing to new artistic forms. She says it is from entering into the "realm of Changing Woman." The Changeless One in us all does bring the change.

Another form includes writing a sacred theatre production that arrived one weekend on retreat with almost non-stop inspired writing. It is *The Monitor and Laughter of the Gods: Saraswati Comes Swingin' Her Hips.* It was produced by Mary Saint-Marie, with the help of many gifted and inspired co-creators, actors and dancers.

Biography and Education

Mary Saint-Marie has lived close to nature mostly in the Northern California mountains since 1974. Nature has been her major essence inspiration.

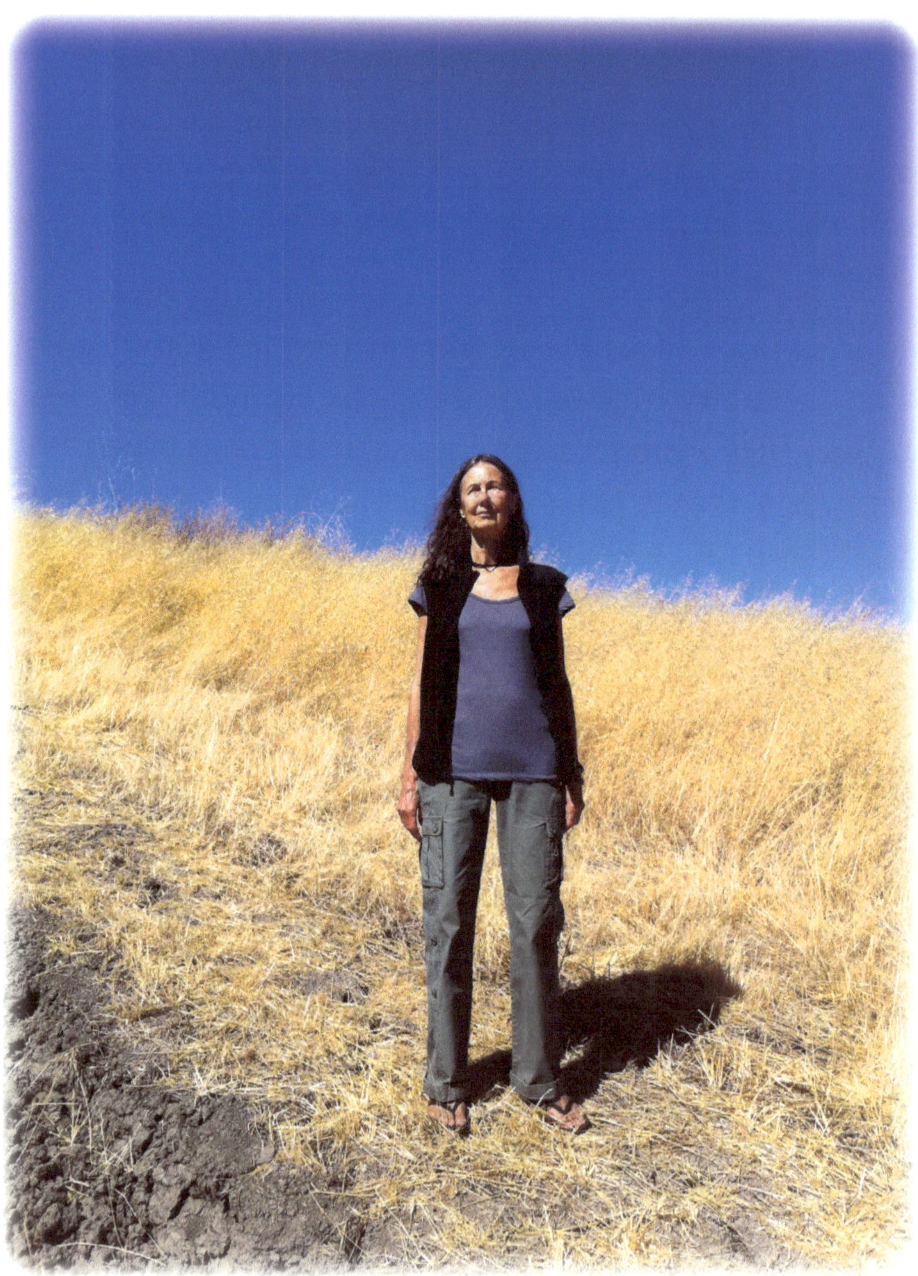

Mary's early life was unusual. She did not speak for her first three years. Rather she sat in silence, smiling into space with her eyes open. She sat on a little stool in the middle of the room. Her mother told her that she was very joyful.

Great was the inspiration of having a pioneering pilot mother in the 40's. She flew in open cockpit doing triple loops while pregnant with Mary. Perhaps this is where Mary first learned about the balance of earth and sky, ground school and flight school. Mary's mother was also a boogie woogie pianist and a dancer, opening the door to a world of creativity.

Then Mary found nature. Nature was her first potent childhood teacher.

Barefoot was her life…running wildly across hot sand dunes in the Texas gulf and through the deep gushing rain in the ditches of Iowa and flying on great vines across ravines of Mississippi and riding sea turtles on an island in the Gulf of Mexico. This sense of freedom in nature was later to be captured in many art forms.

Formal education includes a degree in Education and English, after which Mary spent eight years teaching high school English, Mythology and Communication. She was also coordinator in public educational television at the University of Wisconsin. There she also studied Fine Art. Later Mary was an instructor of English at a two year college in Oregon.

During that time Mary had a spontaneous soul experience/awakening during a head-on car collision that provided the opening to see her life via her soul. As pure joy! Following this opening Mary could see emanations of light radiating around living things. The exalted and numinous experience initiated a new life. Mary was inspired to begin her life as an artist.

Mary bought a Kelty pack and sleeping bag and took one change of clothing and art supplies in 1971 and went overland to Spain, Morocco, Italy, Greece, Crete, Turkey, Iran. Afghanistan, Pakistan, India and Kashmir, where she felt and loved the art, culture, heart and soul of these peoples. Upon her return to the U.S., Mary pioneered her first visionary art exhibitions, long before visionary galleries showed themselves on the art scene. Her subject matter was illumined beings walking out of the sacred landscapes. Her work sold.

Creative Process and Inner Journey

Mary Saint-Marie draws and paints from within, allowing herself to be a vessel for the expression of Beauty and Consciousness. She does not have a preconceived vision of what she will paint. It arrives as she works and allows. Usually there is time spent in nature before beginning another creation. Walking in nature or sitting by a river, lake or waterfall or sitting on the mountain. Being empty.

Mary enters the studio with reverence, lights a candle and goes into the Silence, the Stillness, before beginning a painting. Mary learned over the years that the painting flowed and came "alive" if she would also "be one" with her brushes, paper, colored pigments from the earth, water and on. She realized that they could all communicate with her if she would enter deeply into the Field of Light that is ever present. And the paintings would flow. The paintings combine drawing, painting and printmaking. They are multi-media, multi-technique and multi-dimensional. They are visual prayer.

Mary's mystical (union with presence) and sacred art of the soul reflects her seemingly personal experiences as the Impersonal. The art reflects her inner world of Spirit. She allows the ancient beauty of primordial, primal, archetypal imagery to reflect itself from the background spaces of the mixed media, working ever in reverse.

Mary works with feeling the essence…the holy presence…playing back and forth between the Formless and form, the Invisible and visible, always using the human form as the *temple template of Infinity,* allowing it to reveal from the Timeless.

"It is in the realization of Essence Self that we glimpse our own Star-Stone Essence, our multi-dimensional nature and sometimes even beyond. It is what I playfully call Galactic Shamanism or the marriage of earth and sky. It is love. And it is pure Consciousness. I Am Awareness."

"The Light of Consciousness is the love and the wisdom, the yin and yang of our being, expressed as Beauty. In that, we all become, not only beholders of Beauty, but keepers of Beauty. And, in that, are we all artists."

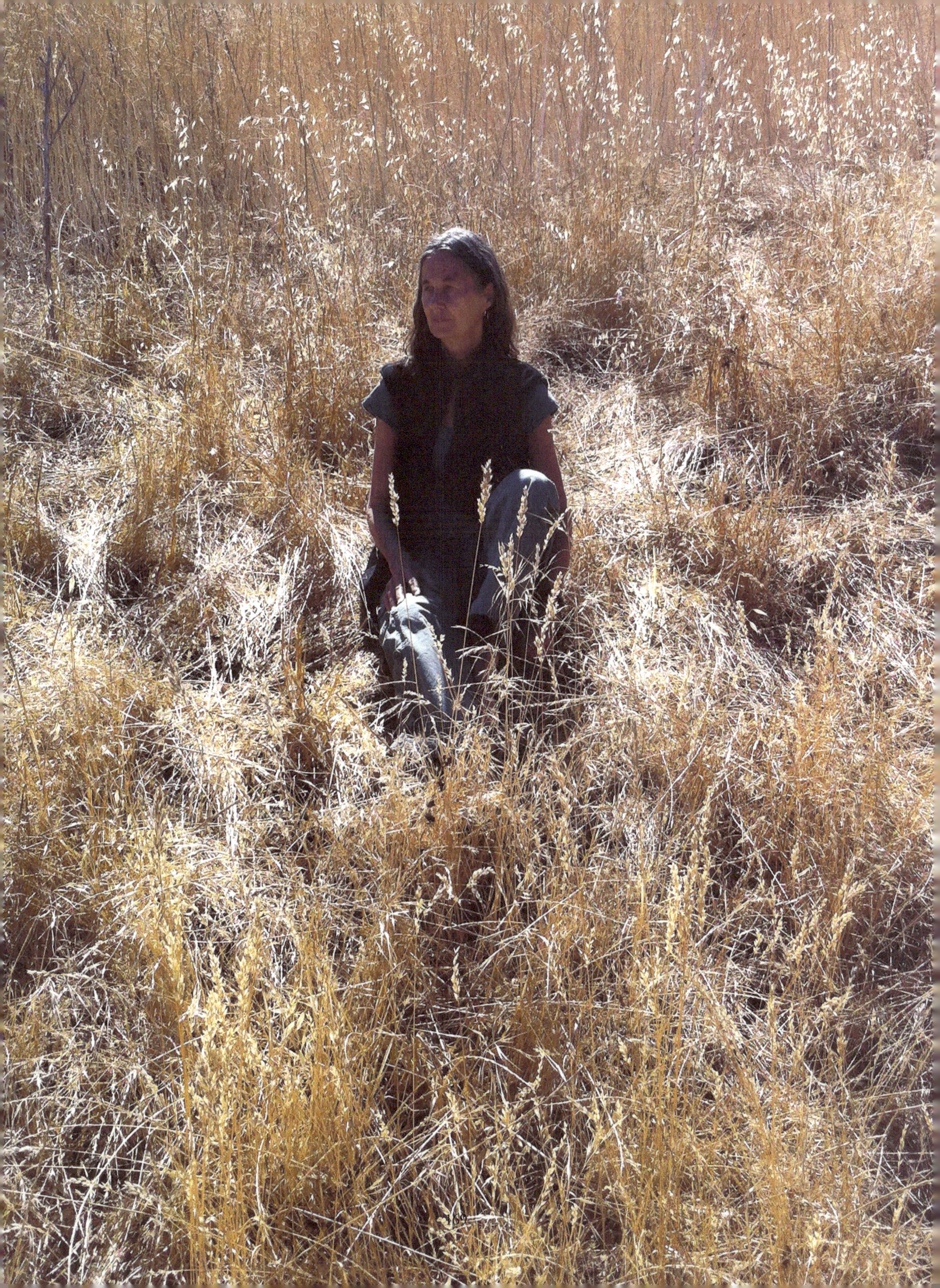

Paintings, Art Exhibits, Soul Sessions and Soul Retreats

www.MarySaintMarie.com
www.EarthCareGlobalTV.com

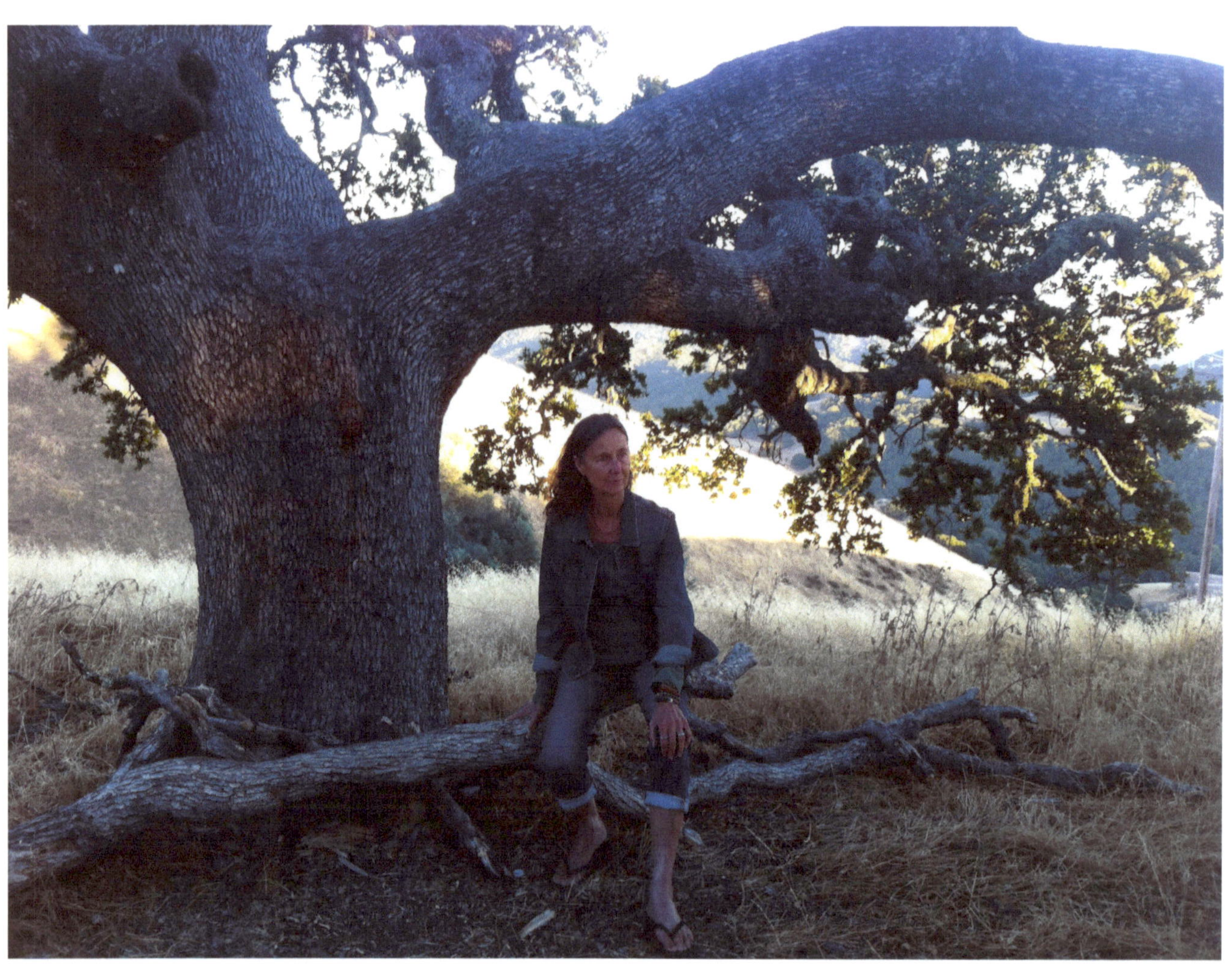

Art of the Soul:
Ancient Beauty Studio by appointment
Original paintings and giclee fine art reproductions available
Bronze sculpture available
Conferences, symposiums, exhibitions

Soul Sessions: For individuals, by phone or in person, or will travel to another town/city if there is a coordinator

Soul Remembering Retreats: For individuals, in person, and lasting 1/2 day

The Holy Sight Workshop: Experiential work for groups

Sounds and Signings of the Soul: Individual initiations into sacred soul sounds and sacred soul movements/dance, that one is in one's soul expression of Life

Journey through the Kingdoms and Journey through the Elements: Individual initiations into feeling, seeing and/or being aware of one's Oneness with Kingdoms and the Elements, that one is in the I Am Awareness in nature

The Sacred Two: Initiation into the ancient yin-yang circle to be aware of the World Birth of Balance, the SHE and HE of Creation, to be aware of the Law of Love…the One come as the Partners in Purpose

SHE…it is…who Remembers: A Sacred Enactment of Ancient Remembering: Multi-media sacred theatre with art, dance, sacred sound, narration, music and shadow effects, from the book *Galactic Shamanism* by Mary Saint-Marie

Recordings: Inquire about purchase of recordings
SHE…it is…who Remembers: A poetic odyssey and narration of a portion of *Galactic Shamanism*
Return to Oneness: Recording of a poetic odyssey into the soul of the animal realm and their rights upon this earth

Poetic Odyssey Readings: Request information

The Monitor and Laughter of the Gods: Saraswati Comes Swingin' Her Hips: This sacred theater was performed in Ashland, Oregon, in 2011. Please inquire about further productions.

EarthCare Global TV: Request information on the vision of a profound unification of global earth care or go to website: www.EarthCareGlobalTV.com

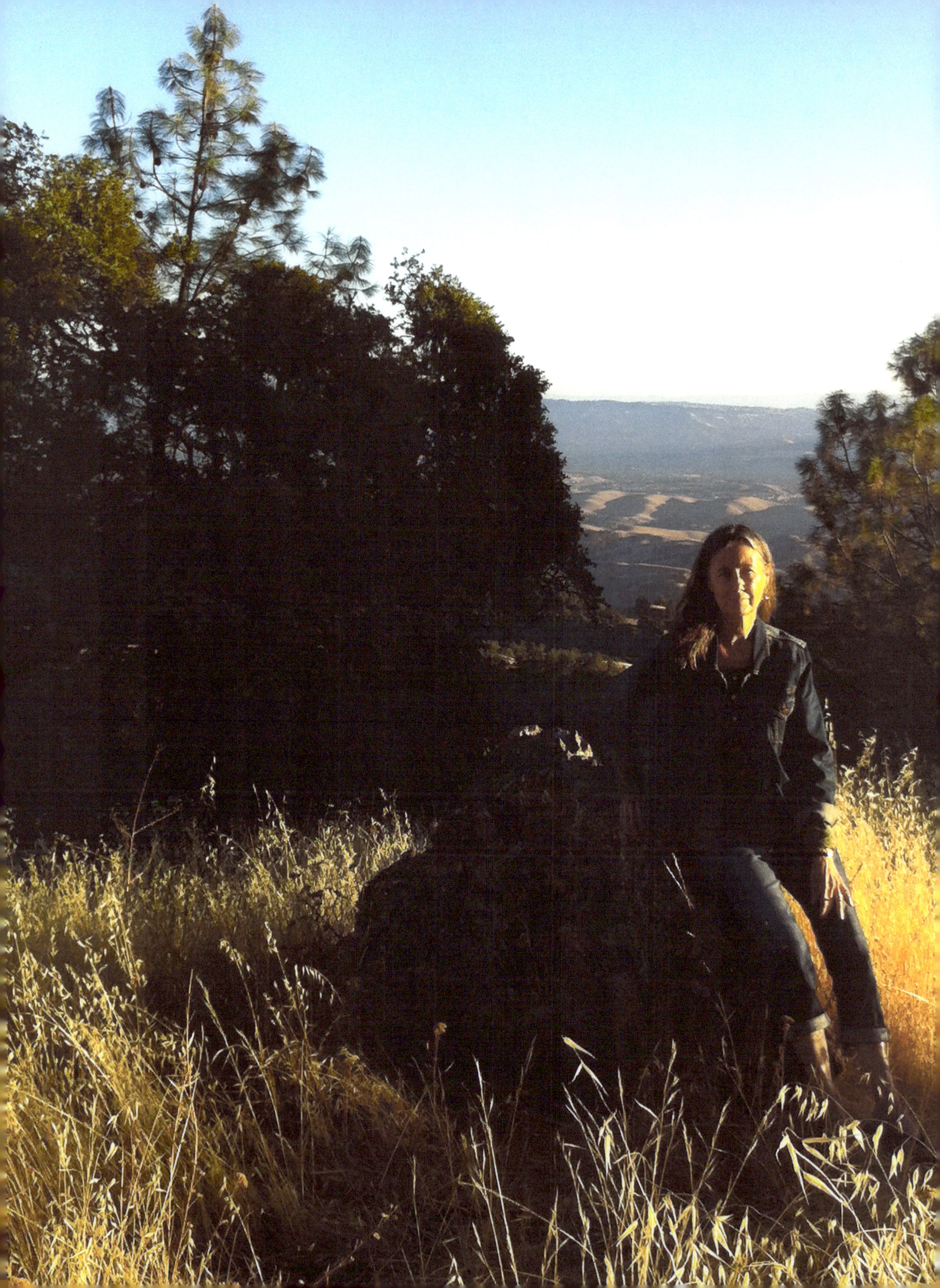

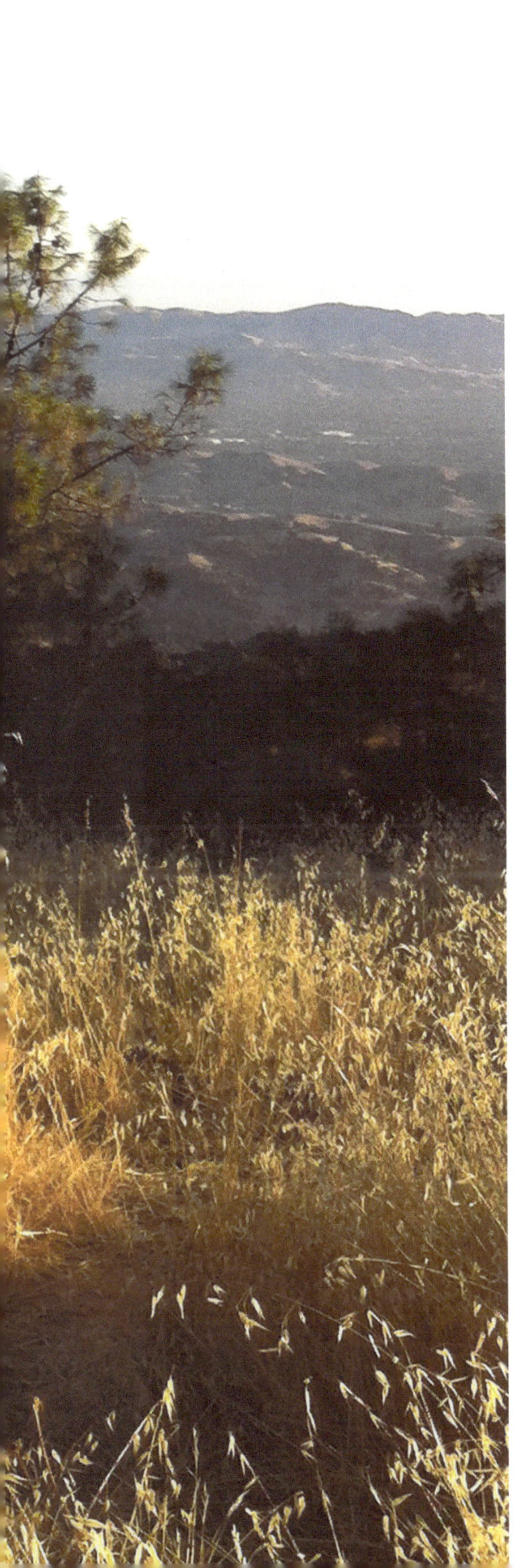

a thousand drunk donkeys

thank you for the gossamer kisses in my heart
every dawn, again and again...

I live for the lovemaking in the night
through every cell...

I would that I could spread that love to everyone,
that tears of joy alone do come...

I would that a thousand drunk donkeys
would bray at my orgies with the eternal...

my orgies of holiness have banished now
my lust of the ages...

o my holiness
only you deserve the name
and you are everywhere...

these lines of love are as raindrops
on parched soil...

www.ingramcontent.com/pod-product-compliance
Lightning Source LLC
LaVergne TN
LVHW070120110826
845147LV00002B/159
* 9 7 8 0 6 1 5 7 7 8 2 1 1 *